Susan Irvine's Rose Gardens

A garden really lives only insofar as it is an
expression of faith, the embodiment of a hope
and a song of praise.

Russell Page
The Education of a Gardener

If, amid the cataclysms of anguish that clamour
around us everywhere nowadays, you declare
that all this babble about beauty and flowers is
a vain impertinence, then I must tell you that
you err, and that your perspectives are false.
Mortal dooms and dynasties are brief things,
but beauty is indestructible and eternal.

Reginald Farrer

By the same author:

Garden of a Thousand Roses: Making a Rose Garden in Australia
A Hillside of Roses
Fragrant Roses (Australia's Best Garden Guides)

Susan Irvine's Rose Gardens

with a description and illustrated list of
Alister Clark roses

Susan Irvine

HYLAND HOUSE

First published in this edition 1997 by
Hyland House Publishing Pty Limited
Hyland House
387–389 Clarendon Street
South Melbourne
Victoria 3205

Garden of a Thousand Roses first published in 1992
A Hillside of Roses first published in 1994

National Library of Australia
Cataloguing-in-publication data:

Irvine, Susan, 1928–
    Susan Irvine's rose gardens.

    Bibliography.
    Includes index.
    ISBN 1 875657 83 5.

    1. Clark, Alister, 1864–1949. 2. Rose culture. 3. Rose culture —
    Victoria — Bendigo Region. 4. Roses — Victoria — Bendigo
    Region — History. 5. Roses — Varieties. I. Irvine, Susan, 1928-
    II. Irvine, Susan, 1928- . A hillside of roses. III. Irvine, Susan,
    1928- . Garden of a thousand roses. IV. Title. V. Title: Rose
    gardens. VI. Title: A hillside of roses. VII. Title: Garden of a
    thousand roses.

635.933372

Illustrated by Peggy Shaw
Colour photographs by Susan Irvine, Garry Aitchison, *Your Garden*,
Lynette Cooke and Janis Nether
Endpapers by Rosemary Manion
Index by Vida Horn
Typeset by Butler Graphics Pty Ltd, Richmond 3121
Printed in Hong Kong by South China Printing Co. Ltd.

Contents

Garden of a Thousand Roses

A Hillside of Roses

List of Illustrations

A Hillside of Roses

(ix)

Alister Clark Roses

'Amy Johnson', 'Australia Felix', 'Baxter Beauty',
'Black Boy', 'Borderer', 'Cherub', 'Cicely
Lascelles', 'Countess of Stradbroke', 'Courier',
'Daydream'

'Diana Allen', 'Dividend', 'Doris Downes', 'Editor
Stewart', 'Fairlie Rede', 'Flying Colours',
'Gladsome', 'Glenara', 'Golden Vision'

'Gwen Nash', 'Jessie Clark', 'Kitty Kininmonth',
'Lady Huntingfield', 'Lorraine Lee', 'Mab
Grimwade', 'Margaret Turnbull', 'Marjory Palmer',
'Mary Guthrie'

'Milkmaid', 'Mrs Albert Nash', 'Mrs Fred Danks',
'Mrs Harold Alston', 'Mrs Harold Brookes', 'Mrs
Maud Alston', 'Mrs Richard Turnbull', 'Nancy
Hayward', 'Peggy Bell'

'Princeps', 'Restless', 'Ringlet', 'Scorcher', 'Sheila
Bellair', 'Squatter's Dream', 'Suitor', 'Sunlit',
'Sunny South', 'Tonner's Fancy', 'Zara
Hore-Ruthven'

Possible Alister Clark Roses

'Cracker', 'Edith Clark', 'Emily Rhodes', 'Herbert
Brunning', 'Janet Morrison', 'Lady Somers',
'Nancy Wilson', 'Nora Cunningham', 'Queen of
Hearts', 'Traverser'

Garden of a Thousand Roses

Making a Rose Garden in Australia

Bleak House.

Preface

This book is the story of the making of a garden. I have not attempted to go into the very complicated history of the development of the rose. This has been done very often and very competently and would be out of place here. The reader wishing to understand something of this complex subject is referred to the incomparable trilogy of Graham Stuart Thomas: *The Old Shrub Roses*, *Shrub Roses of Today* and *Climbing Roses Old and New*. The gardener looking for clear, faithful illustrations as well as scholarly text could not go past *Classic Roses* and *Twentieth Century Roses* by Peter Beales. These two authors form the nucleus of any collection of rose books.

There is often considerable disagreement among the experts concerning nomenclature, classification and, in particular, spelling. Depending on whether the third part of the name is considered to indicate a form, a subspecies or a variety, it may be printed in roman or italic typeface, with an upper or a lower case initial, enclosed by inverted commas or without. The simplest solution, it seems, is to choose one authority and at least be consistent in citation of names. The authority followed throughout this book is the great English rosarian Graham Stuart Thomas.

My warm thanks are due to Peggy Shaw for her delightful black and white watercolours; to Jenni Mather for her excellent colour photographs; to John Nieuwesteeg for his enthusiastic involvement in the search for and the propagating of the Alister Clark roses; to Ruth Rundle, Eve Murray, Maria Fawcett, Tid Alston and all the other gardeners who have so kindly opened their gardens to me and given so generously of rose cuttings; and to Vida Horn who spent many hours carefully reading the text and meticulously checking spelling of botanical names.

If this book conveys something of the joy in store for all those who turn seriously to the growing of roses it will have served its purpose.

To my very dear husband

Yarrow.

Unwanted and Unloved 1

It stood alone, the little bluestone cottage, unoccupied and unloved, by the side of the Calder Highway, which leads from Melbourne to Bendigo. I had passed it every week for five years and wondered idly who owned it and whether it was bluestone. It was so hidden behind thistles, blackberries and long grass that it was hard to tell.

And then one day there was an auction sign on the fence: 'Land for Sale'. Nothing about the house. The agent told me later that they took no account of the house. It was old and decrepit and fit only for the bulldozer.

I had driven past, but turned and went back. There was nobody there, but the doors were open. They could no longer be closed. And two sheep were standing in what I took to be the kitchen.

Four rooms only in the bluestone part of the house, two very tiny with irregular, sloping ceilings and low, wide-silled, multipaned windows. The walls, internal and external, were forty-five centimetres thick and there were big fireplaces in every room. The floors were sound, and on the walls and ceilings the old lining boards had never been painted. Two weatherboard rooms had been added later and here, too, the lining boards were in their original condition, mellowed to a rich mahogany colour. It was indescribably dark and dirty. The windows were broken and cobwebs hung from the ceilings. And I fell in love with it on the spot.

1

I went back to the auction sign and read it carefully. 'Land for Sale. Lot A 170 acres.'

What on earth would I do with sixty-eight hectares — and me with no knowledge of farming and a very demanding job in the city? I resolved to put it out of my mind, banish it as a piece of romantic nonsense.

I did not pass by again for three weeks. I told myself to forget it. The auction would be over and the property sold. Probably a developer had bought it with plans to demolish the cottage.

But when I got there, the sign was still up — no 'Sold' sign pasted over it. I drove on to Castlemaine, where I had a weekender. It was charming and the garden was beginning to be very pretty. I had renovated the house — a quaint old cottage made of handmade bricks complete with cellar, and a dovecot in one corner of the garden which has since been classified by the National Trust. I had bought a pot of *Sternbergia lutea* on the way up from Melbourne and for half an hour I wandered round the garden trying to find a spot to plant it. There was no room left in the little garden. Clearly, I told myself, I needed more land. But not quite sixty-eight hectares.

The previous week I had spent half an hour in the Bookshop of Margareta Webber and had found, quite by chance, *Wild and Old Garden Roses* by Gordon Edwards, with 'Rosa Mundi' on the dust jacket, growing in the author's garden amongst a sea of foxgloves. I had taken it home and pored over it and decided that growing old roses would be the ideal occupation when I retired from my present position. So, of course, I needed more land.

On the way back on Sunday evening I called in again at the little stone cottage. It was a stormy evening and the wind howled through the branches of the huge old pine tree that stood just behind the house. The back door swung disconsolately on its hinges. The sheep had left the kitchen and were huddled in the tumbledown stable which had been built on to the front verandah. No one in his right mind, I told myself, would take on such a task.

But on Monday morning I rang the agent. No, it had not sold. It had been passed in at auction. If I liked to make an offer . . . I explained that I had no use for the sixty-eight hectares. Could I not buy it on four? No, that was not possible, but there was no problem. A local sheep farmer had been leasing the land for years and would be more than happy to continue to do so.

Still unconvinced, I made my offer. Too low, I thought, so that would be that. But that afternoon the agent rang back. The owners were happy to accept the offer and when could I come to Kyneton to sign the papers? I did so that very evening, and Bleak House became mine.

Muscari.

Further Acquaintance 2

I thought of little else all that week. Since the house was unoccupied, I tried to arrange for early settlement. I drove up on Saturday morning filled with antici-pation. It had been raining all the week and during the hour-long drive my windscreen-wipers had been working overtime. As I rounded the bend in the High-way and Bleak House came into sight I was filled with incredulity. Behind the house was a huge lake.

Now I knew I had acted hastily. I had not consulted my financial advisers (who would certainly have advised against it). I had not had a builder look at it. I had not enquired about the carrying capacity of the land, or the quality of the under-ground water or the nature of the soil. But however hasty my decision, I was quite sure I had looked at it carefully enough to have seen a twenty-hectare lake if it had been there. And it definitely had not.

I drove slowly back to Kyneton and went to see the agent. He was apologetic. We should have told you, he said. It's terrible farming land. It floods like this every year, when the winter or spring rains come, and the water lies there for months. Hopeless grazing land.

Worse still, in his eyes, were the old quarries. There were three of them on the property, he said. They had been worked in the early days and the stone taken to Melbourne. Many of the big buildings in the city had been built of Malmsbury bluestone.

With a half-hearted attempt at encouragement, he spoke of historic interest. The cottage itself had been built of stone quarried on the place. But, sounding a note of gloom once more, the quarries were no use now — full of rabbits and snakes. His sympathy for me was patent, and possibly genuine. What would a city woman do with a property such as this?

I bought a pair of gumboots, a sandwich and a tin of gin and tonic and drove back to Bleak House in a state of mounting excitement.

The low carrying capacity of the land might be a matter of some concern to a farmer, but to me it was quite immaterial. But quarries and a lake were riches I had not dreamed of.

I slipped on my gumboots and started off down the paddock. The rain had stopped and the sun had come out. The hills along the skyline were a deep navy blue. And on the lake were black swans, dozens of them. As I got closer, a flock of mountain duck rose slowly into the air and wheeled away across the water in perfect formation.

On the far side of the lake an old road, hand paved with stone, led up into the quarry. It was huge. Towering masses of stone, all covered with soft, grey-green moss and lichen. I found an old hand drill sticking in a block of stone and the remains of an old chimney. Had people lived, as well as worked here, I wondered.

A deep waterhole was overhung by elderberry bushes, and *Rosa canina*, the old dog rose, grew along its margins. Rabbits scuttled away from under my feet.

I skirted the lake and turned back towards the house along the southern boundary of the land. There was another quarry much closer to the house, quite a small one this time. It was shaped like an amphitheatre, huge slabs of stone forming a protective semicircle against the wind.

There and then I formed the notion of a quarry garden, remote, sheltered. I had a vision of it filled with daffodils, tulips, muscari. Rabbits don't eat bulbs. And neither do stock. The paddocks round Castlemaine, where the ruins of the early settlers' cottages were, are filled each year with masses of daffodils. Sheep graze there and rabbits in their thousands but the daffodils come back every spring. Iris, too. I remembered a day in late spring when we had come suddenly on an old ruin at Guildford surrounded by a sea of purple and white iris.

My quarry could be planted with bulbs. They are hardy. They like to be dry in summer and the quarry would be well-drained in winter. It could be fenced in from the sheep and the fences covered with rambling roses — little netting guards would give protection from the rabbits until the roses were high enough — 'Albertine', and 'Félicité et Perpétue', that dear little white rose with the soft pink buds that is to be found round so many of the old houses in this part of Victoria.

In a stone shaped like a giant armchair I sat and ate my sandwich. A misshapen old tree-violet (with a heavenly scent when in flower) overhung my seat, and a couple of magpies had nested in a self-sown hawthorn.

The birds were oblivious of my presence and I counted, in all, from my vantage point above the lake, sixty black swans. There was no house in sight. Only, across the other side of the lake, an old stone ruin and what is known in this part of the world as a shepherd's croft, long since deserted. The highway was far behind me and only the cry of the plovers broke the silence.

It was not just a bluestone cottage I had acquired, but a little piece of Paradise.

Restoration

3

I was brought down to earth a week later when, at his insistence and with deep misgivings, I brought a friend up from Melbourne to inspect my purchase.

We arrived at dusk, and in the fading light the little cottage looked sad and forlorn. The back door shrieked a protest as we pushed it open, and a couple of bats brushed against my face. Inside it was dark, and John hit his head on the lintel of the door into the hall – people really were much shorter a century ago.

There was nothing to see in here, and we went out hastily. Surveying the sea of thistles from the back door, John tried to conceal his incredulity.

'Well,' he said finally, 'sixty-eight hectares so close to a capital city has to increase in value.' No use to talk to a stockbroker of the scent of roses, of moss-covered stone, of wild birds and wetlands!

We talked of other things on the way back to Melbourne.

I had six weeks of holiday then, and resolved to spend them making the house habitable. Impossible to think about the garden until I could at least lock the front door, sleep comfortably at night and cook a meal at the end of a day's toil.

On my very first morning a large snake – I think he was a copperhead – slid away almost from under my feet just outside the back door. So the first priority was to clear away some of the undergrowth from around the house.

I went to see the farmer whose sheep were agisted on the land. 'Yes,' he said with a smile, 'plenty of snakes there. The last tenant used to drape the dead ones over the front fence whenever there was any talk of finding a purchaser for the place. Puts people off, you see.'

I borrowed from him two large rams — large and stout with curling horns, which I regarded with some mistrust but preferred to copperheads. They stayed a fortnight and did a splendid job.

A builder came from Castlemaine, and we approached the question of renovations practically and systematically.

First, he insisted, I had to be able to lock it up.

'Right here on the highway ... a woman on her own ... the prison farm not a mile away ..' (Youth Training Centre is, I think, the preferred euphemism.)

I insisted on restoration, not modernisation. I wanted, above all, to retain the atmosphere which had made me fall in love with the cottage in the first place. So no changes were to be made to the bluestone part. The two weatherboard rooms at the back had been built on later — about 1880, I discovered — and, with their steeply pitched roof, looked rather like a country schoolhouse. The very back room, I deduced from the broken remains of a wooden sink, must have been the kitchen. No stove — that had been purloined long ago. It had one small window only and, since the internal walls were the colour of old mahogany, it was difficult to see one's hand before one's face.

Ivan put in a whole wall of multipaned windows facing east, and another facing north, and high, narrow French doors opening south to a terrace.

Since I spend the least possible amount of time in the kitchen, I decided not to waste this room on such mundane things, and it became the dining room. The sun streamed in in the morning, and I could watch it set over Mt Alexander in the evening. And as the garden progressed in the years that followed, this room became a sheer joy and a vantage point from which to view the whole.

The inner weatherboard room became the kitchen. A huge skylight let in both sun and light. The floor was covered with deep blue ceramic tiles and a tiny room which had housed a tin bath (but had no water or taps!) became a walk-in pantry. A large Scottish slow-combustion stove (my birthday present to myself) ensured that this part of the house at least would always be warm.

All those practical and essential things such as power, plentiful hot water and a very pretty bathroom, were added in the next couple of months.

We had a small dispute about the handmade bricks which made the floor of the front verandah. They were uneven, and broken in places, and Ivan's builder's soul could not contemplate them with any degree of equanimity. They were a blot on his otherwise meticulously finished article. To me, they were in keeping with the shingles which were still to be seen on the verandah under the iron roof and belonged to the bluestone part of the cottage which we had resolved not to alter. They are still there today!

The four bluestone rooms were dark, with one window each and the roof coming down steeply over the verandah. It was difficult to see how this could be changed without altering the character of the whole. Finally, in an inspired moment, I thought of dormer windows in the roof constructed as light wells. We put in three, one for each of the front rooms and one for the central hall, and the inside was transformed. There was one clouded moment when we had a slight altercation with the Shire Engineer who insisted we were putting in upstairs rooms without a Council permit!

The internal walls in this part of the house, too, were old lining boards of the same deep, rich mahogany colour, but here they extended only to the traditional metre, and above that was wallpaper — old, grimy, the pattern no longer visible. I started to strip it and found another layer underneath, and another, and another, and underneath all that was hessian, stretched tight. I did the stripping myself, and, as the hessian came away, revealing the stone walls beneath, the dust of a century filled the cottage for days.

We replaced it with plaster, leaving the lining boards untouched, and I searched Melbourne for Victorian wallpaper. Big open fireplaces, sloping ceilings and window-sills forty centimetres deep lent character to these rooms. In a fit of extravagance I purchased an antique, four-poster bed.

With gardening out of the question until the builders were gone, and with my curiosity aroused, I read through the title-papers carefully to find out what I could about the previous owners of the cottage. 'The Hospital Farm' it was known as in the district. But its original name, given to it when it was built in the late 1850s, had been 'Bleak House'. I decided instantly to revert to the original name. I was very taken by the prospect of having a Dickensian flavour to my rose garden. Not that I really believed that Charles Dickens's novel had much to do with the naming of this little cottage in the Antipodes.

Bleak House was published in 1854 and it is just possible, since it was issued in serial form, that early copies had found their way to the young colony. But I think it much more probable that the property derived its name from the bitter winters, harsh frosts and howling winds that beset it for a large part of each year. I often thought subsequently, when sitting by the fireside and listening to that wind in the pine trees, that if it had not been called 'Bleak House' I would have named it 'Wuthering Heights'.

Seeking information about the original owners, I enquired of the Kyneton Histori-cal Society who sent me to the curator of the Museum, which was housed in a fine old Georgian styled building in Piper Street. Here I learned that the property had belonged to Sarah Ann and James Pennington, who had died at 'a great age' in 1872, she first and he only a few months later, 'probably of a broken heart' said the old lady in charge. Being childless, they had left the farm in perpetuity to the Kyneton Hospital. The Hospital had leased it out over the following one hundred years to a succession of tenant farmers until, in the last few years, with no power connected and no running water, it had been impossible to find a tenant. The Hospital had no money to spend on it, and when the vandals got to work, the decision was taken to sell it. That was where I had come in.

The good-natured curator could tell me no more, but suggested I contact the Kyneton *Guardian*. Here I found an extract from 3 May 1872:

Mr. James Pennington died in Piper St. He came to Victoria in 1839 and was a native of Tasmania and came to Kyneton with Mr. Thornblow, manager of Barfold Station, recently purchased by Sir George Arthur, Governor . . . James Pennington worked for him for many years. He did not believe in banks and hid money in out of the way places. Many expected that some day a large hoard would be found by someone. A roll of 50 or 60 notes — many rotted — stated to have been found by a surveyor's party out Barfold way in a roof of an old hut, was popularly believed to have been hidden by him.

Whatever 'hoard' had been concealed about Bleak House had been discovered long since. All I ever found was a halfpenny with Queen Victoria's head on it!

I was delighted with all this information and went from the *Guardian* office to the Kyneton cemetery. After some searching, I found the headstone — an unexpectedly large and pretentious one, obviously erected at some more recent date:

> In Memory of
> Sarah Ann Pennington
> Died 10th December, 1871
> aged 52
> Also James Pennington
> Died 5th May, 1872
> aged 57 years.

Nothing more. But I was greatly struck by the fact that these two persons who had died, to quote the Curator, at 'a great age' were much the same age as I was then!

In the weeks that followed I had a visit from a bookbinder. I was working in the front garden when the car drew up and a rather fine-looking man asked if he could possibly see the front room. 'You see,' he said, 'my father was born there and I have been so pleased to see the house being restored.'

I had a similar visit from a dear, old lady who told me she had spent holidays there with her grandparents who had farmed the property. Her first job each morning had been to draw two buckets of water from the well and take them into the kitchen to her grandmother. She was delighted to find the old well still there.

Truly we, who think we own things, are only caretakers for a while. I was reminded of a painting on a little house in the Black Forest which I had seen while studying in Germany years ago. I love their custom of painting landscapes and figures on the outside walls of their houses, and sometimes poems and homespun philosophy as well. I had stood in the road and learned this one and resolved to put it, one day, on a house of my own. And now, I felt, the time was ripe:

> Das Haus ist mein,
> Und doch nicht mein.
> Ich geh' hinaus
> Ein andrer kommt herein.
> Ach Gott! Wer wird
> Der letzte sein?

Roughly translated it reads:

> This house is mine
> And yet not mine.
> I shall go
> Another will come.
> Oh god! Who'll
> Be the last one?

It was not practical to paint it on a weatherboard wall, even less so on a stone one. So I had a plaque made by a local sign-writer who also wrote the poem on it.

I took it then to my friend, Peggy Shaw, a very fine watercolourist. With it I took a copy of an illustation from a sixteenth century Book of Hours, depicting, of course, roses. She copied it faithfully and the plaque was hung on the south wall in the courtyard above a little garden which was later planted with paeonies and lavender, and a little golden rose which sprang up of itself, either from a seed brought by a bird, or from a root planted long ago by other hands. I do not know its name to this day.

Clematis.

4 *The Front Garden*

With the builders finally gone and the painter due to start work, I sat down to plan the front garden.

It is tiny. With hundreds of hectares at their disposal, and a beautiful vista stretching away across paddocks to distant hills, with Mt Macedon off to the south and Mt Alexander to the north, the early settlers who had built this cottage had elected to build it facing due west, away from the view, and only seven metres from the front fence. So the area I had, in which to plan my front garden, was no bigger than the average suburban garden — and facing the Calder Highway.

It was bounded on one side by the drive and on the other — barely three metres from the edge of the verandah — by the fence which divided the house block (one could not dignify this jungle with the name of 'garden') from the sheep paddocks. On this fence were an old quince and a gnarled, old apple. I decided to leave them both. Height is important in a garden, and it would be several years before anything I might plant would attain it. And somehow they were a link with the past, with Sarah Ann Pennington and her husband, James, who had lived and worked here a hundred years ago and had made a garden. For there had once been a garden. All along the front fence, made of cyclone wire and in a sad state of disrepair, an

Unwanted and unloved.

Dormer windows in the roof. The silver birches and the hedge of *R. rugosa alba* are in the foreground.

Silver birch and white wisteria in the front garden with a sea of spring forget-me-nots.

(*Left*) 'Maigold' in a mixed border of lupins (on the right), *Penstemon* 'White Swan', iris and scabiosa. (Courtesy *Your Garden*).

An Arthur Rackham-type face leers at 'Golden Showers'.

'New Dawn' and 'Heidekönigin' spilling down a bank.

R. rugosa 'Scabrosa' makes a fine hedge.

'Edna Walling' up a plum
tree.

'Carabella' behind a hedge of
lavender.

An old single paeony.

(*Above*) 'The Edna Walling Rose' (left) and 'Tea Rambler' (right) reach for the sky. (Courtesy *Your Garden*).

(*Right*) The old windmill with climbing 'Meg' and white lychnis in the foreground.

(*Below*) 'Zéphirine Drouhin' (left) and 'Titian' (right) cover the pergola.

old red Gallica rose was pushing through. It had bloomed, amid the thistles and the docks, in January, just after I had taken possession – a deep red old fellow, with a deep rich perfume to match.

And on the corner of the house, when the rams and the builders had done their worst, where no trace of a rose had been before, the purple rambler, 'Veilchenblau', had appeared. In the intervening months 'Veilchenblau' reached the top of the verandah posts. Truly the tenacity and recuperative powers of roses are something to marvel at.

And along the north wall of the house, under a tiny multipaned window, I found, when I started to dig, a narrow bed edged with bricks and in the following October clumps of Christmas lilies (*Lilium candidum*) appeared. They flourished against the protection of the bluestone wall and their heads nodded in at the little low window of my bedroom.

So here I had an area some seven metres by fifteen metres, facing west, with one quince and one apple on the left-hand fence, a red rose across the front and a deep purple one on the corner of the house.

It was essential that the garden be planned before the painter started. In the manner of old cottages the front door provided the only link between house and garden, so a colour scheme had to be chosen which would bring the two together.

The steep roof, coming down low over the verandah, was the dominant feature. So this was where planning had to begin. I do not much like red – either in the house or the garden – and green roofs do nothing for bluestone cottages. The prevailing impression was sombre – bluestone walls and the five dark old pine trees – so finally I decided on a soft, butter yellow, with that wonderful rose, 'Mermaid', climbing up the verandah posts, intertwined with a white wisteria. 'Mermaid' would have a struggle since she would get little sun – none until about 2 p.m. – but I thought that if any rose could succeed here, she would. Besides, she is almost evergreen and flowers throughout the summer.

With her single flowers she is often taken for an old rose and this would be in keeping with the old cottage. Actually, she was bred by the firm of Paul in England in 1917, a daughter of that rampant white climber, *R. bracteata*, so vigorous that it has become almost a weed in some parts of America.

I needed a couple of trees to shade the front rooms from the westerly sun and decided on silver birches – their airy foliage, white trunks and autumn colour were what was needed as contrast to the solidity of the bluestone.

The front fence posed a problem. In a moment of false economy (since much regretted) I decided to leave it there and grew *R. wichuraiana*, the little white, ragged Memorial rose of Japan, right along it, with a hedge of *R. rugosa alba*. Although a ground cover rose, I thought *R. wichuraiana* would also twine itself in and out of the cyclone wire – it might also do away with the necessity to weed under *R. rugosa alba*, which is excessively prickly.

R. rugosa alba has been a wild success. The Rugosas must surely be among the best hedging plants. They grow happily to about two metres, are almost evergreeen, require little or no pruning and never get black spot or mildew. The single forms set brilliant hips, the size and colour of little tomatoes, and the foliage turns gold in late autumn.

Of *R. wichuraiana* I cannot speak so enthusiastically. It flourished. It rushed along the bed under the Rugosas and wound itself in and out of the cyclone wire.

But it did not stop there. It takes root almost wherever it touches the ground, and it came up in the path and in the bed on the other side of it and set off across Council land towards the Calder Highway. Six years later I was still pulling it out and have resolved that the only place to plant it is on the wall of a dam. It would certainly prevent soil erosion and would be a splendid sight during its few brief flowering weeks. But in a garden – NO.

With the frame set – the front hedge and the climbers along the verandah – and the two birches planted, I set to work to plan the rest. There was to be no lawn. Water would always be at a premium and there was, in any case, no room. A path must run, in true cottage garden style, from front gate to front door, and this I decided to edge with miniature roses – 'Green Ice' and 'Orange Cascade' (which is not orange at all, but a soft, warm yellow) because they are so hardy and so floriferous.

At the gate I had planted a forsythia, that herald of the spring, and later I sent to Tasmania for bulbs of chionodoxa, glory of the snow, which blooms at the same time – a deep gentian blue.

The beds were to be edged with muscari and *Narcissus bulbocodium*, with the cheerful little *Sternbergia lutea* and *Zephyranthes candida* for autumn colour. There were to be daffodils and the blue and yellow *Iris xiphium* and clumps of yellow day-lilies – in fact this whole garden was to be yellow, white and blue.

But there was the old red Gallica rose along the front fence. I decided, reluctantly, that he would have to go. Not altogether. I could plant him elsewhere, but he certainly had no place in my yellow, white and blue garden.

But I reckoned, as the saying goes, without my host. I enlisted masculine help and we dug him up – by the barrowful. I gave roots to all my friends, and then to all my acquaintance. Finally we thought we had eliminated him. Next spring, with the Rugosas all in place, up he came again, not in one or two places, but in ten. Six years later I conceded defeat. He is flowering happily in the midst of the white Rugosas and his scent fills the whole garden.

Gallica roses planted on their own roots will do this. They form thickets, spread and multiply, and from every broken root comes a new shoot. 'Jenny Duval', that lovely soft, pink-mauve, eighteenth century rose of unknown origins, has done the same in another part of the garden quite smothering the little pink and white, 'Echo', and the early Tea, 'Jean Ducher'. Ideal, for large, rambling country gardens, but in a small garden Gallicas need to be planted as grafted plants.

The muscari make a carpet now under the Rugosa hedge, with snowflakes, which just appeared one spring. So, too, did an English gooseberry (more of Sarah Ann's legacy?) under the quince tree. It bears a heavy crop, and gooseberry jam is now an annual event. *Clematis montana* was planted to grow through the quince and a hybrid clematis, 'Fair Rosamund' (a pearly white) at the foot of the old apple.

Campanula poscharskyana forms a starry ground cover along the shaded verandah bed and masses of yellow and white violas, which seed themselves each year now, blanket the large, centre bed. The white ajuga is forming a dense cover under the silver birch, together with a soft, apricot-yellow violet, a gift from a friend.

In the centre bed is the double white Rugosa, 'Souvenir de Philémon Cochet', the bright buttercup-yellow *R. foetida lutea*, which came first to English gardens from Asia in the sixteenth century, and the white form of 'Cécile Brunner', the little sweetheart rose.

In the main it was carefully planned, my yellow, white and blue front garden, to bring a new spring, and sunshine, to the sombre old cottage. So with the plans made, I was ready for the painter. He came to see me one Sunday afternoon, ready to start the next day. I gave him a bloom of 'Mermaid'. That was to be the colour of the roof, the shutters on the front windows and the front door. Yes, he understood — and white woodwork on the verandah posts and window frames.

I drove up from Melbourne the following Saturday, filled with excitement and anticipation. As I rounded the bend I almost swerved off the road. There stood my cottage, its roof the colour of those raincoats children are urged to wear to make them visible at a great distance.

The painter was waiting for me, full of pride in his work.

'Johnny,' I said, 'that's not the colour of the rose I gave you!'

'No,' he agreed, looking slightly dashed. 'But, then,' cheering up visibly, 'it'll fade!'

It did. But it took six months.

Iris.

5 *Iris*

It was 'Altissimo' that had first taken me, years earlier, to Kelsall Court on the outskirts of Castlemaine. There it was, clearly visible from the Highway, absolutely covering a three metre trellis with its startling, velvety red single blooms.

I think it was my first acquaintance with a modern, single rose. Influenced, I suppose, by *Rosa canina*, the dear little dog rose, I had thought of single roses as being essentially early ones (I had still to discover the whole fascinating range of species roses) and here was this great flamboyant mass, three metres high and five metres long and bearing no resemblance at all to the deceptively delicate-looking pale pink rose that makes its appearance in paddocks and by roadsides and in my quarries.

I got out of the car to examine it more closely. It formed the boundary between the two enchanting little cottages, one brick and one weatherboard, which made up the whole of Kelsall Court.

And framed in the door of the weatherboard one stood Babs Mair. Stout, white-haired, with a face which fitted the description of Peggotty in *David Copperfield*, having cheeks so red the birds might peck them in preference to apples, a face alive with kindness and good humour. And on her feet were a pair of boots Gertrude

14

Jekyll might have envied. She was one of the first great gardeners I came to know – 'great' in that she lived for her garden, and every green thing she touched lived and flourished.

'Yes,' she nodded. 'It's worth a visit. It's called "Altissimo" and it's not an old rose at all. Fred and I saw it first a year or so ago and planted it to hide an ugly fence.'

They must have been among the first to grow it in this country for I found later that it had been bred in France in 1967.

Babs invited me in for coffee and to see her garden, and this was the first of many visits. In fact, Kelsall Court became a regular stopping place between Castlemaine and Malmsbury.

Babs and Fred were brother and sister. They had moved to the country and bought these two little miners' cottages long before miners' cottages became trendy. Each lived alone but they came together for dinner every evening. They shared an intense love of gardening, a taste for old cottages and for early Australian furniture.

The cottages were tiny. The weatherboard one belonged to Babs, its front verandah, cool and inviting, clad in ornamental grape (cut back hard every winter) and its front fence covered in wisteria.

In the low-ceilinged kitchen where we drank our coffee the wood stove was burning, chintz cushions were on the chairs, pots of geraniums stood in the window and the kettle sang. All that was missing from the Helen Allingham painting was the cat. I looked for him in vain. Babs was a bird-lover.

She and Fred had bought the cottages ten years ago in a very bad state of repair. There was no garden. They stood in a paddock surrounded by those unsightly mullock heaps which characterise old mining towns.

And in these unpromising surroundings they had created an oasis. Each time I called in we walked slowly round the garden to see what was in flower. It was the best course in horticulture I could possibly have had. From Babs I learnt about ground covers. She gave me roots of *Campanula poscharskyana* and *Campanula portenschlagiana,* and of the soft blue prostrate rosemary *Rosmarinus officinalis* 'Prostratus' which trailed down over the retaining wall at the back of the cottage and asks so little care. From Babs I learnt to cover fences, not only with roses but with clematis and jasmine and ornamental grape. Through Babs I came to know Gertrude Jekyll. She lent me that wonderful book *Colour Schemes for the Flower Garden* and the biography by Betty Massingham. Indeed there was much of that grand old gardener (apart from her boots) in Babs herself, in her intimate knowledge of every one of her plants, her generosity, and her total disregard of her ailing body – Babs was crippled with arthritis.

I visited them the week after I had bought Bleak House. Babs had seen it often as she passed up and down the Highway. She had given me so much help to create my little garden in Castlemaine, and I think she was secretly appalled at the thought of my exchanging it for this windswept expanse. However, she set about that very week striking pieces of ornamental grape and honeysuckle.

Fred's reaction was different. 'You will have room for the iris,' he cried with delight.

Years earlier, when he had owned that picturesque stone cottage which is now Badgers' Keep, Fred had dreamed of starting an iris nursery. He had imported high quality stock from America and started out full of hope. Age and ill health had overtaken him and he had given them, some time since, to two green-fingered sisters who lived in an old sandstone cottage in Chewton. They, too, had found the task beyond them and Fred knew that they were now, in their turn, looking for a home for the iris.

The following Saturday − I was still working very hard in Melbourne and had only weekends for Bleak House and the garden − I found myself knocking on Margaret and Helen's front door, a door which opened straight off the footpath and gave no hint of the rambling garden behind, which sloped right down to the banks of Forest Creek, that scene of such frenzied activity during the gold rushes.

I received a very warm welcome. The sisters had planted the whole orchard with iris but the task of looking after them was quite beyond them. Margaret led me out through the tiny kitchen to see for myself.

There they were, in symmetrical beds, under gnarled old apple and pear trees and totally overgrown with weeds. Margaret was apologetic. 'Such beautiful iris,' she said, 'the most wonderful colours. But my back has gone and neither of us can garden any more.'

I arranged to collect them over the next few weeks and each Saturday saw me knocking on that door with a couple of large, green garbage bags, a spade and a fork. And each Saturday I received the same warm welcome − a cup of tea in the kitchen, homemade biscuits, a pot of jam, a jar of dried lavender.

Gradually the iris were moved to Bleak House. There was, of course, no garden there yet, but this was an opportunity not to be missed. So I borrowed a small rotary hoe and dug a strip along the fence. This would provide a temporary home. Their names had been lost long ago and, as they had not been planted in any kind of order, the colours were mixed.

After four or five Saturdays spent in this way I felt I had all the iris I could handle and broached the subject of payment. Margaret looked shocked and Helen, gentle, white-haired Helen, crept away in embarrassment. 'Oh, but we couldn't take *money* for them. We're just so pleased they've found another home.'

I brushed this aside. I spoke of business, of material needs which we all have, of being practical. All to no avail. I felt I had hurt their feelings. Finally, and very tentatively, Margaret mentioned that they *would* love a new carpet in the living room. So it was settled. Necessary phone calls were made and a few weeks later the new carpet, a soft, warm pink, was installed.

Iris are wonderful companions for roses. I am sure I did not know *how* wonderful when I collected them. They don't mind frost and heavy winter rains. They don't mind heat − in fact, they seem to love it. At Bleak House they are never watered. The roses are on a trickle line but there are no outlets for the iris, and they don't seem to mind. Like roses, they like the sun, and like roses they appreciate a handful of lime now and then (except for the water iris).

And they are quite unpalatable to rabbits. When I first planted them in their temporary home the fence consisted of a few old wooden posts and rusted strands of wire. The rabbit population was immense and growing daily (I decided they must all be Catholics).

Fred's iris were all of the tall, bearded variety. Over the years many other iris were added to the garden.

Through those bleak days of July and August when the roses, having been pruned, look as though there is no life in them, the little *Iris unguicularis* (which we used to call by the much simpler name *'stylosa'*) send forth a wealth of powder blue flowers.

There is a white form, too, and a deeper mauve variegated form, but these are harder to come by.

Then in October, when, with the daffodils and narcissi over, the garden seems to hold its breath until the flowering of the Banksias heralds the onset of the rose season, the *Iris pumila* and *Iris innominata* are among the chief joys of the garden. Both come in a wide range of colours, multiply with astonishing speed and need dividing every three years or so.

And then, dignified and stately, come the tall, bearded iris, usually coinciding with the first roses. There were many soft yellow ones among Fred's collection. The yellow roses, which were the last to be introduced to our gardens (none of the species roses from Europe is yellow), are the first to bloom. I planted 'Frühlingsanfang' (Onset of Spring) and 'Frühlingsgold' (Spring Gold) and 'Maigold' as a group. They flower together and abundantly and the bushes spill over the path and intermingle. And with them I planted Fred's yellow iris, not in ones and twos but in dozens. It is one of the sunniest corners of the garden and brings back each spring happy memories of Fred who imported them and Margaret who nurtured them and handed them on.

Sparaxis.

6 *Other People's Gardens*

The front garden had almost planned itself. Given the position of the house, the drive and the front fence, I had only a very small space to play with.

The rest of the 'garden' was quite another matter, consisting as it did of nothing but flat paddocks stretching away for what seemed a vast distance to north and east. No trees except for five old pines, planted, I suppose, as a nostalgic reminder of 'the old country' which was 'home' to the original settlers, and two of the biggest boobyallas (*Myoporum insulare*) I have ever seen, on the south side of the house. One of these blew down in a storm shortly after I moved in, and the other was so infirm that I was persuaded to have it cut down. The gardener who did the cutting left a stump some one and a half metres high. It is a gnarled old stump, and presents an Arthur Rackham-type face to the world – or rather to my back door, where it seemed to watch with derision all of my comings and goings. Over the next weeks I started to plan the garden.

Formal gardens are possible in Australia. Indeed, I think we must be the only gardeners in the world who think we have to make a choice between indigenous and 'exotic' plants. Some of us even go so far as to make it a moral issue, seeing it as a virtue to plant only 'natives' and totally ignoring the great wealth of plant material which botanists, travellers and naturalists have made available to us over the last two hundred years or so.

But the idea of a formal rose garden on the open plains of Central Victoria did seem incongruous. I had visited Cathlaw at New Gisborne the previous year during daffodil time when not only daffodils but also chionodoxa — regarded as a rarity by most Australian gardeners — formed a carpet under towering trees, predominantly oaks, for this is a garden with strong European connections, planned and planted by three women who made frequent trips to England and the Continent.

My most vivid and lasting impression of Cathlaw is of a small space on the east side of the house totally enclosed by a tall, dark, cypress hedge at least three metres high. Within this enclosure was nothing but lawn, save for a small, formal pool, shaped like the Ace of Spades. Around the pool was a bed of brilliant scarlet geums ('Mrs Bradshaw'), startling, against the dark green of the cypress. I felt for a moment that I had stepped into Italy.

No hope of tall, dark cypress hedges on my open plains — they would take years to establish and I wanted results in a hurry! I had a suspicion that 'true' gardeners do not think like this, and I thought of Betty Ross-Watt at Cathlaw who came upon her mother one day aged ninety-four, planting a new tree. She was well aware that it would not flower for fourteen or fifteen years, but to her it was the creation of the garden that was important. Whether she would be there to see it in its maturity was irrelevant.

My mind turned, too, to Bolobek, that most formal and tranquil and restrained of Australian gardens. I thought of the formal little rose garden, surrounded on three sides by three metre high brick walls — mellow old bricks, kept when the original house was demolished — with pear trees espaliered against them and clematis growing through the pears. Rectangular beds and a sundial as a centrepiece, flanked by clipped box balls, little box hedges and *Alchemilla mollis* — a classic English rose garden. But it, too, was in the setting of an English garden, dominated by towering English trees over a century old.

I resolved to pay another visit to Tanglewood, my friend Maria Fawcett's garden at Donvale, not out of any desire to reproduce design, or plantings, or structures, but because it is a garden with which I feel a deep kinship. Both it and Cathlaw are very personal gardens, designed and worked by their owners and evolving over a long period. If you accept Russell Page's dictum that 'a garden really lives only insofar as it is an expression of faith, the embodiment of a hope and a song of praise', then your garden must be a personal creation.

Knowledge of plants will be acquired in many ways, design concepts influenced by many gardens and many gardeners, but if you are to create the sort of garden Russell Page was writing of, a great deal must come from within yourself.

Maria's garden is one such. It is the sort of garden we dream about, the Secret Garden of our childhood, an entirely personal creation yet a source of inspiration and refreshment of the spirit to many. 'You cannot give people happiness,' she said to me on my first visit, 'any more than you can give a bird song — but the garden can give something nothing else gives.'

Her garden covers about one hectare. It could be anywhere, for it is entirely screened from the outside world by tall trees, high fences, tangled hedges of camellias and roses and honeysuckle.

Little paths — not swept, not tidy — twist and turn through forests of camellias — the seedlings are allowed to grow where they will — huge crab-apples (not pruned or shaped) — *Malus*×'Eleyi', with its deep, plum-coloured leaves, in magnificent flower, with the grey foliage of wattles behind it and lilacs as a foreground. Helle-bores have seeded everywhere — no need to weed where they and the forget-me-nots have formed so thick a carpet. There is an old belief that hellebores afford protection from evil spirits, so they are planted at the back door, too.

At the end of the garden is a solid wall of the white Banksia rose, interspersed with *Rosa laevigata* ('The Cherokee Rose'). Brought from China in 1759 it flowers early, as does the Banksia, and is covered in earliest spring with large, single white flowers with superb golden stamens. And growing through them both is a pink honeysuckle. The scent is intoxicating. The ring-tailed possums feast on the young buds — 'but it doesn't matter,' said Maria 'there is enough for all of us'.

The old roses, Gallicas, Albas and Damasks, have long ago outgrown their beds and form great banks. Many have been gifts from friends, so, struck from cuttings, have formed dense thickets. Many of them have no names. To Maria this is immaterial. Their beauty is not enhanced by their being ticketed and labelled.

A mysterious, deep red rose cascades down from the very top of an old apple tree — 'it's a Bach fugue,' said Maria, 'all intertwined'. It is 'Château de Clos Vougeot', described by Graham Stuart Thomas as 'containing all the oldest wine' and by Jack Harkness as 'the dark red rose of our dreams, the darkest red, black as night, to be stroked with the eyes, velvet and voluptuous . . .'

Bulbs grow everywhere. Sparaxis form a carpet at the side door, where they were never planted. A forest of Japanese anemones (*Anemone hupehensis*) is at the back door. Little paths, dotted with English daisies (*Bellis perennis*), lead through tall banks of shrubs. Dragons pop out from behind the leaves of the giant lily, 'Green Goddess', nymphs shelter under overhanging branches, Aladdin jars mark the turning point of a pathway. And everywhere there is the song of birds.

There are wonderful trees in the garden. I go each year in autumn especially to see the persimmon. There are species lilacs from China with most exquisite, pale pink, single blooms — valued not because they are rare, but because they are beautiful.

Rarities for their own sake hold no attraction for Maria, surrounded as she is by daily miracles. The little cherry plum trees are among her favourites, and the magical winter-flowering *Parrotia persica* whose tiny flowers glint in the sun like thousands of rubies. She would certainly say, with Walter de la Mare:

> The lovely in life is the familiar,
> And only the lovelier for continuing strange.

Maria shares her garden, not only with the birds, who are safe and valued here, but also with her Siamese cats (who seem not to be hunters) and even with a fox — and with the many friends who come, as I do, for refreshment of the spirit, a re-charging of batteries. It is a still world that she inhabits, a tranquil and a very beautiful one — far removed from the world of getting and spending, buying and selling, just outside her gates. I am reminded always of the inscription on the tomb-stone of the President of the Bird Protection Society:

> He loved birds and green places and the wind on the heath, and saw the bright-ness of the skirts of God.

Windbreaks and Hedges 7

'Garden rooms', since Sissinghurst has become the Mecca of gardeners the world over, have become fashionable. In fact, I would hazard a guess that, among trendy gardeners (and I leave you to make your own definition of 'trendy gardeners'), their period of being 'in' is almost over and they are in danger of being regarded as a gardening cliché.

I had visited Sissinghurst at the age of twenty-one. Vita Sackville-West was in residence then, but it was as the author of *All Passion Spent* and *The Edwardians* that I saw her, not as one of the world's most creative, sensitive and inspired gardeners. Indeed, in my abysmal ignorance, I don't think I saw gardening as an art at all or even, such was the narrowness of my intellectual horizons, as an occupation to be taken in any way seriously, a gentle indulgence, perhaps, for one's extreme old age.

So it was with no thought of fashion that I designed the Bleak House garden as a series of rooms. Nor did I design it, as all good garden books advise, on paper and all at once. Rather it grew, section by section, the boundaries being pushed out as I felt I could handle a little bit more, or as I came upon a new group of roses or a new irresistible idea.

I had only one thought in mind when the first 'room' was designed: wind protection. For Malmsbury lies on that treeless expanse just north of Woodend over the Great Dividing Range, known to local inhabitants as 'Pleurisy Plains'.

The area to the north of the house, where I planned to plant my first old roses, was the first to receive attention. The sheep were put out and a two metre high fence erected for about a hundred and fifty metres along the Calder Highway frontage where the wind howled in from the west. It was made of treated pine boards, set about ten centimetres apart to allow the wind to pass through rather than its hitting a solid obstacle.

Then it had to be covered. I tried — after considerable thought — ornamental grape on the outside, with roses — 'Lamarque', 'Buff Beauty', 'Nevada' and 'Penelope' — on the inside. It was the least successful of my windbreaks. The grapes looked spectacular in autumn, but came through the fence and twined themselves all round the roses, making pruning a long and tedious job each winter and severely inhibiting the growth of the roses. 'Lamarque', which remains one of my favourite roses, hated the bitter frosts, which cut it back harshly each winter. In fact, the only really successful part of the whole arrangement was 'Buff Beauty', which continues to cover itself with glory each year.

Then I went on a trip to the north-east of Victoria. We were driving along a gravel road in the Buffalo River Valley when we came upon 'American Pillar'. I did not know its name then. I don't think I cared. There it was, a mountain of it, five metres high, dense clusters of lipstick-pink, single flowers, with a white eye, completely covering a little, ruined weatherboard cottage. In retrospect, I strongly suspect that it was the weight of 'American Pillar' that ruined it.

I took masses of cuttings, with no particular intent, and they all struck. It was as I was potting up the dozens of little rooted plants a couple of months later that I realised what a wonderful windbreak it would make — hardy (it had certainly had no attention in the Buffalo valley), dense, quick-growing and impenetrable.

Wilhelm Kordes, the great German rose breeder, describes 'American Pillar' as being of 'a crude colour, lacking in feminine appeal!' And there is an entertaining passage in one of Vita Sackville-West's articles where she describes a neighbour as having planted roses right along his hundred metre boundary fence. She was delighted until they flowered. It was 'American Pillar' and she described it as 'a long, angry, startling streak' which brought tears to her eyes out of 'regret that so fine an idea should not have been more fastidiously carried out'.

I resolved to be more fastidious. I do not dislike 'American Pillar' as she did, but a hundred metres of it along my north fence might be overdoing it somewhat. I had plenty of little plants of the purple rambler 'Veilchenblau' which had sprung up along the front verandah, and plenty of that dear little, very double white rose with the pale pink buds, 'Félicité et Perpétue', which was to become one of my favourites. Named after two Carthaginian martyrs, it is almost evergreen, flowers prodigiously in early summer and flourishes in the windswept gardens of Wales and northern Scotland. I resolved to make a tapestry hedge of the three of them. We erected a cyclone wire frame, using bush poles instead of cut timber, and planted the roses about one and a half metres apart. In three years the support was no longer visible. The roses flower simultaneously and it is a joyous sight each December.

I had used rooted cuttings instead of grafted plants for the sake of economy —
I needed so many. But I realised later that ramblers do extraordinarily well on their
own roots. And there is no problem with suckers coming up from the root-stock.
If they did, they would be virtually impossible to eradicate under that thick,
thorny mass.

So successful was this as a windbreak that I tried another on the south fence,
but there I planted the fence thickly with damsons first, as this possibly faces our
worst wind. The ramblers grow all through the damsons and the rich blue fruit
is a marvellous splash of unexpected colour in autumn long after the roses have
finished. The common hawthorn, too, *Crataegus monogyna*, forms a good support
for a rambler hedge, as do the little cherry plums which seed themselves so readily
and flower so briefly in earliest spring. I never see them without thinking of the
beautiful poem of John Shaw Neilson:

> It is the white Plum Tree
> Seven days fair
> As a bride goes combing
> Her joy of hair.

I find it difficult to believe that someone who wrote with such sensitivity about
birds and flowers should have worked, for a great part of his life, as a labourer
in stone quarries. He should, most certainly, have had a garden.

If I were planting such a hedge again I would probably, with greater experience
and wider choice available to me, use 'Francis E. Lester' in place of 'American Pillar'.
Like so many of our best roses, this was a chance seedling, probably from the Hybrid
Musk rose, 'Kathleen', and named after an American rosarian who rescued as many
of the old roses as he could from the early settlements of the gold rush days in
California. Very bushy and dense, it is literally covered, in early summer, with small,
single roses in clusters, rather like apple blossom, and they have a scent which
fills the garden (completely refuting the surprisingly commonly held misconcep-
tion that the more petals a rose has, the stronger the scent!). Later it sets little
scarlet hips which hang in bunches well into winter.

I planted another section of the Calder Highway fence later, just with 'Albertine'.
Certainly one of the loveliest of all ramblers, it covers itself with soft, salmon-pink
blooms in late spring. Visitors often commented on the scent as soon as they came
in the gate. I have a longstanding love affair with 'Albertine' and find myself putting
in more cuttings every year with no particular purpose in mind. Bred in France
in 1921, she will tolerate very harsh conditions — I planted my first one in a shaded
corner not four metres from the trunk of one of the old pine trees. She flowered
there as well as she did anywhere else and made a rather dreary corner a thing
of beauty. Somehow, when the little cutting-grown plants are potted on, I always
seem to find a spot where I could use another 'Albertine'.

The windbreak fences became for me the chief glory of Bleak House. They do
their job. They have enclosed the garden and divided it into compartments. They
have cut down the wind. For sheer prodigality of bloom there is nothing to equal
them.

There is no need to prune these big ramblers. They could not flower more generously than they do. Unless they are getting out of control, pulling down their

supports or taking up more space than has been allotted to them, they are best left alone to get on with it. If you do need to prune, it is best done straight after flowering as most of them flower on last year's wood.

We get little or no wind from the east and I did not want to block the fine view across the paddocks with a high fence. We had no need to provide a 'borrowed landscape' such as the designers advocate. We had our own.

So I resolved on hedges along the east side of the garden. Buoyed up by the success of *R. rugosa alba* along the front fence — it was into its second year and doing nicely — and seeking some semblance of uniformity, I decided to use another Rugosa here. I wanted a single one. The doubles are lovely but they set no fruit and these great scarlet hips are one of the joys of autumn. 'Fru Dagmar Hastrup' the pale pink single, has splendid hips, but she is probably the lowest growing of the Rugosas, too low to form an effective hedge in this sort of position. And so I decided on what is probably the most vigorous of them all, 'Scabrosa'. It is not my favourite colour — a deep, rose-magenta — but this is tempered by the contrast of the dense, cream-coloured stamens.

I planted twenty of them — and now have more than I can count. I planted grafted plants but the birds have carried the seed from those splendid big hips and they come up each year all over the garden. Some of the seedlings have come more or less true to type — we have had vast numbers of little 'Scabrosas' and little *R. rugosa albas* — but there are also a number of hybrids, some of them quite fine. One in particular, which from its position and its appearance I think is probably a cross between 'Scabrosa' and the deep purple 'Roseraie de l'Haÿ', I have become very fond of. It has flowered consistently for the last four or five years and grown into a fine bush, so fine that I am tempted to go through the necessary procedures and register it.

The Rugosas are among the hardiest of all roses. They seem impervious to wind. They do not object to frost. More than most roses, they tolerate wet feet. I have seen them growing happily in sandy soil at the seaside, lashed by salt-laden winds. They are grown successfully in the very shaded, damp gardens on the slopes of Mt Macedon. In Europe they are used extensively along motorways and in public parks where they receive very little attention.

They strike relatively easily from cuttings, but the problem of suckers then becomes almost insuperable, so that I would never grow them on their own roots except in a paddock or to cover a steep bank, or, with *Rosa wichuraiana*, round the walls of a dam.

A year or so after the planting of the 'Scabrosa' hedge a branch of the National Trust needed a quantity of roses as table decoration for a big function. It was late autumn and a quick walk round the garden convinced me that we had nothing in flower in sufficient quantitites. Finally I picked an armful of 'Scabrosa' hips. The Trust sent me a photograph later, showing those great scarlet berries in a silver bowl on a polished table. They looked superb.

There is an old, single paeony, whose name I do not know. It is exactly the colour of 'Scabrosa' and has the same rich creamy stamens. The two flower together at the very beginning of spring. The paeony is easily propagated from root cuttings. I took a few each year. It was my ambition to grow them all along as a border beneath the 'Scabrosa' hedge.

A climbing 'Iceberg'.
(Drawing by Anita Barley)

Climbing Roses

8

I had taken the advice of Edna Walling and 'defined my boundaries' — at least for this first part of the garden. As time went by they were repeatedly pushed out as a little more of the paddock was taken into the garden. But for this section, my fences were built, my ramblers planted and my Rugosa hedge. Within these boundaries all I had was a flat, bare rectangle of sheep paddock.

The first essential, it seemed to me, in a flat garden is height. In the corner nearest the house, the south-west corner, was an old windmill which was at present the only water supply. Beside it was a tank on a high stand and an old well. I had a second high tank installed, as water was obviously always going to be a problem. On the first of these tank-stands I planted the little creamy-yellow Banksia rose, because it is the first to flower in spring, because I love the dense clusters of tiny roses, because it is thornless and because, being virtually evergreen, it would hide the ugly iron legs of the tank-stand the year round. On the other side of the same stand I planted 'Wedding Day', the first of the many little white single roses I fell in love with. It flowers much later than the Banksia, grows incredibly quickly and covers the tank-stand in glory towards the middle of December. The flowers are followed by clusters of tiny scarlet hips which hang on for months. And here, already, was my first departure from my resolve to concentrate on old roses. 'Wedding Day' was bred in 1950!

With these two I had most of the things I wanted for this prominent position, but no scent. So on the second tank-stand I planted *Wisteria sinensis* and the creamy coloured climbing rose, 'Devoniensis', known also, I expect because of its colour and the texture of the petals, as 'The Magnolia rose'. This flowers simultaneously with the wisteria and almost as early as the Banksia. Like many early Tea roses, it tends to hang its head, so is best planted where one can look up to it and appreciate the rich, full blooms. It has one of the strongest perfumes in the garden, and puts on another lovely display in the autumn. I think this corner was one of the happiest combinations at Bleak House.

We built up the old stone wall around the well, covered the opening with wire mesh to prevent children (or dogs) from falling in and round it we planted a tiny, white double rose which I found growing vigorously in the Daylesford cemetery, and masses of pale yellow iris, with a few mid-blue ones to pick up the colour of the wisteria. On the base of the windmill itself I planted *Clematis montana*, resolving firmly to cut it back each year, before it became entangled with the head.

But all of this so desirable height was in the south-west corner. On the diagonally opposite north-east corner was a gate which led into the paddock. I resolved to take a path from the windmill to the gate with three pergolas built at intervals along it. Here would be support for more climbers.

Fortunately I did not want a straight path, for this is bluestone country and the stone is nowhere very far beneath the surface. So throughout the garden the shape of beds and the route of paths is determined by the position of the huge bluestone slabs, which are quite immovable.

I arranged with a local man to build the pergolas — simple, unpretentious structures, as befits a country garden. The first was something of a disaster. When I had bought Bleak House some of the verandah posts were rotted at the base and some were missing, so I had replaced them all. The old ones were turned and pretty and the builders had stacked them away in the barn for possible future use. They seemed perfect for this purpose.

The verandah roof was very low so the posts were short. I asked the old handyman doing the job to use six of them for the first pergola. 'But set them in concrete,' I said, 'to give extra height, and strength to support the weight of the roses.'

When I returned next weekend there was the first pergola, beautifully constructed and already painted. The posts had been set in concrete, as requested, but *below* ground level. Even I, who am barely one metre sixty tall, had to bend my head to walk under. There was no way that Albert, who was doing the job, could walk through at all, he being something over one metre eighty, but he was quite content to go round!

The painting, too, was a mistake. The white woodwork was very effective for a few years, but by the time the paint needed renewing, the roses had grown so big that painting was impossible. I had to choose between cutting down the roses or leaving the pergolas unpainted. Of course I chose the latter, but later pergolas were built of treated pine and simply oiled.

On the first of these pergolas I planted what is, for many reasons, one of my favourite roses and one I could not possibly do without: the lovely 'Madame Alfred Carrière'. I have searched through every rose book I own in the hope of finding out who she was, this woman who had such a very lovely rose named for her, but I have found no mention of her. Her rose is almost white, with the most delicate pink blush. She blooms from spring to the end of autumn. She is richly scented and the foliage is lush and seems to suffer very little from any disease. She grows over six metres high on a wall at Sissinghurst, and Gertrude Jekyll grew her as a hedge, trained along wires. She is equally happy grown simply as a large, lax bush. She is excellent for picking and, best of all, she will continue to flower happily in semi-shaded conditions. My pergola was shaded almost until noon by the house and the huge old pine tree on its north-east corner. It worried 'Madame Alfred' not a jot!

With her, because the flowers are so exquisite and the associations so rich, I planted 'Souvenir de la Malmaison' — visions of the Empress Josephine and the garden she made round the hunting lodge she so loved — the English, so the story goes, even lifted their embargo on French ships during the Napoleonic wars to allow passage for those ships carrying roses for the garden at Malmaison. Inseparable from it, too, is the name of Pierre-Joseph Redouté, 'the Raphael of Flowers' who spent the greater part of his life painting Josephine's roses; and the Russian Grand Duke who, on his visit to Malmaison some years after Josephine's death, bestowed its name on the delicate pink, richly quartered rose he admired there.

But being transported to the Antipodes was not to her taste. She turned out to be one of the most vexatious, frustrating and infuriating roses in the garden. Like the little girl who had a little curl, when she is good she is superlatively good and when she is bad, (which is every spring) she is horrid. The buds ball and turn brown at the slightest hint of rain or too much sudden heat (which, of course, in Victoria is our typical spring weather) and instead of being a thing of joy she is something we walk past quickly with heads averted, planning to return and cut off every hideous brown bud. But in the autumn, as if to make amends, she puts on the most glorious show, a profusion of palest pink, quartered, scented blooms which would soften the hardest heart. And so I continue to grow her.

On the second pergola I planted 'Albéric Barbier', which proved to be so rampant that a couple of years later we had to roof the pergola to give him adequate support. He puts on a perfectly breathtaking display of creamy-white blooms in early summer. The glossy green foliage is lovely all the year round. In his enthusiasm he climbed in no time to the top of the pergola, over the top and down the other side — a feat which few roses can achieve. Here he became entangled with the beautiful, salmon-pink single climber, 'Meg', which I had planted on the other side. When restrained, he set off instead across the lawn (a euphemism, this, for the paddock grasses we mowed, having insufficient water to maintain a lawn) and I earmarked him for future use as a groundcover. 'Meg' is another of the moderns who looks as if she must have been with us for decades. But romance is in her breeding. Released in England in 1954, she is thought to be one of the offspring of 'Madame Butterfly'.

On the third pergola I decided I must have something which would flower recurrently, so settled for 'Sea Foam', that most versatile of roses, equally happy as a climber (he climbs to the very top of a *Cornus kousa* on the front drive at Bolobek), a ground cover, pegged down to cover banks, or as a big sprawling shrub. The individual blooms are not striking, but he produces them with such generosity, great foaming trusses of them for months on end, and he would be a good foil for the lipstick-pink of 'Zéphirine Drouhin', which I wanted to plant on the other side. Thornless and recurrent flowering, the latter was nevertheless something of a disappointment. She is, like all the Bourbon roses, prone to black spot, but her main trouble was wet feet. The garden slopes almost imperceptibly towards this north-east corner and in our wet winters 'Zéphirine Drouhin' stood with her feet in water for months at a time, something no rose will tolerate. Laying drains in our great shelves of underground rock was a prospect not to be contemplated, but later we raised the bed a foot or so and she responded immediately.

A path must lead somewhere. This one led to the gate into the paddock. To give it added emphasis the path was widened to make a circle in front of the gate, from which other paths were to lead off. In the centre of this circle I placed a very large celadon jar as a focal point. In the jar and round its base I planted the tiny white ground cover rose, 'Snow Carpet'. It lies flat to the ground, has diminutive glossy green leaves and tiny double white roses the size of a five cent piece.

So this part of my garden now had shape and form. To this point I had not needed to have recourse to the big rose nurseries or the commercial growers. I had decided to grow as many of my climbers as possible on their own roots.

Most climbers strike readily from cuttings which can be taken at almost any time of the year – in fact, whenever a kind friend offers them to you. I have found straight after Christmas a good time for these, as long as you water the pots religiously every day and give them some protection from the hot sun. In fact, Boxing Day cuttings of the big ramblers became something of a ritual.

Very fortunately for Victorian gardeners, there is a picturesque, country nursery just outside Castlemaine which specialises in old roses, cottage garden plants and the older varieties of fruit trees. Centred round a four-roomed sandstone cottage built in the gold rush days, Badgers' Keep is surrounded by a true cottage garden: herbs, roses, perennials and fruit trees intermingled, with winding paths, stone walls and a chamomile lawn under a spreading mulberry tree. And it offers a wide selection of old roses grown from cuttings, as well as commercially produced grafted plants. The proprietors are true plantsmen (I wonder whether the feminists would insist on 'plantspersons'?) with an extensive knowledge gleaned over twenty years of running a nursery, a genuine love of plants and gardens and an unwavering insistence on correct nomenclature – all things often lacking in nurseries dedicated simply to profit.

It was from here that I bought all the climbers I needed for this part of the garden. They were healthy little plants, container-grown, and although they take a little while to catch up with the two-year-old, grafted plants available in many nurseries, the end result is immensely satisfying – strong, vigorous plants, and no suckers!

For the rest of the initial planting in this section of the garden I decided to use the grafted plants. Suckers are less of a problem under bushes than under ramblers, and I was still working in Melbourne and was not at Bleak House often enough to cosset too many little plants. This decision made, I sent away for catalogues to the big retail growers, Deane Ross in Adelaide and Roy Rumsey in Sydney.

Nigella (love-in-the-mist).

The First Rose Order 9

'Madame de Sancy de Parabère', 'Baronne Henriette de Snoy', 'Omar Khayám', 'Tricolore de Flandre' – I delighted in their very names, exotic, evocative, conjuring up visions of distant places, other climes, other centuries.

'La Reine Victoria' – soft pink, fragrant cupped blooms named for a young Queen; there is 'Maiden's Blush', known in France as 'Cuisse de Nymphe'; and 'Rosa Mundi', striped and seductive, introduced to our gardens in the sixteenth century and named after the lovely mistress of Henry II. Then there is the beautiful sport of 'Souvenir de la Malmaison' named 'Souvenir de St Anne's', found by Lady Ardilaun in the garden of her castle in Ireland and later cherished and propagated by Lady Moores. Pomp and ceremony enter with 'Cardinal de Richelieu', Minister to Louis XIII for eighteen years, a rich velvety purplish-red; and a hint of something sinister with 'Robert le Diable', a menacing figure in French history and legend. He achieved new fame as the 'hero' of Meyerbeer's spectacular opera which took Paris by storm in 1831. His rose is deep violet, cerise and crimson.

Where does one start with a bare paddock in Australia at one's disposal and such a wealth to choose from? One thing was certain: there would be no place in my garden for 'Frilly Dilly' or 'Sexy Rexy'!

I returned to the volume which had been the catalyst for all of this, Gordon Edwards's *Wild and Old Garden Roses*, and read it again from cover to cover. It is not a textbook. Much as I needed to do so, I learnt nothing of botany from its pages. But I put it down with the conviction that here was a man who had found a great love.

My catalogues arrived from Ross and from Rumsey, both growers who sell direct to the public rather than supplying retail nurseries. Both were informative but I needed fuller information than any catalogue can supply. I needed books. It was no use borrowing them from libraries. I needed to be able to refer to them constantly. I decided on a trip to the Bookshop of Margareta Webber, acknowledged then as Melbourne's leading source of garden books and owned by Neil Robertson, a knowledgeable and dedicated gardener.

From Neil I sought advice. He agreed that a good reference library is an essential, even for an expert gardener. For a novice such as I was, it was a *sine qua non*. And so was born another passion, one that tends to become an addiction and keeps one constantly poor.

I returned home that day with the three volumes of Graham Stuart Thomas, whose name is almost synonymous with old roses: *The Old Shrub Roses, Shrub Roses of Today* and *Climbing Roses Old and New*. In these volumes I found the accumulated knowledge of a lifetime, an intimate acquaintance with the roses themselves and expert advice on how to get the very best results from them. For many years Garden Adviser to the National Trust in England, Thomas has designed and advised on many great gardens, among them what is, perhaps, for rosarians the most inspiring of all, Mottisfont Abbey. Here, sheltered behind the high, mellow, old brick walls that enclosed what was the monks' kitchen garden, Graham Stuart Thomas has designed a garden which is a veritable museum of roses. But I was not to see this until some years later.

These three volumes, the start of my garden library, have remained my bible, despite the fact that gloriously illustrated rose books have come on the market since and I certainly would not be without the English hybridist Peter Beales's *Classic Roses* and *Twentieth Century Roses*. For sheer practical commonsense local knowledge I bought Dr A. S. Thomas's *Growing Roses . . . in Australia*. The Foundation President of the National Rose Society of Australia, there is nothing he does not know about growing roses in our conditions, so very different from those of England. For good reading, I sought for but could not find Nancy Steen's *The Charm of Old Roses*. A New Zealander, she tells of her travels round New Zealand and her search for the roses planted there by the early settlers, especially the missionaries, and of her later travel in Europe and her attempts to identify the roses she had found. Knowing of my interest, a dear friend gave me her copy and it has a place of honour on my shelves.

Equipped with these, I sat down to pore over my catalogues. Before I could begin to fill in an order form I had to decide whether I was going to plant only old roses or a mixture of old and new. All my inclinations were towards the old roses. On analysis, I decided that this was not for purely sentimental or nostalgic reasons. I did not want a formal garden. I did not want roses and bare earth. What I wanted was roses as shrubs, big, generous, exuberant bushes which could hold their own with other shrubs in a border, which would be attractive as shrubs even when not in flower and would not be stiff, bare sticks for a good many months of each year. I wanted bulbs and perennials and ground covers with my roses. I wanted hips in the autumn. I wanted scent. I wanted subtle colours. The orange and vermilion of some of the newer roses I could well do without. And all of these things pointed to old roses. So, for the time being, I passed over the pages in the catalogues devoted to modern roses.

It was at this point, while immersed in rose books and catalogues, that I came home one evening in Melbourne to find among my mail an envelope marked Shire of Kyneton. I pushed it aside – correspondence from the local council is rarely exciting. While preparing the dinner I returned to it and read, with total lack of interest, that the Shire was considering three possible sites for a new municipal tip, the present one having been exhausted. Obviously a routine communication to all ratepayers. There followed three Lot numbers. I dropped the letter into the wastepaper basket. Tips hold a singular lack of interest for me.

It was as I was putting the plates on the table that a terrible thought struck me. Lot 256 was the Lot number of Bleak House. Frantically I retrieved the letter from the wastepaper basket, smoothed it out and read it again. There it was in black and white: Lot No 256. Perhaps I was mistaken about the Lot number of Bleak House. I ran upstairs, tipped all the contents of the Bleak House file on the floor and hunted feverishly for the Title documents.

There was no mistake. This was no routine communication to all ratepayers. Bleak House was under consideration as the possible site for the new tip. I felt sick, furious, indignant and tearful by turns. Could I, in this democratic country, be compelled to hand over, and for such an ignominious purpose, something which had already absorbed so many weeks and months of working and planning, and had already become such a great love, the object of my dreams? The letter spoke of compulsory acquisition and added reassuringly that owners would be compensated.

I reached for the telephone book and rang the Shire Secretary. Yes, he said, it was correct. The relevant authorities had inspected the land some time ago – without my knowledge, I interjected sharply. Yes, that had not then been considered necessary. They had reached the conclusion after inspection that it would be the perfect site for a tip – it was, of the three under consideration, the preferred site. The old quarries, you see, and the swamp – he called it 'swamp' with a note of contempt – that extensive area of wet-land, home to the swans and the mountain duck and the plovers, which I had planned to develop as a safe haven for them. The land was useless, he added, hadn't been farmed successfully for years. And as for the house, it had been established beyond doubt when the Hospital put it on the market, that the house was fit only for the bulldozer.

Had he seen it recently, I asked. Well, no, not in the last twelve months or so, but he'd known the place for forty years, man and boy. And the tone of his voice implied that his knowledge would be far better founded than mine. And he was a Realist, which I clearly was not.

I spoke of the renovation of the house. Yes, well, a touch of paint couldn't remedy those defects. The only sensible solution would be to pull it down and start again.

I spoke of the garden. Nothing, he assured me, would grow on those plains. The soil was no good. There was inadequate water in summer and a deluge every winter. Besides, the place was overrun by rabbits. If I wanted to grow flowers (an unmistakably contemptuous note crept in here), why didn't I take the compensation offered and buy a little block in the Dandenongs?

I spoke of the beauty of the old quarries, and heard, without any possibility of mistake, a snort of incredulous laughter.

Had I been growing pigs instead of roses, I might have got somewhere. As it was, I was obviously wasting my time. From him I got the phone numbers of every member of the Kyneton Council.

Over the next week I rang each in turn. Most did not want to know about it. The site of the tip was obviously a matter of no importance to them. They simply wanted a decision made so that it could go ahead without delay. One or two were vaguely sympathetic but assured me that, much as they would like to help, it was really out of their hands.

My despair knew no bounds. I put away the rose books and catalogues and spent Saturday and Sunday walking over the quarries, picturing them full of abandoned cars, old tyres, household refuse, every kind of filth mankind seems to generate in such unlimited quantities.

A letter arrived from the Shire Secretary. There was no intention of taking the house. I could still live there if I wanted and there would be four hectares or so where I could grow flowers.

Marvellous, I thought. A rose garden overlooking a tip! The perfume of the roses vying with the stench from the tip for ascendancy.

And then I had a visit from a friend, a lawyer. He was sympathetic but carefully non-committal. After lunch we went for a walk over the paddocks, skirted the quarries, climbed through a fence and wandered down to the Campaspe River. The water was clear and shallow and the banks overhung with willows, home to nesting ducks. There are trout in the Campaspe and Bill was watching for rising fish, obviously with an eye to a quiet afternoon's fishing. I was filled with a deep despondency and found it difficult to enter into the spirit of the thing.

A few weeks later I had another letter from the Shire Secretary. It had been determined, he said, by the State Rivers and Water Authority that the site would be unsuitable, as the water from the swamp drained into the Campaspe River and flowed thence to Lake Eppalock which supplied drinking water to Bendigo. It had been decided, in consequence, to take the site adjoining the Kyneton Cemetery for the location of the new tip. He regretted any inconvenience I might have been caused.

It was never discussed between Bill and me and to this day I do not know how it came about. With a feeling of elation I picked up my rose catalogue again, took out a sheet of paper and started writing my first order.

Lobularia maritima.

First Choices 10

The roses I ordered that first year are, for the most part, the ones I would order still if I were starting a new garden. Repeated readings of the books I had bought initially and increasingly frequent additions to my gardening library ensured that.

Among those I love best are the Gallicas, which have been in English gardens for centuries. To be sure, they bloom for only three or four weeks in the year, and for the rest of the time their bushes are not remarkable. But what a glorious flowering it is!

There are such subtle, mysterious colours, blendings of mauve, purple, dusky pink and grey. I would plant together 'Anaïs Ségales', 'Jenny Duval', 'Belle de Crécy', and 'Cardinal de Richelieu'. And I would use nepeta as a border rather than box which seemed too formal for a country garden. The soft mauve flowers and greyish foliage of the nepeta would set off to perfection the colours in the roses and, if cut back after the first flowering, it flowers again after the roses are over.

'Anaïs Ségales' I looked for in vain at first. Nancy Steen had found her growing in abundance near the early settlements in New Zealand, especially near the mission stations, often having survived a hundred years or so of total neglect. I found her finally, but too late to include in this planting.

It was schoolgirl memories of reading and re-reading *The Three Musketeers*, rather than any knowledge of French history, which ensured a place in the garden for 'Cardinal de Richelieu'; that, and his rich, dark purple colouring, described by Graham Stuart Thomas as resembling 'the bloom of a dark grape'. I planted him beside the grey-leaved *Pyrus salicifolia* with *Stachys lanata* syn. *S. byzantina* round his feet, and found him infinitely pleasing.

'Complicata', her large single pink blooms with their golden stamens borne on long, arching canes, needs space. Her origins are unknown, nor can I imagine where the name came from, for she is in appearance one of the least complicated of roses. If she is planted alone as a specimen shrub the effect is arresting.

I could not have a garden without 'Charles de Mills', rich, darkest red and so many-petalled. Like many of the Gallicas, if grown on his own roots he quickly forms a dense thicket. I have envied Nancy Steen her findings of roadside roses in New Zealand and thought that it was only in old cemeteries that we were likely to find such riches. But recently, driving along a country road near Woodend, I came upon a great thicket of 'Charles de Mills' in full flower, and not a house or a garden to be seen.

A rose of great antiquity, found originally in Europe and South-west Asia, *Rosa gallica officinalis* ('The Apothecary's Rose'), brings with it suggestions of walled monastery gardens. Its bright cherry-coloured blooms are borne in dense masses on bushes seldom more than a metre high. Used in medicine it certainly was, perhaps because it retains its scent so well. There are historical associations also, as it is believed to have been the Red Rose of Lancaster.

With it I planted its sport, one of the best loved of all old roses, 'Rosa Mundi'. Of the same cherry colour, it is striped with white and palest pink and is said to have received its name in honour of Rosamund, the lovely mistress of Henry II. Major Lawrence Johnston planted it as a hedge round the kitchen garden at Hidcote – an unforgettable sight.

Then to the Albas. No words can capture the delicious scent, or describe the loveliness of the delicate colouring of these roses, with their matt green foliage. Nor can any gardener ask for more vigorous or long-lived plants than these.

They came into our gardens long ago, and in most cases their origins and dates are unknown. I chose *R. alba maxima* (The Great White Rose), and the pale pink 'Chloris', also known as 'Dew of the Morning'. And at their feet I planted the white form of *Helleborus orientalis* and a variegated ajuga (*Ajuga reptans* 'Variegata').

'Königin von Dänemarck' grows to two metres. Her delicate pink flowers and soft grey-green foliage look splendid against a stone wall. I planted her against the side of the house and each year for three years a diminutive pardalote came and built her nest in a little hole in the stone just behind her. With her I planted 'Félicité Parmentier' and the ivory-coloured 'Madame Legras de St Germain' and, of course, 'Great Maiden's Blush', which has been in English gardens since before the fifteenth century. And if you have visited Sissinghurst, you cannot see 'Madame Plantier' without remembering how she grows to the top of the old apple trees in the orchard there.

The Damasks quickly became favourites. Their very light green, fresh, young foliage is one of the earliest delights of spring. An eminent scientist of my acquaintance recently grubbed out all his Tea roses and replaced them with Damasks,

'Clair Matin' as a pillar rose with *Chrysanthemum ptarmiciflorum* and *Pyrus salicifolia* as a background to 'News'.

Our first pond with *Iris kaempferi*. The white rose is 'Swany'.

'Clair Matin' with foxgloves.

Little Portion with 'Mrs Herbert Stevens' on the arch.

Little Portion with 'Swany' in the foreground.

'Daydream' not 'Pliable' — enough for a maypole — with Little Portion in the background.

because he is convinced that the flocks of cockatoos which beset our gardens in spring do not find the Damask foliage to their taste, whereas they appear to regard the young reddish foliage of the Teas as a gourmet's delight.

'Ispahan' I love. It is one of the first to flower and produces its soft pink, deliciously fragrant blooms over a long period. And it seemed to mind less than most the harsh conditions of the plains of Central Victoria. And 'Leda' or 'The Painted Damask', with its pale pink blooms each outlined in crimson — best in the front of the border, as the bush seldom grows above a metre.

I included 'Kazanlik' (*R. damascena trigintipetala*) for its history. It was grown in great quantities in Bulgaria for the making of attar of roses. I found it something of a disappointment. The bush is straggly and the pale pink roses not remarkable. I have never found time for the making of potpourri and, in any case, to me even the scent of 'Kazanlik' is surpassed by that of others. I think I would agree with Gordon Edwards who dismissed it with the blunt statement: 'It has no garden value.'

I could not agree with him, however, about 'Quatre Saisons' (*R. damascena bifera*) which, he said, produces 'very fragrant double flowers of poor quality' and 'qualifies as ancient history — pre-Roman — rather than as garden value'. Perhaps it is happier in our warmer climate, for I could nearly always find a flower on it from early summer to autumn — soft pink, simple, rather ragged flowers of great charm. I cannot speak so warmly of its sport, 'Quatre Saisons Blanc Mousseux', whose white flowers I found sparse and often discoloured, perhaps by the heat.

Despite its historical associations, I was disappointed, too, in *R. damascena versicolor*, known as 'York and Lancaster'. I found it straggly and the pink and white flowers undistinguished and washed-out compared with those of 'Rosa Mundi'. Perhaps it is happier in England, or needs better conditions than I could give it. I saw a splendid bush of it at Hidcote.

'Hebe's Lip', I must confess, I ordered for the name alone. When my roses finally arrived and I unpacked them, I found 'Hebe's Lip' in a sad state. The scion had quite broken off from the understock. I was about to discard it, but on an impulse put the scion in as a cutting in the traditional mixture of three parts coarse sand to one part of wet peat moss. I watched it carefully for a few months. It did not turn black, but neither did it show any sign of making new roots. I pushed it to the back of the shelf in the glasshouse and, after a while, forgot about it. It was the following winter before I looked at it again and there, through the drainage holes at the bottom of the pot, protruded little white roots. I planted it out the following spring (fifteen months after its arrival) and it rewarded me a few months later with two little creamy-white blooms edged in deep rose. Like a delicate child (or a sheep which has gone astray) it has received ever since very favoured treatment and has responded accordingly.

But the undoubted Queen of the Damasks is 'Madame Hardy'. Indeed she is regarded by many rosarians as the loveliest of all white roses. The flowers are a good size, very full, and pure white with a distinctive green button eye, and they are carried profusely on a shrub which easily attains a height of one and a half metres. I never see a bush of 'Madame Hardy' without thinking of the English rosarian, Peter Beales, who said he would gladly exchange a whole field of 'Iceberg' for one bloom of 'Madame Hardy'.

Then there are the Centifolias — the Rose of a Hundred Petals, the Cabbage Rose, the Painter's Rose — great, gaunt, straggly, thorny bushes many of them, but such full, tightly packed, rich blooms, and such a fragrance!

Some of them, like the deep magenta-coloured 'Tour de Malakoff', which can grow to over two metres, really need some sort of support — a wall, or a tree, or a tripod — and he is certainly sturdy enough to have a clematis growing through him. And some of them, like the adorable 'de Meaux' and 'Petite de Hollande' are almost miniatures — suitable for growing in a container. *R. centifolia variegata* with the charming popular name of 'Village Maid' is one of the loveliest of the variegated roses — softest pink and white irregular stripes, and the flowers borne in great clusters on long arching branches which really do need to be shortened back in July if they are not to trail on the ground with the weight of the flowers.

And a place of honour must surely be reserved for 'Fantin-Latour', that mystery rose who came from we know not where. Suffice it to say that it is aptly named for the great French painter, for it is the very epitome of romance.

And here I thought I should stop in that my first year. The Mosses and early Tea roses, the Hybrid Perpetuals and Hybrid Musks would have to wait for another twelve months. For I was still working full-time in Melbourne with only weekends and occasional holidays to devote to my garden, and it would take every bit of time I had to transform my sheep paddock into prepared beds before the roses arrived in mid-winter.

Crab-apple.

Preliminaries

11

There was much to be done before the roses arrived in June. I had read enough to know that my virgin soil had to be deeply dug, and manure added (if available), in plenty of time for it to break down before planting time. So I enlisted the help of Albert, the old fellow who had built the pergolas, and we set to work.

Across the bottom of the garden, the north boundary, was a huge pile of rocks. They were big rocks, too big for Albert and me to move. The ground everywhere was full of stone and I suppose that, years ago, this paddock had once been ploughed and the stones put in a heap, as they were thrown up, to be out of the way.

They were very much in our way now, and posed a problem. In the end we decided they would have to stay there but we would move those we could and form them into a raised rock garden. This we did over the next couple of weekends and were tolerably pleased with our efforts.

But this was not the whole situation. The rocks were so big that we had pockets fifty to sixty centimeters deep which would have to be filled with soil.

With a touching faith in the local suppliers and a total ignorance of the varying types of topsoil, I ordered a load from a local landscape supplier. It rained the day it was delivered and then followed three very hot days. It was heavy black soil and, by the time we came to work it the following Saturday, it had set like concrete. So this was not the answer. There had to be a better way.

My mind went back to Cathlaw. On my first visit there, as Betty Ross-Watt showed me round the garden, I had remarked on the many very pretty ponds. She had laughed. 'Yes,' she said, 'my mother was the garden designer and she was always making new beds. It was too expensive to buy topsoil so whenever we wanted more we just dug a new pond!'

Here was our solution. So Albert and I set to work and dug our first pond in the middle of our rock garden. We dug it as deep as we could. Then we selected the flattest pieces of stone and lined it, setting the stone in concrete to which we added a waterproofing compound and some dark grey colouring matter.

I wanted a rose to grow round the pond so I added to my initial rose order two plants of the Rugosa ground cover rose, *R. paulii*. It grows horizontally and is pro-digiously prickly which makes training it something of an ordeal. But it bears a mass of very pretty, pure white, single flowers with golden stamens. Unfortunately it is one of the few Rugosas which does not flower recurrently, but the foliage is handsome and it is as hardy as all its relations and I was delighted with it. At the back of the pond against the fence I planted several clumps of lad's love (*Artemisia abrotanum*); its grey-green foliage made a good foil for the white roses and it is hardy enough to need very little attention beyond a hard cut back each year.

Then I made the most terrible mistake – one I paid for dearly for years to follow. I hired a fellow with a rotary hoe and got him to dig my beds for me. He did a splendid job, digging deep and thoroughly and exercising exemplary restraint when his hoe struck rock.

But country gardens are full of weed. My most prevalent ones were bindweed (for which I came to harbour the most intense hatred), twitch – a near relative of couch, docks and sorrel. Every piece of every one of them cut up by the rotary hoe took root and flourished. I had committed the elementary mistake of not poison-ing the weeds first.

I attacked them, too late, with the gardener's best friend and indispensable ally, Round-up, which acts through the chlorophyll in the foliage and leaves no residual poison in the soil. I do not like using poisons. In fact, I hate it, but after a year or so of painstaking hand-weeding I decided to compromise and bought my first five litres of Round-up. It worked well on the sorrel and I discovered that sorrel is also somewhat discouraged by generous applications of lime. Round-up works less well on well-established docks, which I concluded really have to be weeded out. It appears to work well on couch and bindweed but these are so deep-rooted that over and over again I found, just as I dared to hope they were gone, they would emerge triumphantly once again. I came upon a marvellous little book at this time called *The Labours of Forty-eight Years of William Lawson*, published in London in 1618. It contained, amongst other pearls of wisdom, the following:

> The Gardner had not need be an idle or lazie lubber, for so your Orchard will not prosper. There will ever be something to doe. Weeds are alwaise growing.

Here was the voice of experience!

Hand-weeding and deep mulching became a routine. I started with a magnificent supply of old cow manure. The hospital's last tenant at Bleak House before it became uninhabitable was a farmer who had conducted a Jersey stud. There was an old tumbledown barn across from the house and in this, so I was reliably informed, he had housed his bulls. I concluded he must have been a 'lazie lubber' for he had never bothered to clean out his barn and by the time he left the property, discouraged understandably by the lack of water and power and the dilapidated state of the fences, the manure was over a metre deep.

The builders had shaken their heads at the sight of it, condemned the barn as beyond repair and suggested putting a match to the whole thing. This suggestion I had firmly repudiated, for this was to me a treasure richer than gold.

Painstakingly Albert and I barrowed it on to the beds. It took many weekends, for the barn was a good size. Indeed I did not reach the end of it for over two years. But it gave the roses a wonderful start.

One other thing I wanted to do before the roses came was to plant a few trees. Not many, for roses like an open sunny position – they must have at least four or five hours of sun each day – and I could not afford to plant trees which might, in time, grow huge and block the sun. But I wanted a group on the western corner – no one really wants our harsh western sun – and I wanted to screen out the Calder Highway as much as possible. The five big pine trees which were there when I bought the property were all on the south and east sides of the house. To the north, where the main rose garden was to be, there was only one aged mis-shapen willow, broken and battered by a century of storms. I engaged a local tree-lopper (I'm sure he would not have laid claim to the title of 'tree-surgeon') with the colourful name of Paddy McGuinness, to cut out the dead wood and restore it to some semblance of symmetry. Paddy turned out to be just as his name suggested. Cheerful and charming, he hacked away with a will and my poor old willow was in no time reduced to a forlorn-looking, three metre high stump. In Paddy's defence I must add that within twelve months it had shot and grown prodigiously and no longer had any real need of the evergreen climber *Rosa × fortuneana* which I had planted hastily to hide its nakedness.

To link this part of the garden with the adjoining front garden I bought (being always impatient) two advanced silver birches (*Betula pendula*). These I planted in the corner near the windmill. A couple of weeks later I bought a potted rose from a local nursery and in the pot were six diminutive self-sown birch seedlings. Rather than throw them away, I planted them – straight into the ground – in the vicinity of the two advanced trees. If even one survived, I thought, it would form an attractive little group. All six survived and flourished mightily. Within eighteen months they had overtaken the advanced trees and it became a delightful little copse.

Influenced by Maria, I planted, in the western corner, two *Parrotia persica* and in this corner also two golden ashes (*Fraxinus excelsior* 'Aurea'). Then, as a specimen tree, and in memory of very happy student days in Germany, I planted a linden (*Tilia × europaea*). It did not like our hot, dry summers and made deplorably slow progress.

I had been given, the Christmas before, by a dear friend and valued colleague three lemon-scented gums (*Eucalyptus citriodora*). The accompanying card read: 'You have educated my three daughters. Please plant these in the new garden and call them Mary, Elizabeth and Catherine.' I was delighted. It is, I think, my favourite among the eucalypts. The avenue of them which leads from the gate to the house at Cruden Farm outside Melbourne must be one of the loveliest entries to any Australian property.

I had misgivings about them in our climate, but planted them and hoped. My misgivings proved justified for they did not survive our first severe frosts. I planted three crab-apples in their place — *Malus ioensis* 'Plena', *Malus* 'Gorgeous' and the bronze-leaved *Malus* 'Lemoinei'. These grew better than any other trees I planted and gave blossom in spring, fruit in summer and glorious colour in autumn. They happily tolerated our wet, cold winters and the hot, dry summers — and, an added bonus, they belong to the Rosaceae family.

Little Portion.
(Drawing by Jenny Phillips)

Little Portion 12

Small things have a particular appeal, and small plants tend to get lost in a large garden. I wanted, somewhere in the broad expanse of hectares I had acquired, a miniature garden – somewhere for miniature roses, tiny bulbs (crocus, species tulips, miniature narcissi) and for English primroses and auriculas which needed the sheltered, semi-shaded conditions I could at present certainly not provide.

And so I set about planning my Miniature Garden. It would have to be enclosed, both for aesthetic reasons and to break the force of the winds which howl across the plains of the Central Highlands. How to achieve this quickly was the problem.

Some weeks earlier I had decided, one still, sunny afternoon, to walk round the entire perimeter of my sixty-eight hectares. There was a narrow frontage to the Malmsbury East Road, which runs parallel to the Calder Highway from Malmsbury to Kyneton. Here, adjoining my land, I had found an old stone ruin which had once been a substantial home. And beside it, still intact, the shepherd's croft I had glimpsed from the quarry on that first afternoon. Made of bluestone with a shingled roof, it consisted of two rooms only, one door and three windows and a tiny corner fireplace. It measured in all six metres by four. Here was the perfect centrepiece for my miniature garden but there were problems: firstly, it did not belong to me, and secondly, it was a full twenty minutes' walk from the house. Out of the question.

The more I thought about it, the more perfect it seemed. Such a building would give the atmosphere I needed at one stroke. I had the bluestone. The old quarries were full of it. Cut pieces in all sizes, just as they had been chipped from the big blocks a hundred years ago. And I had heard of an English stonemason near Castlemaine. Perhaps he might agree to undertake the building of a replica.

Vic not only agreed. He was positively enthusiastic. So we measured the little building and made rough drawings. He brought his front-end loader and we started collecting stone.

Doors and windows posed a problem. New ones would be entirely out of place. Old ones, the size we wanted, were not easy to come by.

It was at this stage that I made a trip one morning to Castlemaine. On the outskirts of the town I had to pass a little old miner's cottage, the sort that abounded in this area and around Maldon in the early mining days. It was entirely unspoiled, even to its picket fence and iron lace and the huge old oak tree that overhung the verandah. The renovators had passed it by. I tried to buy it once from the white-haired old fellow who owned it, but he had simply shaken his head and asked, 'And where would I live then?'

I had watched it ever since in my goings and comings, and my friend, Ian Hargrave, a painter who specialised in painting watercolours of the old buildings in the area, had painted it for me. I have the painting still.

On this day, as I looked across, I saw, to my dismay and consternation, workmen throwing down sheets of iron from the roof. I braked sharply, turned, and drove back. It was being demolished to make way for four 'cluster houses'. Another link with Castlemaine's early history was gone. As I turned away I noticed the windows stacked near the gate.

'What are you doing with those?' I asked. 'To the tip, love,' said the workman in charge. And so I bought, for $10 each, three little windows, the front and the back door and, on an impulse, the old slate front doorstep, worn with the footsteps of a hundred years.

A month or so later our little stone cottage was complete and stood, isolated and exposed, in the middle of what was still no more than a paddock. An unwonted heavy snow fall a week later made it look, as a friend told me, like something straight out of Siberia. I worried then about the effect of snow on the garden, but soon discovered that its thick, soft blanket does a great deal less damage than frost.

By the following spring an area behind the cottage had been enclosed by high lattice fencing and work on the garden began.

In the back corner we built, with the stone left over from the cottage, a corner seat which I planted thickly with thyme. Lost in contemplation of the spicy scent which would be released by sitting on thyme, I quite overlooked the fact that the bees like it too.

The rest of the stone was used to form edges for the raised beds, built formally round a square, all the paths being paved with old, handmade bricks. A pretty old wooden garden seat made a warm, sheltered spot just outside the back door. It later became a favourite venue for predinner Scotch.

Water was still a problem, so we put a tank at the back of the cottage to catch the run-off from its roof. We painted it olive green, bound wire netting tightly round it and planted the pink, single rose 'Sparrieshoop' to cover it. 'Sparrieshoop' — the name comes from the north German town where the Kordes family have bred so many of their famous roses, roses which do exceptionally well for us here in Victoria — perhaps because they have been bred in a climate not unlike our own, with hot summers and very cold winters. Like 'Mermaid', 'Sparrieshoop' looks like an old rose although it was released in 1953. Unlike the old, single species roses though, it flowers throughout the summer.

I have to confess to a liking for good garden sculpture and used, as a centrepiece for my Miniature Garden, a slender, ascetic-looking madonna, work of the well-known sculptor Hans Knorr, originally from Bavaria. I had bought it some years earlier when he had owned a gallery at Emerald in the Dandenongs.

Miniature roses lend themselves to formality so I resolved to try a miniature form of posts and chains. The posts were barely a metre high and about two metres apart. To climb along the chains I selected the miniature climbers 'Candy Cane' (single, lipstick-pink), 'Climbing Jackie' (white), 'Red Cascade' and 'Baby Jayne' with mauve-pink double flowers like the patterns on old muslins.

Miniatures make excellent standards, so I planted standard 'Mary Marshall' and 'The Fairy' in big tubs beside my garden seat. The climbing form of 'Cécile Brunner' was put either side of an arch at the end of the garden. Although certainly not a miniature, its tiny flowers were right in this context, and it is more than capable of attaining the required height. For the same reasons, the first of the Noisette roses, 'Champney's Pink Cluster' was chosen to cover an archway over the front door.

The roses for the beds (which had been raised up to ensure adequate drainage in our very wet winters) were chosen with two things in mind. I had decided on a basically pink and white colour scheme, soft against the grey stone of the walls. And I wanted roses which would look at home in what was essentially an old rose garden.

Rosa chinensis minima was a must. Miniature roses are a modern development, but this one has been cultivated in China for thousands of years and is in the parentage of many modern miniatures. In colour it is softest pink. There are not many single miniatures, so I planted three each of 'Simplex' (single white), and 'Wee Beth' (an Australian-bred single, apricot pink). 'Dresden Doll' had to be included. It is a miniature Moss rose, and 'Popcorn', a diminutive semi-single white which reminds me of the flowers of feverfew. For contrast I added 'Baby Fauraux' (deep purple) and 'Antique Rose', the dusty magenta-pink of old ladies' bonnets.

These little roses do need some attention to ensure the continuous blooming of which they are capable. I gave them a mulch of stable manure mixed with straw and a handful of blood and bone with ten per cent potash added in the spring. Even so they appreciated an occasional foliar feed and they do need adequate water. We installed a trickle watering system both to conserve water and to avoid wetting the leaves. Black spot looks unsightly on the little roses, and to avoid it some spraying seems to be inevitable. Pruning is no trouble, however. They can be severely treated each winter — with the shears, if you like.

As ground covers I used in the main a variety of low-growing thymes: *Thymus* 'Albus', *T.* 'Coccineus', *T.* 'Lars Hall' and, probably my favourite, the woolly thyme (*T. pseudolanuginosus*); also alyssum (*Lobularia maritima*). All seeded themselves generously and in no time made a fragrant carpet among the brick paving.

The tiny bulbs came up through the ground covers each year: *Cyclamen hederifolium* and *Cyclamen coum* for autumn colour, and in the spring, before the roses come into bloom, English primroses, auriculas, crocus and species tulips. Also a tiny, miniature aquilegia (*Aquilegia bertolinii*) and a variety of small iris: *Iris setosa nana*, *Iris gracilipes* and *Iris graminea*.

On the high lattice which surrounded this little formal area *Rosa banksiae lutea* and *R. banksiae banksiae* (the white, violet perfumed, double form) formed a thick cover very quickly.

The Miniature Garden became a feature of Bleak House. Over the years the cottage itself has filled many purposes, as toolshed, as potting shed, for a while as a horticultural bookshop before a larger space was needed.

A winding path with mixed borders on either side links it to the main house and it was here that the botanical artist, Jenny Phillips, sat for many hours doing a delightful black and white drawing of the cottage, which we later used to print a bookplate.

It was in its second spring that a friend from Melbourne who had recently returned from a holiday in the Cotswolds saw the cottage and fell instantly in love with it.

'Does it have a name?' she asked. No, it did not.

'I have just had the holiday of my life in a little cottage just like it. Would you call it Little Portion?'

So Little Portion it has remained.

Daffodils 13

A Queenslander by birth, I shall never forget my first spring in Victoria. I had grown up in a garden of frangipani and hibiscus, the great scarlet umbrellas of the poincianas, banana palms, and mangoes to be picked from the edge of the verandah.

My mother had grown, with difficulty, in the coolest part of the garden, a few freesias, which she loved, but really we had no seasons. The garden was green and lush throughout the year so that I was totally unprepared for the glory that is spring in a cold climate, the reawakening, the burgeoning, the fresh young leaves and, above all, the carpets of bulbs. I resolved then and there that, if I ever had a garden of my own, I would grow bulbs, hundreds and thousands of bulbs.

The year before I bought Bleak House I had gone to Kyneton to visit a friend in hospital. Having arrived early, I had a few minutes to wait. In the garden I found a birdbath with a small bronze plaque with the inscription:

Mrs E. Murray

The joy of her garden

Has been our gain.

I asked the Sister-in-charge about Mrs Murray. She had a wonderful garden, I was told, and opened it each year at the time of the Kyneton Daffodil Festival in aid of the Hospital. The birdbath and plaque were a small gesture of thanks from the Hospital for years of support.

I missed the Festival the following year, taken up entirely with the initial work on Bleak House. But the following spring I determined to visit Eve Murray's garden.

I had to go through Kyneton and the whole little township was dressed for the Daffodil Festival; daffodils in beds all along the main streets; daffodils adorning every shop window; girls in long skirts, offering daffodils to all the visitors – in one case with a glass of sherry as well. I asked directions to Langley, which is a few kilometres out of the town, but I hardly needed to refer to them as there was a steady stream of cars going in the same direction. Murray's Road itself is lined thickly with daffodils. Not a thin ribbon of daffodils, but great sheets of gold under the gum trees which formed a canopy. They looked as much at home, I thought, as any of Wordsworth's daffodils.

The drive was packed with cars, and at the gate were collection boxes in aid of the Hospital. Little of the garden is visible from the gate, as one enters from the back, but as I came round the corner of the house I caught my breath.

The garden slopes away from the house down to a huge dam, and the slope was a sea of daffodils. Daffodils of every size, shape and colour, more varities than I had ever dreamed might exist, and not a dozen or so of each variety but hundreds. The garden covers an area of one and a half to two hectares. At the base of the slope, Eve had planted, some forty-five years ago, an oak wood. All of the trees were grown from acorns, picked up wherever she could find them and included a holm oak grown from an acorn found in the Adelaide Botanic Gardens. And the oak wood, too, was thickly planted with daffodils.

Afternoon tea was served on the verandah overlooking the garden, and here I met Eve Murray – in a wheelchair: tiny, white-haired, over eighty, with laughing eyes, a penetrating gaze and an absolutely indomitable spirit. Eve had come to Langley as a bride in 1931 to a house set in a paddock. She had immediately set about making a garden, at first watering her trees with buckets of water. A bore was put in in 1938, but the big dam not until 1960. I asked her when she had started gardening – 'from the moment I was born', she said. 'And I used to steal cuttings through the fences on the way home from school.'

A hedge of lilac and a low stone wall divide the garden horizontally. Above this, she told me, was intended to be 'a tidy garden' and below it, 'just fun'. But some-how it never quite worked out that way, and I think the whole garden became fun – a labour of love which has given intense pleasure to hundreds of people.

Eve's special interest in daffodils goes back a long way. Initially her aim had been to breed a pink daffodil and in this she succeeded. Unfortunately she seldom bothered to register the names of the daffodils she bred. Her own favourite among them is 'Philippa', white with a cream trumpet and named after her little grand-daughter. There was a splendid white one on display the day I visited the garden – 'Nell Robinson'.

There were hard times – drought, when there was no water to spare for the garden, for this is also a large sheep property. There was fire through the garden in 1944 which destroyed a lot of trees. And of latter years there has been illness.

Looking at the imposing trees enclosing the garden today, the enormous Judas tree (*Cercis siliquastrum*) grown from seed, the beautiful blue *Cedrus atlantica* f. *glauca* and the tall deodars, the almonds, the itea with its long greenish-yellow catkins, it is difficult to believe that fire wrought such destruction.

I stood on the verandah, looking down on the sea of gold stretching down to the dam, which was Eve's life's work. Among the daffodils were literally thousands of deep blue muscari and two magnificent white magnolias (*Magnolia stellata* and another I could not name). And over to the right, in startling contrast to the traditional yellows, whites and blues of spring, was a bed of brilliant scarlet tulips. I have never liked scarlet as a colour, and usually avoid planting scarlet flowers in the garden, but on this afternoon I went home, thumbed through all my bulb catalogues and ordered thirty *Tulipa fosteriana* 'Red Emperor' for the next year.

Bulbs, I was convinced, were the perfect companions for my roses. They would provide colour in the spring, long before the roses sent forth their first buds, and, if I chose carefully, I could have autumn-flowering bulbs also, when the old roses were finished.

A good many bulbs like the same open, sunny position as roses do, and if I carried out my scheme of watering with a trickle system, I could have an emitter for each rose and let the bulbs have the dry conditions they need in summer.

I had bought some bulbs from Eve Murray's garden (in aid of the Kyneton Hospital) — some twenty or thirty — but this would go nowhere in the space I wanted to fill. I needed to acquire them by the hundred — or by the thousand.

All through this part of Victoria — the Gold Centre — are the remains of little cottages — some rough stone, some weatherboard — built in the booming gold rush days when these little villages were busy, bustling townships, and long since abandoned. Often a little cluster of old fruit trees is the only sign that here was once a cottage. And under the fruit trees are nearly always bulbs — jonquils and daffodils and snowflakes. Often, after a hundred years of neglect, of never being lifted, the daffodils have become double and sometimes tinged with green. These I loved.

There was one particular little weatherboard cottage I passed often. Deserted long since, its windows were broken and the door hung disconsolately on one hinge. But, improbably, the brilliant lipstick-pink climbing rose, 'Nancy Hayward', still flowered bravely on the derelict verandah posts and over the verandah roof right up to the chimney. And the ground was carpeted each spring by daffodils. Here was the sort of supply I needed.

So I set out to find the owner of the cottage, if, indeed, there was one. Enquiries at the local general store elicited a flood of information. It belonged to old Mrs Miller. Her husband had died some years back and anyhow they hadn't lived in that cottage for twenty years. Lived in the village, she did, with a pack of savage dogs. The storekeeper shook his head. Eccentric, she was. Some said — and he made an expressive gesture of his hand towards his forehead. Well, he concluded, no one went there if they didn't have to. Against his will, he gave me directions to her cottage and, clearly puzzled, added further emphatic warnings about the dogs.

I went to visit her the following Saturday. Her cottage stood alone at the end of the village. With difficulty I unbound the wire from the front gate and went up the steps to the front door. As I did so, the dogs emerged from round the back — a mangy, underfed, snarling pack. I was profoundly thankful for the fence which divided off the front garden.

I knocked loudly, realising as I did so that probably no one ever came to the front door. There was no response. I tried again. And again. Just as I was about to give up — wild horses would not have got me to the back door, for that would have meant braving the dogs — round the corner of the house came the dirtiest human being I had ever encountered. She was dressed in rags, a man's old felt hat pulled low over her forehead and men's old boots on her feet, hostility written all over her.

Abruptly she asked my business. 'You own the old cottage at the other end of the village?' I asked.

'And what if I do?' came the reply.

I explained that I was making a garden and I wanted to plant daffodils. Could I buy some of her bulbs?

She half turned away, and there was such a long pause I thought I was going to get no answer at all. Finally it came in what amounted to a snarl: 'I don't want your money.'

I tried again. I explained that they were expensive to buy from nurseries and I needed a lot. I loved the old simple ones, especially the double ones, better than the sophisticated, developed varieties. I was prepared to offer her a fair price. Even as I said it, I was aware that money was not her chief concern. Perhaps she still loved the old cottage. Perhaps its garden had been important to her.

Again a pause. Finally — 'You can 'ave the bulbs. But I don't want your money.'

I asked if there was, then, something I could do for her.

'You can bring me a bucket o' bulbs,' she said as she turned away.

I took a collection of cartons with me and, for four hours, I dug bulbs — mostly daffodils, a few jonquils. There were old roses along the front fence and I took some cuttings. 'Félicité et Perpétue' was growing over an old shed. It turns up in many of the old gardens in this part of Victoria. I suppose, since it strikes so easily from cuttings, that it was given from hand to hand in the early days.

My cartons full, and loaded into the car, I dug a 'bucket o' bulbs' for old Mrs Miller. Then I went back to the general store. The storekeeper was incredulous.

'You never went up there?' he asked.

I assured him that I had indeed and asked if Mrs Miller ever came to the shop. 'Now and again', was the response. I asked what sort of things she bought.

'Chocolate biscuits,' came the prompt reply. 'Always chocolate biscuits.'

So I bought a whole carton of chocolate biscuits. Not being anxious to encounter either Mrs Miller or her dogs again, I deposited the carton and the 'bucket o' bulbs' at the front door and fled.

The following year — with more beds to fill — I went back. She remembered me and was almost cordial.

'You take as many as you like,' she said. And, yes, she wouldn't mind a few more herself.

This time, when I took them to her (together with another carton of chocolate biscuits) I planted them for her — thickly, along the edge of the front verandah. I did not see her again, nor did I try to, but each year, as I pass her cottage in spring, I am glad to see the daffodils still in bloom.

And as I look at them in my own garden, flowering more abundantly each year, I wonder afresh about old Mrs Miller. Perhaps, like Eve Murray, she had gone as a bride to that little cottage and the daffodils and the roses along the fence had been planted when she was young and her heart full of dreams.

Yarrow.

Water 14

Water, it was apparent from the outset, would be a matter of prime concern. And it was a problem which would have to be tackled sooner rather than later. Malmsbury has an annual rainfall of approximately 70 centimetres, and most of it falls in the winter. The summers are long, and dry, and hot, and farming activities in the area are all geared to 'the autumn break' which comes, as a rule, towards the end of March. So the summer months are critical for a garden.

Bleak House is too far out to be served by the town supply and when I bought the property the only water came from the old windmill beside the house. This was sweet water and perfectly adequate for domestic use, but it would never do for a large garden.

Water transforms a landscape. When the lake came up in the winter, the view over the paddocks was splendid. But in the summer, when the lake had dried up and the grass turned brown, the eye sought the relief of water. And there was none. So I thought in terms of dams and contacted a local bulldozer driver to discuss putting in a dam, not too far from the garden, to serve both practical and aesthetic purposes.

I had one very good neighbour, Norman Ward, who owned an imposing four-storied bluestone mill between Bleak House and Kyneton. Norm's family had owned the mill since 1860, and Norm, having lived and farmed here all his life, was regarded as an authority on most rural matters. He came to visit me the day the bulldozer driver came. When he heard of the projected dam, he shook his head and said with the innate conservatism of farmers the world over, 'It's not dam country. It's bore country. Nobody round here goes in for dams.'

Now bores may be very efficient but they do nothing for the landscape. I had a mental vision of a sheet of water (with waterlilies, of course) surrounded by trees and water iris, a veritable oasis in the midst of the plains.

Finally we compromised. Noel Jennings (a treasure beyond price, and the only artistic bulldozer driver of my acquaintance) would build a small dam, a $500 dam, and I would get in touch with a contractor who would put down a bore.

As it must be done in the summer while the ground is dry, work began on the dam immediately. Simultaneously, the contractor arrived to put down the bore. Bores cost so much per metre, so, as there is no way of knowing in advance how deep they will have to go before they strike water, there is no way of estimating the cost. I spent an anxious morning, rushing from dam to bore and watching the progress of both.

The bulldozer struck rock and shale at a depth of about three metres, so could go no deeper. The clay was put back, the topsoil neatly piled up for future use, the biggest rocks – and they were very big – strategically placed round the banks. I had my first dam.

The bore struck water at about thirty metres, quite a good flow, and later analysis proved it to be sweet and suitable for stock or garden.

An electrically-driven pressure pump was installed at the bore head and a petrol-driven one (to give two strings to the bow in case of electrical failure) on the banks of the (still dry) dam. A plumber was called in to take the water from the electric pump to taps all round the garden and I felt that I was ready to face the next summer.

Water was, without doubt, the biggest expenditure involved in setting up the garden. And I was by no means finished. Trickle lines would have to be installed in all garden beds as they were constructed. Sprinklers are really not feasible under my conditions. They use far too much water, a good deal of which goes where it is not needed, and it evaporates quickly if used during the day. Furthermore, overhead watering does encourage black spot in roses.

The following weekend, with my mind still running very much on water, I went for an evening walk in the biggest of the quarries. I loved the solitude, the great moss-covered boulders, the view towards Mt Macedon and to the back of the house. And there, in the midst of the quarry, I came upon a hitherto undiscovered waterhole. This was January, and a stone thrown into the water indicated that it was still very deep. Round the margin were elderberry bushes (*Sambucus nigra*) with their flat ivory coloured flower heads and clusters of berries, some of which were just now starting to turn black. And there was *Rosa canina*, the little dog rose, which must have escaped from gardens in the early days and has become something of a pest to farmers. I regarded it as anything but a pest. Here, ready-made, was the vision I had had in my mind's eye when I decided to put in a dam. It was, of course, too far from the house to be of any practical use, nor could it be seen until one stumbled upon it, but it was, in itself, beautiful. And perhaps it indicated the presence of a spring.

A touch of formality — 'Crépuscule' on the left, a weeping standard of 'Orange Cascade' and 'Paul Transon' on the right.

'Raubritter' hanging down over a stone wall.

'Irish Rich Marbled' with yellow foxgloves.

A group of the Hybrid Musk rose 'Vanity'.

Modern roses in a shrub border. 'Dearest' is to the left of *Chrysanthemum ptarmiciflorum* with a foxglove and chives in the foreground.

My two blue heelers, good mates, affectionate and excitable, great chasers of rabbits, accompanied me on all walks. The little bitch loved water so, with her usual precipitateness, she plunged in. Now this waterhole was formed by quarrying, so the banks all round were of steep stone. Cara, her desire for a swim gratified, found she could not scramble up the sheer stone banks. Willy, a goodtime boy if ever there was one, lay on a flat stone at the top and watched, offering no assistance. By lying flat on a rock, I finally managed to seize her front paws and haul her out, though there was an anxious moment when I felt she was about to haul me in.

I thought about that waterhole all the way home. This was exactly what I wanted in my 'extended landscape', but close to the house. If water could be held all summer in the quarry, then why not on the flat ground which became a lake each winter.

Remembering the role of the State Rivers and Water Authority in the matter of the tip, I contacted them and asked for advice. They could not have been more helpful — even when they found my purpose in all this was far from utilitarian. They assumed initially that I wanted to drain the land and use it for farming purposes. This, they explained, would be very expensive. Quite the reverse was what I had in mind. I wanted to keep the water, so that the waterbirds, instead of flying away each summer when the lake dried up, might be persuaded to make their homes there, in a safe haven.

They tested the soil, examined the ground thoroughly and advised me finally that if I built a chain of waterholes across the lake the water could probably be retained and, an added bonus, the winter flooding would be reduced.

So Noel Jennings was consulted again. Had he been born half a century later, I feel sure he would have done a course and qualified as a Landscape Architect. He was a practising one in any case.

He constructed an enormous waterhole in the middle of the now dry lake. It had bays and inlets and a large island for the birds to nest on. And in the middle of the job Noel came up to the house one day to report that, in the midst of a dry hot February, he had become bogged. He had, indeed, struck a spring and water seeped in, slowly and steadily throughout March — to my infinite satisfaction.

In the autumn we planted the edges — this was a lake, not a dam, so no need to worry about the effects of roots on a dam wall — with several varieties of willow: the weeping willow (*Salix babylonica*), the tortured willow (*Salix matsudana* 'Tortuosa'), the pussy willow (*Salix caprea*) and the basket willow (*Salix viminalis*), which grows all along the banks of the Campaspe River.

But I wanted trees on the island also, and getting there posed a problem. So I bought, the following spring, a small rowing boat. With difficulty, for I have no natural talents in this direction, I learnt to row it. Long spring evenings were spent, planting up the island.

Full of optimism I planted a swamp cypress (*Taxodium distichum*) but, sadly, it did not survive the first summer. A seedling apple did much better and several roots of *Rosa indica major*, often regarded as a form of *R. chinensis*. Much used as a rootstock in the early days, it has survived in many of our country cemeteries, defying all efforts of Shire workers 'cleaning up' to eradicate it. *Rosa multiflora*, also, seemed impervious to drought, flood, frost, sun and wind. Graham Stuart Thomas, in his delightful book *A Garden of Roses* wrote of it that 'on account of its dense, arching, but bushy growth and ease of cultivation, it is used to prevent soil erosion and as a crash-barrier on motorways.' He added that 'its heps provide nourishment for birds'. What more could one ask? It flourished on the island and I hope that, by now, the birds are indeed feeding on the heps.

In my early experiments with herbs as ground covers among the roses, I had planted, seduced by its fern-like foliage and flat white flower heads, some roots of the common achillea, (*Achillea millefolium*). To my eternal sorrow, it proved to be all but ineradicable. In my efforts to discourage it, I weeded it out by the armful and transported much of it to the island. Here it could (and did) ramp away to its heart's content.

The walk to the lake at sunset on summer Sunday evenings became something of a ritual over the next couple of years. I would set out (accompanied by the heelers, of course) row across to the island, and water, with buckets, all that was planted there. The dogs loved it, swimming across and then landing, wet and dirty, in the boat asking to be rowed back.

Later we put in another dam near the smallest of the quarries, which is not far from the house, and another bore with a windmill — always with the hope that here, some day, there would be a garden in a quarry. I planted a blue cedar (*Cedrus atlantica* f. *glauca*) and two deodars (*Cedrus deodara*). Hugh Johnson, in his invaluable *Encyclopedia of Trees*, states that they usually take twenty years to reach a height of thirteen metres, but I reminded myself of the wonderful story of Thomas Jefferson who decided, at the age of eighty, to plant an avenue of oaks. The head gardener, when consulted, suggested tentatively, with Jefferson's age in mind, that oaks took a very long time to reach maturity. 'Right,' said Jefferson, 'then you'd better start this afternoon.'

Neither of these big waterholes was close enough to be of any use for the garden. They were intended for the birds (and incidentally for the sheep we agisted to keep the grass down and prevent it from becoming a fire hazard in the summer) and for their contribution to the landscape.

Much later, as the garden was extended, I put in a very big dam for watering purposes and installed another petrol-driven pump. It had a small island in it with a crab-apple tree (*Malus spectabilis* this time) and daffodils, and we planted self-sown seedlings of the white Rugosa rose, gathered up from all round the garden, round its margin. In the spring after this dam was constructed, the first black swans stayed and brought up their cygnets.

Candytuft.

Mosses and Noisettes 15

I did, after all, order some Moss roses in that first year. For many people they and the Centifolias are the ones that first come to mind when one mentions 'old roses'. Small wonder that they so closely resemble each other for the Common Moss, introduced into England from the Continent early in the eighteenth century, is thought to have been a sport of *R. centifolia*.

With admirable restraint, and influenced, perhaps, by the disparaging remarks I had read about their being sprawling, lanky plants of dubious garden value, I limited myself, in this first order, to seven. And a truly masculine collection they were.

Into the very feminine company of Duchesses, Queens, Countesses and Madames who inhabited my garden I proposed now to introduce 'Général Kléber', 'James Mitchell', 'Henri Martin', 'Alfred de Dalmas', 'William Lobb', 'Chapeau de Napoléon' – and the exquisite 'Madame Louis Lévéque'.

Released, most of them, in the 1850s and 1860s, they were beloved by the Victorians, by gardeners, painters, embroidresses, and the makers of picture post-cards and valentines.

Historical associations and the exotic winged buds which resemble a cockaded hat made 'Chapeau de Napoléon' a 'must'. It is often classed not as a Moss but as a Centifolia; indeed its proper name is *R. centifolia cristata*. The brownish-green moss enhances the beauty of the silvery pink buds and the flowers fade to a lilac-pink as they age. Strange, that such an enchanting rose should be a chance seedling. It was discovered, so Graham Stuart Thomas tells us, in the crevice of an old wall at Fribourg in Switzerland.

Beside it I planted 'Général Kléber', named for the General whom Napoleon left behind to look after his army in Egypt. If ever a rose deserved the name of a beautiful woman it is this one. The fragrant flowers are the clearest, softest pink. Gordon Edwards describes it as 'mother-of-pearl pink'. They are produced on a bushy plant with fresh, green foliage and the buds are endowed with ample moss. I only wish it flowered for longer.

'James Mitchell' makes an attractive bush with long, arching canes and a profusion of small, tight pink flowers, each with a button eye. 'Henri Martin' is a clear and striking crimson – a great splash of colour. And 'William Lobb' is one of the very richest, a deep crimson-purple which fades to soft lavender. The bush is lanky and uncontrolled and, as it will grow to two and a half metres, it really needs some support, either from other plants or from a tripod. I have seen it looking positively splendid at Kiftsgate, intertwined with the rambler, 'Albertine', against a mellow old brick wall.

'Alfred de Dalmas' and 'Madame Louis Lévêque' have the great virtue of being recurrent flowering. Both soft pink, and both sweetly scented, they are worthy of a place in any garden.

Having gone so far as to include the Mosses, I decided to order, in addition, some of the Noisette roses. I did want some recurrent flowering roses included in this first planting.

There is (as always) some disagreement about the origins of the Noisettes, but the most generally accepted version is that the original one was 'Champney's Pink Cluster', the rose I planted over the front door of Little Portion. This originated in 1802 on the property of a wealthy rice grower from South Carolina, John Champney, who was also a keen gardener. His rose was the result (most probably) of a cross, whether intentional or not, between *R. moschata* and the China rose, 'Old Blush', also known as 'Parsons' Pink'. It bears great clusters of semi-double, highly perfumed little soft pink roses, and will climb to a height of four to five metres.

John Champney's neighbour in Carolina was one Philippe Noisette, a member of a family of Parisian rosarians, and he sent seedlings of the original rose to France. From these seedlings stems the family of Noisette roses, still highly prized by gardeners today.

Two of them I would include in that small (but sometimes varying) group of roses which I could not possibly be without. 'Lamarque' I had fallen in love with some years earlier. In the garden of Helen Vellacott in Castlemaine it grows right to the top of a giant *Magnolia grandiflora* and fills the whole garden with its distinctive, slightly lemony fragrance. It produces its creamy-white flowers over a period of many months, and the fresh green foliage is in itself beautiful.

'Madame Alfred Carrière' I met for the first time in that same garden. It is an old garden, a rambling country garden where things grow over and into one another, and the ground is a carpet of bulbs in the spring. Birds nest here and an old weeping elm whose branches come right down to the ground makes a secret place beloved by children. 'Madame Alfred Carrière' was already a very Senior Citizen when I first met her here, but the great bush, three metres wide and four metres high, was simply covered in softest blush-pink blooms which fade to white in the sunshine and scent the whole garden. She grew here in semi-shade under tall trees where the books say roses do not flourish. 'Madame Alfred' defied them all.

I had taken cuttings from this old bush the year before and they had grown. I resolved to plant the tiny bushes along the south side of the high carport I had had built beside the house — a carport with an attic and a gabled roof which was in keeping with the old house. The little roses got only an hour or so of early morning sun and the full blast of the south wind, but they reached the top of the attic over the carport within three years and were a never-ending source of delight. Each year at pruning time I find myself putting in cuttings for no better reason than that it seems such a wicked waste to throw away so much potential beauty. And, as with my many cuttings of 'Albertine', there always seems to be another corner just suited to 'Madame Alfred', or another friend who has not yet realised what a treasure she is.

'Desprez à fleur jaune', soft buff yellow with apricot-pink overtones, and 'Alister Stella Gray', creamy-yellow paling to white, battled manfully with the cold wet winters and became great favourites.

'Maréchal Niel' I had no luck with, although I tried twice. I think he really did find the Malmsbury winters too much for him. They say in England he must be grown under glass. He struggled valiantly each time for a year or two and produced a few lovely soft yellow, scented blooms. I had put him to grow over a shade house so that one could look up at him from underneath. Had he flourished the effect would have been all that I desired, but each winter he grew pale and wan and finally gave up the ghost.

'Aimée Vibert' I could not enthuse over. The little pink buds are charming, as are the clusters of small white roses, but she does die in the most unattractive fashion and it is essential to cut off the bunches of brown heads which spoil the whole effect — a difficult task to keep up in a large garden. Perhaps my dislike of her was influenced by other factors. She played a key role in one of my most conspicuous garden failures.

In an old garden magazine I had come upon a picture of a maypole made of roses. It was enchanting. This was a splendid way to grow climbers. So I set about designing one. I chose a sheltered spot — as sheltered as I could provide. It had an old cypress on the south side at the foot of which I had planted 'Bloomfield Courage' and 'Wedding Day'. The dark green of the cypress provided the ideal foil for the dark red and white of the clusters of single roses. A Rugosa hedge gave some shelter from the west and on the east there was the shadehouse which bounded the projected Yellow Garden.

We set a large bush pole firmly in the ground as a centrepost and from it took eight wires to the circumference of a circle. These were attached to steel posts driven right into the ground. The area underneath was paved with bluestone set on black plastic and sand as I was sure that once the roses grew it would be quite impossible to weed underneath.

There was nothing wrong with the construction, but the whole thing never worked as I had intended. In the first place I think I chose the wrong roses. 'Aimée Vibert' simply refused to grow up the wires. She preferred to make a large shrub. 'Daydream's' canes were not sufficiently pliable and 'Shot Silk', which came to me from the grower as a climber, turned out to be bush after all. The only one that did as she was meant to do was *Rosa* × *leonida*, formerly known as 'Marie Leonida'. Released in 1842 and thought to be a hybrid between *R. bracteata* and *R. laevigata*, she has long pliable canes, glossy dark green foliage and very double rounded creamy-white roses.

In addition to the fact that I think I chose the wrong roses — ramblers would have been far more appropriate — I think, being in the middle of a 'lawn' and hence not part of a trickle system, they never got enough of either food or water. I am sure that the idea was feasible and I would love to try it again with the benefit of experience.

So 'Aimée Vibert' was not popular on this account. Added to this, it was she who harboured my first snake in the garden.

I was going to Melbourne and went down to turn off the tap near 'Aimée Vibert' and there, in front of her, basking in the late afternoon sun, was a large copperhead. I stopped dead. The first essential was to put the dogs away. Cara, who chased anything that moved, was sure to be as silly about snakes as she was about waterholes and magpies. I called them in my most peremptory fashion and succeeded in shutting them both in the kitchen.

I had been presented with a shotgun — a Winchester .410 — it being, I was informed, an essential piece of equipment for one who made a practice of walking in snake-infested quarries. Now I have no natural affinity with guns and always have to stop and think which eye it is I have to close to look along the barrel! I took it down now and loaded it deliberately and with exaggerated care, hoping all the while that by the time I returned the snake would have gone.

But there he lay, watching me, I felt sure, with an intuitive knowledge of my intentions. I had owned the gun for two years or more and never used it except for some target practice in the paddock, shooting at a kerosene tin which I invariably missed. I hated the thought of killing anything. I tried to see the copperhead through D. H. Lawrence's eyes. I tried to envisage the beauty of the one that came to his water-trough to drink and he 'in pyjamas for the heat'. But I thought instead of Cara and Willy and the final line of Kenneth Mackenzie's poem 'and in its mouth it carries death'. Strengthened in my resolve, I put the gun to my shoulder, closed I'm not sure which eye — possibly both — and pulled the trigger. As the little puff of smoke and cloud of dust cleared away I saw, to my utter astonishment, that this time I had hit my target.

Daffodils.

The Yellow Garden 16

It was *R. foetida bicolor* which was responsible for the birth of the Yellow Garden. When I first saw a bush of it, with its bright green foliage and mass of little single roses with petals bright coppery-scarlet on top and soft, butterscotch-yellow underneath, it was a case of love at first sight. I simply had to have it.

Why it is familiarly known as 'Austrian Copper' is a mystery to me. It is a sport of the almost equally enchanting *R. foetida*, known as the 'Austrian Briar', whose flowers are like little enamelled buttercups. Both appear to have had their origins somewhere in western Asia — certainly not in Austria. Perhaps they were brought in stages from one part of the Ottoman Empire to another in the way that many plants have travelled along the Old Silk Road from China to Persia. Neither can I hazard a guess as to why they are called *'foetida'* for their scent, while by no means your usual rose scent, I find in no way unpleasant.

The decision had been taken. I had to find a place for both of them somewhere in the garden, but those brilliant yellows from the East have no affinity with the soft pinks, the rosy-purples and deep wine colours of the old European roses.

There was nothing for it. I would have to extend the garden and make a special place for them.

I had been thinking for some time that I needed a shadehouse. Every owner of a fairly large garden comes to this conclusion sooner or later. Plants are needed in quantity — not in ones or twos. And buying twenty of this and thirty of that from nurseries is out of the question. Propagating becomes an essential part of running the garden. I wanted something quite simple — just somewhere out of the hot sun to put cuttings and plants which were too small to be planted out yet. Plastic tunnels — while no doubt very functional — are anathema to me. I wanted something which would merge into the garden.

So I decided to place the Yellow Garden to the north of the Miniature Garden. A lattice fence was already in place there and would form the southern boundary and — with Albert's invaluable assistance — I erected my shadehouse to cut the Yellow Garden off on the western side. We made it of bush poles and treated pine lattice, like three pergolas in the shape of a rectangle with the centre and the long eastern side open. It was thus protected from north, south and west winds (we got all three!) but open to the morning sun. We roofed it with lattice and, rather than using shade-cloth, I planted that dear little white rambler, 'Félicité et Perpétue' round three sides of it. Dean Hole refers to it as 'Félicité Perpétuelle' (a most appropriate name) and speaks of it 'climbing heavenwards in emblematic beauty'. It quickly formed a dense cover, looked breath-taking each spring and, being almost evergreen, afforded protection not only from the hot sun but also from winter frosts. I gave the whole structure a touch of formality by planting four pencil pines in the inner corners and, in the open centre, a one and a half metre weeping standard 'Orange Cascade', the little miniature rose I had used in the front garden which is not orange at all but a deep golden yellow.

In my yellow garden I planted two each of *R. foetida* and *R. foetida bicolor* and one of the double form, *R. foetida persiana*. Quite in keeping with them is the dramatic red 'Geranium', a seedling of the species rose *R. moyesii*, and raised by the Royal Horticultural Society at Wisley. That great rosarian, Roy Shepherd, described *R. moyesii* as being 'one of the most desirable of all rose species in blossom, colour, foliage and fruits'. 'Geranium' is very like its parent. Its single deep scarlet flowers made it the ideal companion for *R. foetida bicolor* and, after a brilliant flowering, it produces equally brilliant flagon-shaped, scarlet hips which hang on right into winter.

Here, too, I found a home for 'Mutabilis', sometimes thought to be a species rose but probably an old chance hybrid from a Chinese garden. It is unlike any other rose. The buds are vivid orange, then open to a single, soft yellow rose which, as it ages, goes through pink to quite deep red. It flowers continuously, so that at almost any time all colours are on the bush simultaneously. I found it did not much like our harsh frosts and did better later when the garden had grown up a little and it had some shelter from a young apple tree. At the foot of that same apple I planted one of the loveliest of all red roses (I had almost written *the* loveliest of all red roses, but then I thought of 'Charles de Mills') 'Château de Clos Vougeot', which I had grown to love in Maria's garden.

I had an ambition to grow *R. × hemisphaerica*, 'The Sulphur Rose', but it proved to be a piece of arrant folly. The combination of our harsh conditions and my inexperience discouraged it utterly and, after producing one or two miserable flowers, it gave up the ghost entirely.

I covered the eastern fence, against the paddocks, with the evergreen *R. laevigata* ('The Cherokee Rose'). It took a couple of winters before it adapted to the cold, but then proceeded to produce masses of its pure single white blooms with their golden stamens early in each spring, and its glossy, dark green leaves formed a dense, if thorny, cover for the fence. In front of it I planted hundreds (literally) of the soft mauve-blue iris which we used to call 'Iris stylosa' but is now *Iris unguicularis*. They made a patch of colour when most things are dormant in mid-winter.

White agapanthus lined the main path and I found their green seed-heads were a wonderful foil for the scarlet hips of 'Geranium' and for the less showy, but nonetheless very effective, hips of *R. alba semi-plena*. For the same reasons I planted two of the little white Rugosa rose, 'Schneezwerg' (Snow Dwarf).

The area needed trees. I decided on four quinces (*Cydonia oblonga*). Their blush-pink, single blooms must be one of the loveliest of all spring blossoms and fortunately they come well before my scarlet and yellow roses. As an added bonus, their glowing golden fruits hang like great globes in the trees in late summer.

Apricot-coloured roses were at home here, too: 'The Alchemist' with its great flat quartered blooms; 'Crépuscule', the delightful little rich apricot Noisette rose, constantly in flower but appreciating some frost protection; 'Paul Transon', a copper-coloured hybrid of that very versatile *R. wichuraiana*, which my English books said 'might sometimes repeat in autumn', but which unfailingly does so for us; and that strange, milk coffee-coloured modern, 'Julia's Rose', which I found much more rewarding as a climber than as a bush. I put four of the great, scarlet, single climbing rose, 'Altissimo', to grow through 'Félicité et Perpétue' on the shadehouse.

The Yellow Garden, having been started more or less as an afterthought, became a much loved part of the garden. Scarlet 'Red Emperor' tulips were planted here; cherry-coloured ixias, found along the roadside at Taradale; the scarlet *Haemanthus coccineus*, whose huge, strap-like leaves have earned it the name of 'elephant's ears', flowered for a year or so but then mysteriously disappeared; the snake's head iris (*Hermodactylus tuberosus*) with its strange olive-green and black flowers; the barber's pole oxalis with its starry white flowers and cheerful red and white striped buds (definitely not invasive).

White daffodils were planted here and the white form of muscari; the white lychnis (*Lychnis coronaria* 'Alba') with its silvery-grey foliage; *Spiloxene capensis*, whose strange, star-like flowers with a brown and green stripe on the undersurface of the petals unfold in bright sunshine while you watch them.

In parts of the Yellow Garden were great slabs of moss-covered rock with only pockets of soil between. I wound the path in and out around them, filled the pockets with compost and planted yellow and orange and rust-coloured day-lilies (*Hemerocallis*). All were gifts from friends' gardens and I never knew their names, but they flourished and multiplied and made a brave show every summer, with a very minimum of care.

And then there were the great spotted orange tiger lilies (*Lilium tigrinum*), which shrieked at everything else in the garden. I had never liked them but had been given a quantity the previous year and had spent at least an hour wandering round the garden with the bulbs in a bucket, wondering what on earth I could do with them. Finally, in desperation, and consoling myself with the thought that they might not be noticed there, I planted them at the very back of the rockery. They flowered, of course, triumphantly, right beside the soft pink climber, 'Blossom Time'. It was not to be tolerated. They would have to go.

And then I went to Smeaton. I was looking, as usual, for roses planted in old gardens. I had seen pictures of the old, five-storied bluestone mill and heard stories of its garden. It had been built in 1860 on the banks of Birch Creek by a man named Anderson, who had had the forethought to plant the banks of the stream with oaks — they are towering giants today, and provide a perfect setting for the old stone building. And Andersons had lived and gardened there ever since.

I climbed the hill and pushed open the picket gate between two towering poplars. In true cottage garden fashion the path led straight to the front door. But this was no contrived, reproduction cottage garden. This was the genuine article, the result of one hundred years of gardening by one family. The path was narrow and plants spilled over in generous profusion, reducing it sometimes to little over half a metre in width. Love-in-the-mist was here, and daisies, violas and hollyhocks, sweet peas on a high trellis, flowering as they seemed to do when I was a child, and lavateras, their delicate petals acquiring an almost luminous quality in the shade of a giant liquidambar. This seemed to disprove all the theories about liquidambars being unsuitable in gardens as they rob the soil to too great an extent, for cottage plants clustered all about its feet. Currants, red and black, were there in plenty, and gooseberries, conjuring up smells of country cooking and visions of pantry shelves laden with bottles of preserved fruit and jams. And there was a twisted old Granny Smith, its branches weighed down with the weight of its fruit. I'm sure it is seldom pruned.

Lynette Anderson was interested in my quest. Yes, they had old roses, some of them dating back to the building of the house. This was in the gold rush days. It had been intended that the house, like the mill, should be built of local stone, but in all the excitement consequent upon the discovery of gold, this was put off and a weatherboard house built instead. Looking at the pretty roof-line, the wide verandah across the front, the curving bargeboards and big chimneys, I could not feel that much had been lost.

The roses were growing, in the way old roses look best, among cottage plants. Some were flowering at the time of my visit, although the very old ones were over. It is unimportant, in a garden such as this, if they flower only in the spring. Surrounded by lavenders, nepetas, dianthus and herbs, they fade into the background once their flowering period is over, until their hips appear. They were known to Lynette seldom by their registered names, but rather by the names of their donors, so that the garden was full of daily reminders of friends and relatives. I was given cuttings of a little pink rose, known simply as 'Auntie Clark's Rose', and a deep, purplish-crimson Moss rose, not in flower at the time but described at teatime as having 'the colour of Noel Coward's jacket on this record-cover'. It turned out to be 'William Lobb', known in our gardens since 1855 but quite the latest thing, I suppose, when this gnarled old bush was planted.

We had tea in the high-ceilinged dining room on a cedar table with a white linen cloth. It was hand-embroidered with flowers and seemed to bring the garden right into the house. Then, through the window, I saw the tiger lilies, a whole army of them. Tall and arrogant, they tossed their tawny heads above a sea of golden and orange marigolds and yellow daisies — and here, in the right company, they looked splendid.

So my tiger lilies, too, found a home in the Yellow Garden. But in place of the marigolds (I like neither the feel nor the scent of them), I planted cream, yellow and orange eschscholzias. They seed themselves and come back year after year. If I had made its acquaintance at that time, I would also have planted the soft yellow *Anthemis* 'E. C. Buxton'. But I did not meet her until some years later.

Vase of daisies.

Louie Wilson's Legacy 17

The Yellow Garden had benefited from my visit to Smeaton but it was, in fact, quite another quest which had first taken me to this sleepy, forgotten little goldfields town.

In a book entitled *Historic Gardens of Victoria* by Peter Watts, which came out in 1983, I had come upon a short account of Camnethan Homestead near Smeaton. It was described as a garden 'full of reminders of past glory' and 'one of the most elaborate small gardens known to have existed in Victoria'.

The accompanying photograph showed a straight central path edged in box leading to a cottage with a roof-line very like that of Bleak House and, to the left of the path, the most enchanting summerhouse – circular with Gothic arches.

Garden structures fascinate me and I am congenitally unable to resist anything which bears any resemblance to a Gothic arch. I was, in addition, still very much exercised as to how much formality can successfully be introduced into an Australian country garden without its becoming incongruous. I determined to seek out Camnethan Homestead.

Smeaton is in Central Victoria, not very far from Ballarat and about an hour's drive from Malmsbury. The town is tiny. A little bridge leads over the river near the Andersons' mill. There are a few fine old buildings, the Post Office and a General

Store and not much else. I enquired at both the Post Office and the store, but no-one had heard of Camnethan and I did not know the name of the present occupant. Any mention of a fine old garden met with looks of puzzlement and dubious shakings of the head. I drove unsuccessfully round the outskirts of the town and finally, with no feeling of optimism, approached a large woman out hosing her garden, a brilliant affair of orange and scarlet Hybrid Teas, marigolds and zinnias. Concrete edges enclosed geometrically shaped beds, colourful pots lined the concrete drive and a pair of large concrete emus presided over the whole.

I mentioned Camnethan. To my surprise she nodded her head. 'Yes,' she said, 'old Louie Wilson's place. Lives out there by herself. Never comes into the town now. She's well over ninety.' Camnethan, she informed me, lay some miles outside the town but, she assured me, with a rather pitying smile and a glance full of pride at her own creation, there was no garden there.

I drove, according to her directions, along an unpromising dirt track and came ultimately to a wire gate hanging loose on its hinges with the name 'Camnethan' just decipherable on a wooden board. It looked as though my informant might have been right. It was difficult to believe that here had once been a notable garden. An overgrown tree-lined drive led round to the back of the house. No sign of a vehicle in the tumbledown shed. Not even a dog or the dusty white hens usually found pecking round the back yard of an Australian farmhouse.

However, a knock on the back door was answered by a tiny, white-haired, smiling old woman who introduced herself simply as 'Louie' and, despite the fact that I was a complete stranger, welcomed me in. Louie was deaf, so it was with difficulty that I got her to understand that I had read about her garden and was interested in old roses.

She shook her head sadly and explained that there was no garden left. She was ninety-five years old and the garden had been made by her late husband's grandfather. On a hasty calculation I estimated that that put it back well into the last century. Louie was a newcomer to the property, she explained. She had lived here only for the last twenty-five years! For a long time now there had been no one here except herself, no one to tend the garden.

However, she had some photographs of the garden as it had been. She looked in vain through all the drawers in her desk but finally had to abandon the search. I prevailed upon her to let me see, instead, what remained of the garden.

We had to go through the main part of the house, which was clearly no longer in use – faded, water-stained wallpapers, lace curtains yellow with age, antimacassars, tasselled velvet cushions, marks of damp on the ceilings and family portraits on the wall. It was hard to open the front door with its huge old iron key and rusty bolts. But when it finally swung open there, bathed in afternoon sunlight, was the garden – a desolate jungle of long grass and tangled vines, the remains of a large wooden arch lying across the path, and twisted wire frames which must once have been supports for roses. Truly a garden is a fragile thing.

But there, in the middle, in full and glorious flower, was one of the loveliest yellow roses I have seen. The flower was full and quartered, the softest creamy-yellow and on a bush now at least two metres high and as many wide, the scent of the flowers heavy on the late afternoon air. My first thought was that this was 'Cloth of Gold'. But it was autumn, and 'Cloth of Gold' flowers only in the spring.

Louie was happy for me to take cuttings of it, and of the only other surviving rose, a cheerful cherry-red with Tea rose foliage, which was also in full flower on a bush the size of a small tree. This one, Louie said, gave her great joy as she was too old now to go into the garden, but could see it from the window.

The remains of paths were there, an ingenious twisted wire basket used to support, I surmised, some sort of trailing plant, a weeping rose, perhaps. A wild tangle of Banksia rose and honeysuckle scrambled through two old apple trees and, under a twisted pear tree, was a huge patch of bright yellow *Sternbergia lutea*. I picked a big bunch to put in a bowl by the fire where Louie could see and enjoy them. She said there were still thousands of bulbs in the spring.

The next day I wrote to Louie, thanking her for her hospitality and for the rose cuttings. A week later came a letter from her. She had found the photographs and enclosed them with the letter.

They revealed a world long since gone — ladies in long dresses holding decorative parasols, the creator of the garden, proud and portly, with watch-chain and top hat. There were rose arches and arbours, paths edged in box or lavender (from the black and white photograph it was difficult to tell which). And here was the Gothic summerhouse, and roses looped along chains — and there in the middle what must have been my creamy-yellow rose. Here was formality indeed, in the midst of farming country in the very early days of Victoria. And somehow in no way incongruous.

My cuttings took and grew. Later I had knowledgeable visitors to the garden — Deane Ross and Walter Duncan, the big rose growers from South Australia — who both looked at my yellow rose and said, without hesitation, 'Cloth of Gold'. Now I have come upon several roses which are listed in English books as spring-flowering only, yet flower again for us, in our warmer climate, in autumn. Yet I have bought subsequently, from different growers, plants of 'Cloth of Gold' and they flower in spring only, while my rose from Camnethan continues to give a glorious display every autumn. So I call it simply 'Louie Wilson'.

I built my Gothic summerhouse in the paddock beyond the garden — but a summerhouse with a difference. I had it constructed as camouflage round an outdoor toilet and clothed it with the yellow 'Aviateur Blériot', pure white 'Silver Moon' and the creamy 'Albéric Barbier'. In front of them I planted a thick belt of shasta daisies (*Chrysanthemum maximum*).

Again we needed more topsoil. So, in the true Cathlaw tradition, we dug a second pond in a natural depression under the huge old pine tree at the back of the house. I wanted to line it in stone and for once I employed a self-styled 'expert' to do the job. He did a fine job, but I could not persuade him that a fountain would be out of place in a country garden (I had visions of rushing out, in French fashion, to turn it on every time a car drew up at the gate). So despite my emphatic rejection of the whole idea, he left a small hole in the stone floor — in case I should change my mind. In consequence of this the pond always leaked.

I planted the margins with *Iris kaempferi* (the Japanese water iris) in delicate shades of pink, blue and mauve, with white for contrast and deep purple for strength. They stood in water all the winter and we never watered them in summer and for me they were always the climax of the iris season, their great flat, saucer-shaped blooms coming, as they do, after the tall bearded iris are over. And on one corner

I planted a huge clump of Maria's soft, tan-coloured *Iris louisiana*. Behind them I planted blue agapanthus to give colour in the summer months when the iris were over, and behind that again, inspired by Camnethan, roses on chains.

A trip to a demolition yard at Talbot — another of those forgotten little Central Victorian towns — yielded a good supply of beautiful old turned verandah posts. We used four of them here in a semicircle behind the pond and slung heavy chains between.

Rampant climbers would be out of place here — pillar roses were what was needed. On the outer two I planted the bright pink, almost thornless, recurrent flowering Bourbon rose, 'Zéphirine Drouhin', and on the inner two the softer pink, again almost thornless, recurrent 'Clair Matin'. Behind and between them I put the grey-leaved *Chrysanthemum ptarmiciflorum*. I had been given plants from a friend's garden and loved the grey foliage against the pink. The first year after I planted it I cut off all the flowers before they opened in order to preserve the compact shape of the bushes. I had assumed, also, that it would be similar to *Chrysanthemum harad-janii* which has an insignificant gaudy yellow flower which detracts greatly from the beauty of the grey foliage, and would quite ruin my pink and grey colour scheme. Fortunately I missed a piece and it delighted me with clusters of little white daisy-like flowers.

Since then it has produced each year clouds of pure white blossom which are a perfect foil for the roses, especially for the soft pink of 'Clair Matin', and for the deep purples of 'Cardinal de Richelieu' and 'Hippolyte' nearby. It is frost-resistant and propagates relatively easily, though I never get a one hundred per cent strike, so I pot up replacement plants each year.

I was delighted with this corner of the garden and bought, in one of those 'antique' shops which have sprung up recently in every Australian country town, an old pine church pew — more at home in this country setting than scrolled iron work or classic teak. This was placed strategically under the old pine tree where one could sit, on summer afternoons, and watch the reflections of the iris in the water. And in the centre of the pond, on a moss-covered rock, I placed the little figure of a mermaid, shrouded in her own long hair, her hands clasped about her knees, the very essence of youth, and simplicity and gentleness. She was bought in a moment of reckless extravagance, the work of a sculptress friend of mine. The young model was Judith, my daughter's closest friend throughout her school days. She gives a focus and, for me, an added dimension to this corner of the garden, and is a constant source of joy.

Some Modern Roses 18

A path was needed to link Little Portion to the main house for, due largely to my inability to envisage the final layout and design the garden on paper and all at once, the little cottage stood, initially, rather like the proverbial shag on a rock, with the Miniature Garden behind it and a broad expanse of what not even the most charitable of persons could call 'lawn' in front.

Lawn, I decided quite early in the piece, was an impossibility on the plains of Central Victoria. Pictures of those velvety emerald swards in English garden books filled me alternately with despair and envy. There was barely enough water for the garden, certainly none to maintain lawns through those terrible burning January and February days. Added to this, the seed from the paddock grasses was blown continually into the garden, so that we waged sporadic war with dock, dandelions, capeweed, thistles and sorrel, and the only green parts of the 'lawn' in summer were those where clover had taken a firm hold. I remember reading, with joy, an article by Tommy Garnett where he urged Australians to cease, in this respect, emulating English gardeners and to regard their lawns as annuals.

So when I decided to run a broad path, a generous path where two people could walk comfortably abreast, from the house to Little Portion I was not destroying an expanse of potentially beautiful lawn. I would love to have paved that path, which was forced to curve, as usual, round the moss-covered boulders, with old handmade bricks such as I had used in the Miniature Garden, but the expense was prohibitive, so in the end I settled for scoria. It looked cheerful against the sombre grey of the bluestone buildings and weathered, in time, to a warm rust colour.

I made wide beds on each side of the path, and, in the interests of having colour for as much of the year as possible and cut flowers for the house, I decided to opt here for some modern roses.

In choosing these I started from a position of abysmal ignorance. While I had read extensively about the old shrub roses I had totally neglected the enormously wide field of modern Hybrid Teas. Essentially what I wanted was some pink and white roses, with the occasional dark red, which would bloom without cessation from November till the end of May! What I ended up with was a collection of largely 1960s and 1970s roses including, as might be expected, a couple of inspired choices and some horrible mistakes.

There can be no gardener anywhere in the world who has not heard of 'Iceberg', 'the rose of the century'. Trouble-free, ever-blooming, long-lasting, it was my first choice among the whites, despite Peter Beales's rather scathing dismissal! 'Virgo' and 'Mt Shasta' were planted here and they are excellent, but in no way exciting. The really inspired choice among the whites was 'Swany'. The flower closely resembles that of 'Sea Foam' but, instead of growing tall, it forms a wide, procumbent shrub and it really does flower for months on end with a very minimum of attention beyond the cutting off of deadheads.

I have to confess to a soft spot for 'Queen Elizabeth'. I love her long, pointed buds and she is so tall that she is ideal at the back of a border where her awkward, ungainly legs can be hidden by lower growing perennials. My mother had grown 'Dainty Bess' when I was a child. I suppose she would be classed now as a 'nostalgia rose'. Certainly she is that for me. She produces her soft pink, single blooms with their striking reddish-brown stamens over a long period, although the bush is seldom robust. I was pleased, too, with 'First Love' and her offspring, 'Pink Parfait', a Floribunda in several shades of pink.

The most successful of the reds was undoubtedly 'Elmshorn', named after the first nursery established by that famous family of Kordes in 1887. As tall as 'Queen Elizabeth' it, too, is happy at the back of a border where it can be relied upon to produce its clusters of cherry-red blooms from spring until the end of autumn. The dark red 'Europeana' I found plain dull, and 'Eye Paint' and 'Old Master', two of Sam McGredy's 'hand-painted' roses, were certainly not for me. They performed well, and were striking and unusual so that they often attracted the attention of visitors to the garden, but to me they seem a crude and clumsy attempt to do what the old striped roses do so charmingly.

These roses were all planted on the north side of the path. On the south side, in an attempt to break the cold south wind, I planted five crab-apples. The few I had already planted had done better than any other trees with the exception of the birches. So, being on a good thing, I decided to stick to it. Especially as they had the additional qualification of belonging to the Rosaceae family. I chose two *Malus* 'Lemoinei' for the contrast of the dark, reddish-purple foliage and wine-red flowers, two *Malus spectabilis* — blush pink flowers and little yellow apples — and the irresistible *Malus ioensis* 'Plena'.

Behind the crab-apples I planted a hedge of 'Stanwell Perpetual'. One day I shall amuse myself by making a list of the great roses which have started life as chance seedlings or sports. The list will be headed by this one and by the exquisite 'Souvenir de St Anne's'. There is a delightful story – the veracity of which I am not prepared to guarantee – that 'Stanwell Perpetual' was found as a seedling under a hedge in Somerset. Certain it is that most of the Spinosissimas (syn. Pimpinellifolias), the Scotch Burnet roses, have vast numbers of little black hips and do set a vast amount of seed. 'Stanwell', however, sets no seed and is sterile. It is thought to be a cross between *R. spinosissima* and *R. damascena semperflorens*. We do know that it was released in 1838 by a nurseryman called Lee who had his nursery where London airport now is. Growing well over a metre high, it makes a sprawling shrub with grey-green, ferny foliage, and produces in spring and autumn great numbers of palest pink, flat, many-petalled flowers with a delicious scent. It needs little care and no pruning save for the removal of dead wood, and is sufficiently dense to make an ideal hedge.

Fascinated by the description, I planted beside Little Portion two or tree plants of 'Wichmoss', released in 1911 and listed as a climbing Moss rose. Certainly the moss was plentiful, but I found the little cream flowers rather sparse and undistinguished and hardly worthy of the prominent place I had given it. The Miniature Garden was extended by the addition on the south side of a hedge of a dear little pink rose given me as cuttings by Nesta Mackellar.

High on a hill above the little township of Kyneton stands Woodside, one of the early bluestone homes which lend character to the district. Probably it had been built at about the same time as Bleak House, but by a rather more affluent person. The original owner, Captain Lavender, had come to Victoria from Maria Island off the coast of Tasmania, where he had been in charge of the penal settlement, and the property was known in the town as 'Lavender's old place', although Miss Mackellar had owned it for many years.

Approached by a long drive lined by dark old pines, it is surrounded by a rambling country garden separated from the farmland beyond by a hedge which had long since outgrown its allotted height and width. The old house, low and sprawling, its verandah clothed in climbing roses (now unpruned), was dignified still. High ceilings, French doors, marble fireplaces and cedar architraves lent an air of elegance which age could not detract from. Persian carpets, mahogany furniture, faded linen chair covers, solid family silver completed the picture.

And here Nesta Mackellar, in her late eighties, lived alone. And here she bred thoroughbred horses, racehorses, for which she cherished a passionate love, although she never had a bet on a race. On the south side of the garden was a gate in the hedge opening into the paddocks. There Nesta Mackellar had had a stone seat built where there was a view down to the Campaspe River and the Kyneton Racecourse beyond. Here she was sitting on the day I called about the roses, her binoculars in her hand, watching her horse, King Barak, on the track below. The race successfully over, we went round the garden.

The little pink rose must have been planted originally as a hedge round the kitchen garden. My cuttings took and made a hedge once more. It never grew above a metre in height and produced masses of small, mid-pink fragrant blooms, cup-shaped and borne in clusters – possibly it was one of the Poulsen roses, but I never had any confirmation of this, so called it simply 'Nesta Mackellar'. I never walk past it without thinking of that white-haired, dignified, independent old lady.

Having planted my modern roses, I addressed myself for the first time, seriously, to the question of spraying. This occupies a lengthy chapter in every book on rose growing, yet there are arguments against it. In the first place I had too many roses and not enough time to contemplate a regular spraying programme. In the second place I had a deep-rooted antipathy to filling the garden with poison every ten days or so. In the third place I was trying to encourage the birds. I would never persuade them that the garden was a haven for them if I regularly destroyed all the insects. So I made a firm resolution that, except in a dire emergency, I would not spray.

I had read a good deal about companion planting and about herbs so resolved instead to underplant my modern roses (the old ones seem, with the exception of the Bourbons and the Hybrid Perpetuals, to be less susceptible) with herbs. It could certainly do no harm and might possibly do some good.

So I planted big clumps of chives (*Allium schoenoprasum*) — the cone-shaped mauve flower heads were ideal with pink roses — and spring onions. I had planted pink and white single hollyhocks near 'Queen Elizabeth'. The tall heads of garlic (*Allium sativum*) reached almost as high and created quite an architectural effect, reminding me always of the onion towers on the churches in the south of Germany. Garlic chives (*Allium tuberosum*) produced umbels of little white florets and scattered abundant seed — too abundant sometimes. Different thymes were used as ground covers and the bulbs pushed up happily through the carpet they made. The enchanting blue-green lacy foliage of rue (*Ruta graveolens*) was perfect, but I tried always to cut off the acid yellow flowers.

In my little cottage in Castlemaine with its pocket-handkerchief garden I had had a chamomile lawn. I had used the English chamomile, *Anthemis nobilis*. Hours of patient weeding were needed to establish it and anything so labour intensive was out of the question at Bleak House. But I did want to plant chamomile. Its reputation as an insect repellent made it a 'must' and its tiny white daisy-like flowers and fine feathery foliage made it ideal as a ground cover under roses. It thrived among the modern roses and almost reconciled me to 'Eye Paint' with its brilliant vermilion single flowers with their white eye.

I would love to have planted a rosemary hedge, partly for the scent, partly for the legends surrounding it, such as the one which claims that rosemary will never grow taller than the height of Christ. But I really had no place for any more hedges, so settled instead for planting rosemary in three big old coppers — one of the few things I grew successfully in tubs as it is so drought-resistant it does not mind if you forget to water it. I much prefer the pale misty blue flowers of the old rosemary (*Rosmarinus officinalis*) to the 'improved' variety, 'Blue Lagoon', with its much deeper blue. Prostrate rosemary (*R. officinalis* 'Prostratus') quickly formed an edging to some of the beds and spilled over on to the paths, softening the edges and scenting the garden when trodden on.

I had read that parsley is 'helpful to roses in the garden'. I am not sure in what way this helpfulness manifests itself, but certainly the crisp green of its curly leaves made it an excellent ground cover, especially under tall white roses.

Winter savory (*Satureia montana*) was tough, didn't mind the heat or the dryness, seeded itself quickly into the paths and went on happily year after year. And the bees simply loved it.

Borage (*Borago officinalis*) and feverfew (*Chrysanthemum parthenium*) flourished and established colonies in all corners of the garden. For its name alone, I planted lady's bedstraw (*Galium verum*), but it proved far too invasive and had to be removed – not without difficulty. I planted it instead under a vigorous contorted willow where it ramped away and quickly formed a large, soft mat, fit for any lady's bed on a hot summer's day.

How effective all this was in combating diseases of the rose I do not know. Whether useful or not, my herbs were beautiful. Certainly we suffered from black spot from time to time but never in plague proportions. Mildew was almost unknown to us and when friends from Melbourne were wringing their hands over plagues of thrip in the spring, we were relatively untroubled.

The birds came each year to the garden and nested there. Albert delighted me one Christmas when he appeared with a pretty little bird-feeder on a high post, which allowed us to feed them out of reach of the cats – and of Cara, whose favourite pastime it was to chase the magpies, although I am convinced that both she and they knew that she had no chance of success. Each year they nested in the huge old pine tree at the back of the house. I know of no lovelier sound than the call of the magpie on a spring morning. And I think they did a good job with the aphids.

The crab-apples on the south side were a huge success. They grew apace and were soon sufficiently sturdy for me to plant clematis to grow through them. They also set quantities of seed and I found little crab-apples coming up where they were least expected.

One came up in the middle of the path, just on the corner where it curved round the side of Little Portion. It was beautifully placed in front of two mossy boulders and a clump of white nerines. But as it grew larger, squeezing between it and the increasingly rampant 'Wichmoss' became a real problem. One or the other would have to go.

I was delighted one day by a visit from Jean Galbraith, botanist, lecturer, author and, above all, an inspired and impassioned gardener. As she pushed past the thorny arms of 'Wichmoss', stretched across the path, I apologised for the crab, explaining (quite unnecessarily) that it was a self-sown seedling and that I had been promising myself for months to move it.

'Why?' she demanded.

'It's in the middle of the path,' I said, stating the obvious.

'Well, then,' came the crisp reply, 'move the path!'

Penstemon.

19 *Some Early Tea Roses*

Quite early in my life as a rose gardener, I fell deeply and irrevocably in love with the early Tea roses. Most of them originated in France and, one and all, they have that air of elegance and sophistication we associate with things Parisian.

The first to be planted in the garden was 'Safrano'. He was first released in France in 1839, but the old cottage where I found him, rising out of a sea of thistles and dock, was a far cry from Paris. It was no more than a tumbledown shack made largely of galvanised iron and apparently held together by wire and pieces of baler twine. Across the back of the house, where once had been a verandah, was a large area enclosed by wire netting, an approximation to an aviary. In this were housed vast numbers of budgerigars and canaries. The old fellow who lived there sold them to eke out his existence. It stood in the midst of an old, overgrown garden – wild iris and daffodils, twisted old apple and pear trees, and across the front verandah, two metres high and as far across, was a fine bush of 'Safrano'. I did not know its name when I first found it, the late afternoon sun shining through its reddish foliage and lighting up the masses of blooms, the colour of rich dairy cream with just a hint of apricot.

70

The old chap was happy to give me cuttings — they were amongst my first successes, the result of much loving tender care. They rewarded me with a great profusion of bloom every spring and autumn. With a sense of nostalgia I paid a visit to the cottage recently, only to find it gone. The old fellow had won the lottery. With a desire, I suppose, to erase the memories of his former poverty, he had torn down the old cottage and built a brand new brick veneer. 'Safrano' was gone, and in its place was a row of standard 'Peace' and 'Blue Moon' on either side of the concrete front path. A hedge of photinia completed the picture, the old fruit trees having been consigned to the bonfire. Filled with sadness, I went home and, in protest, put in two large pots of cuttings of 'Safrano', my own bushes being by now large enough.

Gradually I added more Tea roses to the garden, although I found them more delicate than some of the others, and it needed care and constant vigilance to get them through our harsh winters.

I bought a simple soil-testing kit and found my soil to be slightly on the acid side of normal. I had suspected this from the steadily increasing stands of sorrel in the garden. So I bought large bags of lime and distributed it according to a regular timetable. This, together with twice yearly applications of blood and bone with ten percent of sulphate of potash added, gradually improved the soil. What there was of my topsoil was good and heavy but there was not a great deal of it. Albert built three huge compost bins out behind the barn and we religiously put all green weeds and vegetable matter from the kitchen into them. Rose prunings were burned and the ash added to the compost. All of this undoubtedly helped, but most effective, I think, were the truck loads of mulch I regularly collected from the racing stables in Kyneton.

Kyneton has a picturesque small racecourse and in its vicinity were two good trainers. The winters being so bleak, the horses are stabled on winter nights. The straw, with fresh manure, is swept out each morning, and the trainers were only too happy if someone came and carted it away. So I mulched, especially my Tea roses, with five to ten centimetres of straw and manure which the earthworms gradually carried down into the soil.

Ideal for a pillar or a pergola or on the verandah posts is the beautiful pure white 'Sombreuil'. Graham Thomas wrote of it that it is 'to be treasured for all time'. I certainly treasured mine and it repaid me by producing its wonderful, flat, very double blooms for months on end. Their perfectly heavenly scent on a spring morning is one of the glories of the garden. I grew it as a climber and gave it a pergola to climb over, but it never reached above two metres.

'Souvenir de Madame Léonie Viennot' was a horse of a different colour. Robust and vigorous, she attained a height of three metres in her first year and produced a mass of soft apricot double roses with copper tonings and a strong scent. The cuttings I took in her second year all struck with no need for the tender care I had lavished on 'Safrano'.

I planted three of 'Marie van Houtte', although *R. bracteata* later smothered one of them. She is a rich cream, heavily flushed with pink, and is generous with her very fragrant blooms, and sturdier than many of her relatives. She looks splendid with the little cream and pink eschscholzias as an underplanting. It does need constant vigilance to keep the dominant orange ones away and I found I had to pull them out regularly and throw them on the compost heap.

'Maman Cochet', again from France, and a daughter of 'Marie van Houtte', grows tall and angular but produces her slightly blowsy, untidy blooms in generous abundance. In the same bed I grew 'Baronne Henriette de Snoy'. I think I would have grown her for her name alone — how I wish I knew who the Baronne was. Her many virtues, however, rendered this piece of folly uncalled for. A daughter of that wonderful full, creamy-apricot 'Gloire de Dijon', she has all the virtues of her parent: full form, delicious perfume, frequent flowering. She does like a warm spot and rather resents heavy pruning, but is equally at home in the garden or in a large pot on a terrace. I grow her always with the soft pink violas round her feet, and she gives me infinite pleasure.

'Gloire de Dijon', herself a daughter of 'Souvenir de la Malmaison' is a 'must'. She does need support, as, with encouragement and a little pampering, she can be persuaded to reach a height of five metres.

With 'Général Galliéni', bred, again, in France in 1899 and named after the first Governor of Madagascar after it had become part of the French Empire, I had infinite trouble and no real success. He should have been a tough old fellow — his namesake is also reputed to have been responsible later for the defence of Paris at the beginning of World War I — but he resented the first hint of frost and, although I nursed him back to health each spring, he never really flourished. This was a bitter disappointment as I have seen him standing tall and sturdy in other gardens and I love his strange, irregularly shaped blooms, ranging in colour from buff, through various shades of pink, to deep red. I planted some of the old red and green alstroemeria with him and it throve as the Général languished. It had brought itself to the garden — another of Sarah Ann's legacies, perhaps — and I was somewhat alarmed to read later that, a native of South America, it so loves our climate that it has, in some places, escaped from gardens and taken on the nature of a weed. Certainly the yellow and orange varieties (*Alstroemeria aurantiaca*) grow wild on Mt Macedon, great sheets of gold and flame colour — perfectly splendid, but not beloved by the owners of the gardens.

It was while on holiday in Tasmania that I heard a romantic story of a red, red rose — reputedly an early Tea rose — the first rose ever to come to Tasmania. It had been brought out on a sailing ship from the famous old garden of Montacute in England to be planted in the garden of a grand old home built in the early days of the colony somewhere near Hollow Tree in central Tasmania, and named Montacute in memory of the owner's English home.

I could find no first-hand news of the old home, so set out one morning to look for it. We took the road which leads from Bothwell to Hamilton. Hollow Tree is no more than a name on a signpost. There was certainly no sign of Montacute, but there was an imposing old sandstone home overlooking the valley, so we drove in to make enquiries. In the big stone barn, Des Hallett was crutching sheep.

He was the fifth generation of his family to live in this home, and it transpired that he also owned Montacute. He told us how his great-uncle had bought it in 1905. He had driven to the auction in horse and buggy and arrived too late. So he offered the successful bidder $1000 and Montacute became his.

'There was a garden once,' Des Hallett said, 'but there's nothing now.' However, he gave us instructions. There is no road leading to Montacute and we had to drive across paddocks. The rough track seemed to go on for ever and we had opened and closed four gates and were quite sure that we had missed the way, when suddenly, high on a hill, we saw a church spire. Below it, in a valley, on the banks of a stream, lay Montacute.

The little church was well maintained, and all the headstones in the churchyard bore the name of Hallett, except for one right at the gate inscribed William Langdon.

The house was a different story. Quite deserted, shingles missing from the roof and the grand old fanlight over the panelled front door shattered, French doors standing open and the fine staircase dangerously broken, it spoke of loneliness and desolation. The remains of an orchard were there – huge pear trees and seedling apples and plums, and the foliage of what must have been a sea of daffodils in the spring – and the remnants of a high stone wall which surrounded the garden. Of roses there was no trace. Some of them are incredibly tough and resilient, so we searched all along the creek bank and through the long grass but could find nothing except for the little pink dog rose that grows wild all over Tasmania.

When I got home I searched for information about Montacute. It had been built, I discovered, in 1834 by Captain William Langdon. He was a sea captain, master of the *Lusitania* and prominent in the shipping world of early Tasmania.

He had been born in the Vicarage of Montacute in England, after which he named his new home. He took up two thousand two hundred hectares on the Clyde near Bothwell in 1823 and brought out between sixty and seventy persons from England. He imported stud cattle, horses, sheep and pigs, also deer and hunting dogs, pheasants and partridge. Birds for his aviary included the blackbird, thrush, goldfinch and skylark. He brought trees and shrubs, including a willow grown from a cutting taken from Napoleon's grave – and he brought roses.

The whole settlement was enclosed by a high sandstone wall. Blacks and bushrangers represented a constant threat. In 1855 William Langdon had built the little church and had it dedicated by the first Anglican Bishop of Tasmania.

Gertrude Jekyll, writing in 1904 of Montacute in England, said: 'Wonderful are those great stone houses of the early English Renaissance (it was built towards the end of the sixteenth century by Sir Edward Phelips) wonderful in their bold grasp and sudden assertion of new possibilities of domestic architecture.'

I wonder what she would have said of Montacute in Australia, this once charming and dignified home with its lovely gardens, its orchards and deer-park, set down in the midst of a strange and frightening land representing, with its little stone church, a tiny piece of the England William Langdon had known and loved. Wonderful, indeed.

It was a disappointment to find no roses at Montacute. We had no real clues to the identity of the rumoured red rose. The suggestion that it was an early Tea rose I did not take very seriously, for 'Adam' is usually accepted as the earliest of the Teas and he was bred in 1833. Most of them date from the end of the nineteenth century. It was more likely to have been an old Gallica.

We had taken a new road back to Ross and all thoughts of the red rose were driven abruptly from my mind when, round a bend, we came upon one of the most beautiful plants of 'Lady Hillingdon' that I have seen. At least two metres high and just as wide, she covered the wall of an old stone barn – a mass of golden roses. We got out to admire her. She has the same rich plum-coloured foliage as 'Safrano', lit up now by the setting sun. And her scent – a scent which Graham Thomas describes as 'the fragrance of a newly opened packet of tea with a hint of apricots' — filled the evening air. 'Lady Hillingdon' is one of the few early Teas which did not originate in France. She is English, bred by Lowe and Shawyer in 1910, the climbing form being a sport released in 1917. How warmly she must have been welcomed during those dark days of World War I!

Standing by the roadside I planned a new corner of the garden. Of course, she must be planted beside 'Safrano' and the underplanting must be blue: nepeta as basic ground cover; deepest blue Dutch iris for spring — I had a mental picture of them against the new red spring foliage of the roses — *Polemonium caeruleum* with its cup-shaped blue flowers and pretty leaves; the dwarf-growing electric-blue *Penstemon heterophyllus* and big clumps of what is, perhaps, my favourite among the geraniums, *Geranium himalayense* which produces its violet-blue flowers all through the summer.

A splash of scarlet from 'Geranium'.

'Louie Wilson'

The famous old Gallica rose 'Charles de Mills'.

The climbing rose 'New Dawn'.

'The Apothecary's Rose' with tall bearded iris.

'Blossom Time' — always in flower.

(*Right*) The Nursery went forward.

(*Below* The house at Glenara with *R. banksiae lutea*, wisteria and 'Cramoisi Supérieur'.

'Sparrieshoop' and iris in the front garden.

'Kitty Kininmonth' covering an archway.

(*Left*) The Alister Clark garden. Inside the garden is 'Daydream' with the summerhouse in the background. (Barbara Strange).

(*Below*) The Bookshop with the stump of the old willow and *R. banksiae lutea* in the background.

'Lady Hillingdon' with *Nepeta* 'Blue Hills Giant'.

'Lorraine Lee' took Australia by storm.

'Reine de Centfeuilles' planted as a hedge with *Digitalis* × *mertonensis*.

Violas.

The Hybrid Musk Roses 20

'Penelope', 'Cornelia', 'Felicia', 'Thisbe', 'Moonlight' and 'Pax' – their very names conjure up pictures of old gardens, of Victorian times, of ladies in long skirts and picture hats, of portly old gentlemen with snowy beards and watch-chains. Yet these roses are not so very old. They belong, most of them, to the first quarter of this century. But they are a godsend to those of today's gardeners who have a leaning towards nostalgia and who want to plant 'old roses', but want them to flower more than once a year. They are just old enough to sneak into the old rose category and yet they have the capacity to flower not only abundantly but continuously.

The passion for 'old roses' was at its peak in this country in the 1970s, the Heritage Rose Society being founded, thanks to the untiring efforts of Trevor Nottle in South Australia, in 1978. Then, for a time, specialist rose nurseries were full of Gallicas, Damasks, Albas and Mosses. But the average Australian gardener – even the fortunate one – has only a quarter of an hectare or so at his disposal, and before long even those with an abiding passion for old roses were looking for a longer flowering period. It was then that the Hybrid Musks came into their own. Big, generous shrubs, most of them, up to two metres high and as much across, with

75

subtle colours and strong perfume and, most importantly, the ability to flower for months on end — great trusses of flowers forty to sixty centimetres across and bearing fifteen to twenty individual heads of bloom.

What more could any gardener want? At about the same time cottage gardens came, very sensibly, into vogue. 'Very sensibly' because they fill the needs of the home gardener who wants colour and variety in his quarter of an hectare, and who loves to potter and experiment and plant seeds and take cuttings and whose home, in any case, would not lend itself to the setting of a formal garden. The Hybrid Musks are perfect for cottage gardens, for mixed borders, for growing with holly-hocks and penstemons, snapdragons and foxgloves, honeysuckle and paeonies.

I had planted six or seven 'Buff Beauties' and the same number of 'Penelope' along my western boundary fence before I was aware of the manifold virtues of the Hybrid Musks. But they had done all that I had expected of them and more. They quickly outstripped 'Lamarque' (who hated our bleak winters) and 'Nevada' (who never looked really robust for me) and became the outstanding feature of that part of the garden. In the spring they covered themselves with glory and in the autumn the sight of 'Buff Beauty' against the russet, red and gold of the ornamental grapevine on the fence was quite unforgettable.

And then, one spring, I visited Heide, the sculpture park and garden at Bulleen, and realised that 'Penelope' was capable of even more than I asked of her. For here she was trained as a climber over a rose arch in the kitchen garden — and she was quite breathtaking.

A copy of *Rebels and Precursors*, given to me a few Christmases previously, had been my introduction to Heide and to John and Sunday Reed and the company of artists and writers they had gathered round them in an old, weatherboard farm-house set in six hectares of paddocks which sloped down to the Yarra River near Heidelberg.

While John, with Sidney Nolan, Max Harris, Albert Tucker, Joy Hester and Arthur Boyd had painted and written, philosophised and argued, Sunday, brilliant, witty, elegant Sunday, who neither painted nor wrote, had created a garden. And this was, for her, and for the many people who visit it still, just another form of artistic expression.

With a total disregard for conventional and accepted concepts of garden design, she planted fruit trees, roses, vegetables and herbs in glorious profusion. Silver-beet grows amongst the wallflowers, lavender rubs shoulders with green peppers, zucchini vines trail among the roses.

And 'Penelope', on her rose arch, looks down on a tangle of soapwort, valerian, feverfew and mulleins. And further over, in the garden of the old house itself, she climbs, in company with wisteria, over a mellow brick wall.

Clearly the Hybrid Musks, vigorous and versatile, were worthy of far closer attention than I had, to date, given them.

They are one of the many legacies left to gardeners by the English clergy of Victorian times — times when the clergy had leisure to indulge in fox-hunting, quail shooting, fly-fishing — and gardening.

All his life the Rev. Joseph Pemberton had loved roses. 'I was raised in a rose atmosphere and loved the rose when a child in petticoats,' he wrote. He grew up in a garden — the sort of garden where standard roses grew in a walled kitchen garden among the gooseberries and currants. He learnt to bud roses at the age of twelve. When taken to church on Sundays as a small boy he vied with the elderly gentleman in the next pew as to who had the finest rose in his buttonhole.

With his father, he regularly visited the rose shows at the Crystal Palace. And each November, when he went back to school, he took with him a flower of 'Souvenir de la Malmaison' in an empty barley sugar tin. This served as a constant reminder of home and all that it meant and it was taken home again, brown and battered from constant fingering, at Christmas time.

He started showing roses in 1875 and continued to do so for the next thirty years. In his retirement he devoted himself entirely to the breeding of roses.

In his very readable and scholarly book *Roses — their History, Development and Cultivation*, published in 1908, he devotes a chapter to hybridisation and cross-breeding. He lists the roses he found useful in his breeding programme — initially 'Trier' and 'Aglaia' both with *R. moschata* and *R. multiflora* in their parentage. He gives clear and detailed instructions for the amateur, would-be rose breeder, encouraging him to 'take it up seriously and he will find in it a recreation of deepest interest'. Certainly the Rev. Pemberton found in it both interest and success. There is little trace of the original Musk rose in his Hybrid Musks for he crossed his original parents with a succession of Teas, Hybrid Teas and Hybrid Perpetuals and, to use the words of Peter Beales 'he came up with a complete breakthrough — a distinct strain of long-flowering, shrub roses, with substantial flowers borne in clusters and in quantities equal to those of Polyanthas'.

Joseph Pemberton was inspired, perhaps, by his fellow cleric, the Rev. Reynolds Hole, Dean of Rochester. Inaugural President of the Royal National Rose Society, he is known to rosarians the world over. Kindly and genial, he found in gardening, and in roses in particular, his chief passion in life. He gives, in *The Six of Spades*, a delightful picture of the English country clergyman of the time:

I cut a bouquet of the last roses of autumn ('Dijon's Glory', generous 'Jules Margottin', brave 'Maréchal Vaillant' and fair 'Souvenir de Malmaison') inter-mixing a few bits of hardy ferns and of feathers from the Pampas grass. After breakfast, writing a sermon with part of my posy before me . . . I refreshed myself twice by peeping into my little houses, by a hasty survey of my treasures, in vinery, greenhouse and stove. For luncheon, I had a luscious, Beurré D'Aman-lis pear, which I consolidated with a brace of dry biscuits, and medicated with a glass of sherry. In the afternoon I had a dig in my kitchen-garden, which made me feel as though I could swarm up the greasiest pole, and eat the leg of mutton afterwards; and then in my parochial walk I took two portions of the bouquet aforesaid, and two small bunches of grapes, to four of my sick folk; and I would that a certain earnest and eloquent London preacher, who told us that we clergy were not to entertain the desire of becoming good gardeners — I would that he had seen the smiles which welcomed both flowers and fruit.

Dean Hole planned and organised the first National Rose Show and travelled the length and breadth of England looking at gardens, talking to gardeners and encouraging local communities to establish their own flower shows. His first and most famous book, *A Book about Roses*, appeared in 1869. It was warmly received and widely read. So famous was he in his own time that when, on one occasion, he turned up unannounced to see the roses at Belvoir Castle, the home of the Duke of Rutland, the Head Gardener, when he learned the identity of his guest, so wished to honour him that he did the only thing that came to mind and shouted to the under-gardeners: 'Turn on the fountains, turn on the fountains!'

And there were, among the English clergy, others who left their mark and for whom roses became an abiding passion. There was Bishop Darlington, author himself of a book entitled simply *Roses* which appeared in 1911. One of the Hybrid Musks (but not one of Pemberton's) is named after him. And the Rev. Foster-Melliar wrote in 1910 *The Book of the Rose*. He was a great exhibitor and for him showing roses was more rewarding than breeding them.

Fortunately for posterity these men of the cloth considered rose growing, and gardening in general, as an occupation commensurate with their calling. The curate in Dean Hole's book, *The Six of Spades*, quotes, in justification of the time spent in his garden, the Book of Genesis, Chapter 2, Verse 8: 'And the Lord planted a garden eastward in Eden and there He put the man whom He had formed.' And he concludes his dissertation on the joys of gardening with talk of 'the Christian gardeners who hear "the voice of the Lord God, walking in the garden" '.

So with heartfelt thanks to these clerics-cum-rosarians, I planted 'Bishop Darlington'. I put him in the same bed as 'Safrano', whom he somewhat resembles, being a semi-single of a most delicate creamy-apricot. 'Cornelia' and 'Felicia' are both of Pemberton's breeding. 'Cornelia' forms a big shrub, one and a half metres wide and just as high. She bears great heads of small apricot-pink blooms in splendid contrast to her bronze foliage. She looks fine beside the soft yellow of 'Buff Beauty' and with an under-planting of blue: *Veronica teucrium* and *Veronica gentianoides* whose leaves form a dense weed-suppressing mat; some of Fred's tall bearded iris; bog sage (*Salvia uliginosa*) with its sky-blue flowers and its tolerance of almost any garden conditions.

'Felicia' needs to be planted in a group of at least three and warrants a bed almost to herself. She was bred in 1928, the result of a cross between 'Trier' and the much-loved 'Ophelia'. She forms a bush something over a metre in height and breadth and bears soft, salmon-pink blooms continuously. I planted seven plants in a circular bed with the deeper apricot climber, 'Souvenir de Madame Léonie Viennot' on a tripod as a centrepiece. For underplanting I used *Geum rivale* 'Leonard', the exquisite white sage (*Salvia transcaucasica*) and *Salvia sclarea* with its delicate white, mauve and pink-tinted flowers – an annual, this last one, but it sometimes sets seed and is, in any case, worth planting every year, for there is nothing like it for sheer delicacy of colour.

'Autumn Delight', not one of Pemberton's and of unknown parentage, became one of my favourites. Its semi-single flowers are the essence of simplicity – softest creamy-yellow, fading to white, with golden stamens. The foliage is a deep, polished green. In the same bed I planted 'Pax'. This is one of Pemberton's earliest and again bred from 'Trier'. It produces big clusters of pure white, nearly single blooms with amber stamens and it reaches a height of two metres. With Cathlaw in mind, I surrounded it with the scarlet *Geum*, 'Mrs Bradshaw'.

'Vanity' I resisted for a number of years. It makes a big, sprawling, untidy bush with rather sparse foliage and I found its hot pink difficult to place. Finally, because of my ever-deepening affection for all its friends and relations, I succumbed and planted two together with an underplanting of blue, mauve and silver: the grey-leaved *Chrysanthemum haradjanii* and blue violas at ground level, and *Campanula latiloba*, which blooms all summer through and sends its spires of lavender-blue blooms right up through the rose. It spreads quickly and forms a dense mat. And from Suzanne Price, who specialises in small and rare bulbs, I got bulbs of *Oxalis hirta* (small but not rare), which produces little open flowers like lavender jewels in autumn, is very hardy, multiplies quickly but is not at all invasive.

I remembered Christopher Lloyd and his six metre hedge of 'Penelope', all struck from cuttings, and resolved to try propagating the Hybrid Musks myself as they really warrant planting in large groups. Without exception they struck easily and as I gloated over my little new plants as I potted them up I found myself thinking again of Dean Hole and his 'dear little cuttings, so bravely upright in their thumb-pots; so charmingly conceited at having roots of their own!'

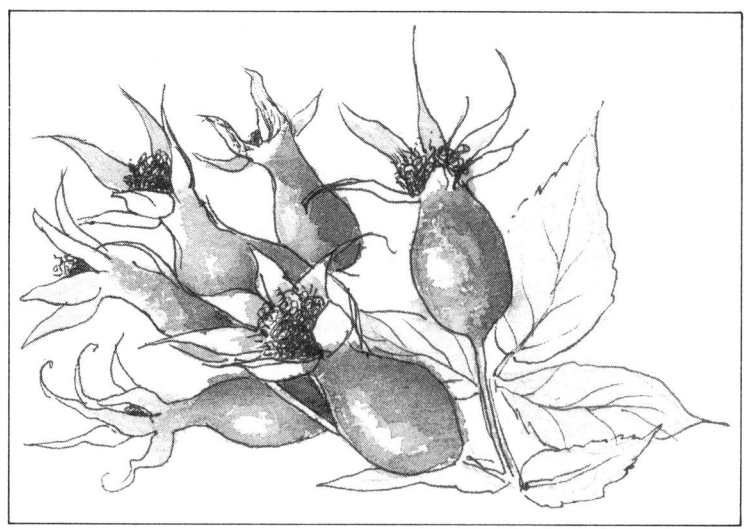

Rose hips.

21

Species Roses in the Orchard

At the end of 1982 the farmer who had been agisting his sheep on my sixty-eight hectares decided he no longer needed the land, having bought another property adjoining his own. So I had to face the problem of what was to be done with this (to me) great expanse of grazing land. Ungrazed, it quickly becomes a bushfire hazard, so stock of some kind there had to be.

After much consideration I decided that the best solution was to build a small cottage and to put in a tenant who would, as a part-time occupation, look after the land, stocking it, either with his own sheep or mine. He might even be persuaded to lend a hand in the garden.

The cottage was built of stone from the property as Little Portion had been, and much thought was given to designing it in such a way that it would fit into the landscape and not be too much at variance with Bleak House itself. So well did we succeed in this that I had a visit one day, as the roof was going on, from Norm Ward from the big mill. He had just had an indignant phone call from a neighbour who had lived in the area all his life to say that 'the little old stone cottage north of Bleak House was being demolished and something should be done about it!'

We called it Satis, the name of Miss Haversham's house in *Great Expectations* — partly because I liked the idea of adding to the Dickensian flavour of the property, and partly because it was 'enough' — enough of building, enough of expansion, and in itself enough — no frills but cosy and comfortable — enough.

Between Satis and the end of the garden was one-third of an hectare of empty paddock. I did not want to extend the garden. The fence was already covered in ramblers. Trees, I decided, would form a pleasing link between the garden and the cottage. And, if trees, then why not fruit trees? And so an orchard was planned.

This was apple country and apples would obviously do well. Pears and plums were in all the old gardens in the area and I had seen big old walnut trees bearing heavy crops in Kyneton, eight and a half kilometres away. Apricots and peaches did not do well, but medlars did and quinces.

And so I planned an orchard on formal lines, with the trees in rows about six metres apart. I planted three varieties of pears and three of plums (I was especially attracted to one with the marvellous name of 'Sultan's Blood'!); walnuts and almonds, olives, quinces and medlars; one nectarine (as an experiment and because I love them, but it never fruited) and a great variety of apples.

In my choice of these last I was guided by my friend Ian Hargrave. Ian lived half an hour's drive north of Malmsbury at Harcourt in the granite belt, in the midst of Victoria's apple-growing district. Here he had a sixteen hectare apple orchard, an enchanting old granite house built by his grandfather, a rambling country garden and a small nursery. Peacocks and pheasants roamed the garden; the most prolific 'Nancy Hayward' rose I have ever seen adorned the front verandah; and in a small outbuilding, now a gallery, hung a collection of Ian's water colours. He loved this part of Victoria and he painted the early settlers' cottages, the old pubs and barns of the district — many of them now demolished. In the intervals between painting, collecting antiques and playing the very beautiful old harpsichord before the open fire in his living room, he gardened.

On his advice I planted Jonathans, Red Delicious, Golden Delicious, Stewart's Seedling, Five Crowns, Cox's Orange Pippin, and, from Clive Winmill at Badger's Keep, one with the inexplicable name of 'Winter Banana'.

Right on the fence-line, after a great deal of thought and with many misgivings, I planted a row of the Leyland cypress (× *Cupressocyparis leylandii*) to form both a windbreak and a visual break.

I had decided not to prune my fruit trees except for the removal of old wood and badly crossing branches. I could never possibly use a fraction of the fruit they, when mature, would produce. Blossom and fine-looking trees were my objective.

Just at this time a friend, seeing my young orchard, presented me with half a dozen Chinese silky chickens and half a dozen ducks — beautiful ducks they were, with bronze feathers and deep turquoise green heads. They would add a splendid touch, free-ranging among the trees.

The very first night we lost one to a marauding fox who had crossed the paddocks from the quarries. Willy was obviously not taking his duties as a watchdog seriously enough, so both chickens and ducks would have to be shut up at night. Henhouses are traditionally unlovely things and I was loath to spoil the appearance of my orchard. After lengthy consultation with Albert, I decided we would have two A-frame houses, painted charcoal grey and planted with the climbing rose, 'Paul's Scarlet', one for the hens, one for the ducks. Albert set to work with a will and by nightfall the first one was up and painted. Enticed by a handful of wheat, the ducks went in happily and seemed to accept this as home.

I was reminded again of Cathlaw as we dug the pond for them. But we wanted water this time, not topsoil. It was a good-sized pond. We lined it with plastic and Albert and I paved it with flat stone from the quarries, set in cement. With the cement we mixed a waterproofing compound and dark grey colouring matter and were well pleased with the result. The margins were planted thickly with blue agapanthus and yellow cannas and a couple of big clumps of pampas grass which would provide shelter for the ducks and a nesting place should the spirit move them. This done, we filled the pond with water and stood back and watched with great satisfaction as the enthusiastic ducks took their first swim.

I was very taken that spring with *Rosa canina*, the little pale pink dog rose which grows wild in the quarries. The birds had dropped seed in the garden, too, and it came up in unwanted places. Despite its delicate flowers and colourful hips, it is really not for the garden, being a thorny, awkward, tangled shrub, and yet I wanted it somewhere (other than in the quarries), both for its beauty and for its historic significance, it being the commonest of the wild roses native to Britain and Europe.

So I dug a couple of seedlings out of the garden and planted them in the orchard. And this was the beginning of a collection of species roses. I had left a generous space between trees, so decided to plant a row of species roses between each two rows of trees, so that I had roses and trees alternately. Here it would not matter if they grew large and untidy. There would be no need to prune them and they could grow as they would do in the wild.

So began a new love affair. There is something very appealing about the species roses – the freshness and simplicity of the small, single blooms, and the thought that they are today as they have been for many thousands of years, long before the birth of Christ. Many of them have colourful hips, some of them beautiful foliage and some of them wonderful autumn colour. They originated in Britain, in Europe, in the USA and Canada, in Asia and in the Middle East. Strange that none of them is native to the southern hemisphere, and yet they are quite at home when planted here.

I chose with care, but my choice was, by necessity, limited by commerical availability. At the top of my list was *R. willmottiae* from western China. I had never seen it growing, but had read descriptions of its fine, bluish-tinted foliage, plum-purple stems and small lilac-pink flowers. More importantly, I had just finished reading Audrey le Lievre's *Miss Willmott of Warley Place*, a fascinating account of the life of that inspired and eccentric gardener for whom the rose was named when it was brought to England in 1904. I have only once handled a copy of her great book, *The Genus Rosa*, the culmination of her life's work, but some of the wonderfully detailed watercolours which she commissioned Alfred Parsons to paint were made available to us again in 1987 by Graham Stuart Thomas in his book *A Garden of Roses*.

Next came *Rosa farreri persetosa*, again from China, chosen partly for its name, 'The Threepenny bit Rose', and partly because of a picture I had seen of the long arching canes weighed down with tiny, mauve-pink flowers. Since for newer generations of gardeners a 'threepenny bit' is no longer a concept, I expect this delightful name will fall into disuse. 'The One-cent Rose' does not have the same charm!

It was some of the American roses which provided spectacular autumn colour in the orchard. *Rosa setigera* ('The Prairie Rose') which has its origins in the USA and in Canada, forms a big sprawling bush with cerise-pink fragrant blooms and fewer thorns than most. *Rosa woodsii fendleri* has attractive ferny foliage, lilac-pink flowers with soft golden stamens, followed by clusters of red hips. And, most spectacular of them all, *Rosa virginiana* with red-tinted stems, bright pink flowers with yellow stamens and autumn foliage that turns from gold to flame red, to orange, to purple and every shade in between.

Rosa sweginzowii from north-west China I chose for its hips – orange-red, shaped like little flagons, comparable only with those of *Rosa moyesii* and its hybrids.

Rosa glauca which, when I planted it, was known as '*Rosa rubrifolia*', is the landscape architect and flower arranger's dream – not for its flowers, which are the usual lilac-pink and quite undistinguished, but for the wonderful purplish colour of its stems, its bluish-grey foliage and its spectacular hips. At a distance, in autumn, it resembles quite strikingly *Crataegus tanacetifolia* (also, of course, a member of the Rosaceae family).

I think it was the thorns which earned *Rosa sericea pteracantha* a place in the collection. As it comes from Mt Omei in China it was known for a long time as '*R. omeiensis pteracantha*'. Much easier are the popular names, 'The Wing-thorn Rose' or 'The Maltese Cross Rose' – the latter because it is a rarity in having only four petals. The tiny pure white roses are delightful, but the thorns are the real feature – huge, elongated and blood-red they make it a formidable bush. It is best planted where it will catch the rays of the setting sun.

Two shorter, suckering, thicketing roses, both from North America and Canada, form great decorative clumps. *Rosa blanda* produces pink flowers, larger than most of the species roses and it is almost thornless. *Rosa nitida* is another of those with glorious autumn colouring. Its bright pink flowers are followed by round red hips.

I planted two great climbers in the orchard, but since there was nothing for them to climb on in that flat expanse they just formed great, sprawling mounds. *Rosa brunonii* (The Himalayan Musk Rose) will climb twelve to fifteen metres up trees, where its clusters of little white fragrant blooms, admirably set off by its grey-green foliage, hang down in great festoons. Alas, there was no opportunity for such a display here, but it performed admirably nevertheless. *Rosa moschata*, with its haunting, musky scent, flowered in early summer and often again in autumn. Coming from southern Europe and the Middle East, perhaps it was more at home in Australia than in the colder climate of England where it first made its appearance during the reign of Henry VIII.

No collection of species roses would be complete without at least one of the pale yellow ones from China. So I planted *R. hugonis*, brought to Europe in 1900 by Father Hugh, a French missionary. The ferny foliage sets off the tiny, soft buttercup yellow flowers, which are followed later by rather inconspicuous reddish-black hips. *R. primula*, also from northern China and Turkestan, has long arching canes, set with creamy yellow flowers. The foliage is said to carry the scent of incense, hence its popular name, 'The Incense Rose'. I cannot honestly say I have noticed it.

I have left *R. eglanteria* till last – eglantine, the sweet briar of England, sung by Shakespeare, conjuring up memories of English hedgerows and country byways. Its bright pink roses in clusters are followed by brilliant scarlet hips which hang on into the winter, and the foliage, when crushed, has a scent of apples – so much so that at Mottisfont Abbey, the great rose garden planned by Graham Stuart Thomas in the early 1970s, *R. eglanteria* is planted behind the seats around the fountain which forms the centrepiece of the garden so that 'whichever way the wind blows, the sweet apple aroma will reach the seated occupants'.

So the orchard became much more than a collection of fruit trees. Here were gathered together roses from far-flung corners of the globe and from times far distant from our own.

Many of these big sprawling bushes with their fine foliage and tiny single blooms bear little resemblance to their descendants, the roses of today. For Australians this has a special importance. We have no species roses of our own but where modern roses with their often opulent flowers look ill-at-ease with our Australian native plants, these old species roses look at home. They open up new possibilities for gardeners who have devoted themselves mainly to Australian natives and have thought that, for them, roses were out of the question.

The Chinese silkies and the ducks flourished. At one stage the duck population reached thirty! They never did nest under the pampas grass provided for them, but preferred instead the inner recesses of the mounds of *R. moschata* and *R. brunonii* or the honeysuckle we had planted along the orchard side of the fence to mingle with the rambling roses on the garden side.

Helleborus.

My Introduction to Alister Clark 22

It was some time in early 1983 – just after I had retired in Melbourne and was revelling in being able to work full-time at Bleak House – that I had a momentous visit from Tommy Garnett.

We had met briefly some ten years earlier, when we were both involved in education, but since then, although I was a regular reader of his wide-ranging articles in the weekly gardening supplement in the *Age*, Melbourne's leading daily newspaper, I had had no personal contact with him.

I had visited his fascinating garden at Blackwood, The Garden of St Erth, started when he was still Headmaster of Geelong Grammar School, and carried on with legendary vigour, enthusiasm and botanical knowledge in his retirement. A real plantsman's garden, this one, extending over some four hectares deep in the Wombat Forest. As well as a European garden, with an extensive collection of exotic plants, all meticulously labelled, there are informal Australian gardens where native plants grow in the bushland setting which they love. There are roses and clematis, an orchard, and a kitchen garden which supports the entire extended family, an alpine garden, a herb garden, a section devoted to iris and one to sorbus, a rare collection of cistus — Tommy's interests in the plant kingdom are extensive indeed and his knowledge encyclopaedic.

He had been interested, he said, in what I had been doing at Bleak House and had come to have a look for himself and to talk to me about Alister Clark, about whom he was writing a book.

I find it hard now to credit, following eight years of reading and searching, after immersing myself in his diaries and articles, that at that time his name meant nothing to me. Tommy, however, was not surprised. It meant nothing to most Australians. And yet Alister Clark was the greatest rose-breeder this country has ever known — the only one to have won international acclaim.

He was born at Bulla, on the outskirts of Melbourne, in a wonderful old home called Glenara, painted by Von Guérard, classified by the National Trust and listed on the Historic Buildings Register. And it was here, after being educated in England and Scotland and later at Cambridge, that he lived for most of his life. His interests were wide and, since although he studied law he never practised, he had leisure to pursue them. His marriage certificate, when he married Edith Rhodes in New Zealand, listed his profession simply as 'gentleman'.

He was a fine horseman. There are many photographs in the family archives of Alister in riding or hunting gear. His diaries in the earlier years speak of hunt meetings when he was Master of the Hunt, of polo matches and the ponies he regularly brought from New Zealand after holidays spent there with Edie. He owned and bred racehorses and was founding President of the Moonee Valley Race Club. His portrait hangs in the Committee Room to this day and the Alister Clark Stakes is run each year in the spring.

He was a keen golfer, a foundation member of Royal Melbourne, and his diary entries tell frequently of trips to Cranbourne to play golf with his great friend Albert Nash on his private golf course. After a morning's golf he frequently returned to Glenara to spend the afternoon ferreting — rabbits were always a problem. He was a fly-fisherman and an excellent amateur photographer, as photographs of his in the family collection testify. He had a keen social conscience and was a Justice of the Peace and served on the local Council. He was one of the first to grow grapes for wine in this part of Victoria.

But what was of greatest importance to me — and perhaps to Alister himself — was that he maintained and extended the fine garden started in his father's time and there he bred daffodils and some one hundred and thirty-five roses — many of them bred especially to suit Australian conditions.

Glenara lies in a gully, protected and warm, and Alister embarked on his career as a breeder of roses with a specific object in mind. He wanted to breed roses which would flower throughout the year. He had observed which roses did best in the mild climates of the Mediterranean and Ireland, and he had nurserymen scour Europe for the roses listed by the great English gardener, William Robinson, as the best garden roses.

This is important, for Alister was interested in producing, not prize exhibition blooms, but roses which would do well in the garden, what he called 'decorative roses'.

Unfortunately for rosarians, the book in which he kept records of his breeding programme was left out in the rain one night towards the end of his long life and ruined, so the parentage of many of his roses remains unknown. We do know, however, that he used extensively the great vigorous white climber, *Rosa gigantea*, from Burma and the Himalayas, which, under favourable conditions, will climb to a height of twelve metres. At the time this was a breakthrough. Horace McFarland, president of the American Rose Society, writing of Alister Clark says: 'Only in Australia has the rampant *Rosa gigantea* proved amenable to the hybridizer, so that its progeny get into commerce.'

Using *Rosa gigantea* Alister produced vigorous climbers, many of which bloomed very early. Best known is, perhaps, 'Jessie Clark', named after his niece and, of course, a second-generation gigantea hybrid, 'Lorraine Lee'. This last-named flowers so prolifically that W. H. Dunnallan, writing in the *Rose Annual* of 1932 could say that a bunch of 'Lorraine Lee' was shown at every meeting of the National Rose Society for twenty consecutive months.

It is easy to see why such a rose took Australia by storm. Hedges of 'Lorraine Lee' were planted all over Melbourne and Adelaide. E. W. Hackett, a South Australian nurseryman, wrote in his 1934 Catalogue that in the ten years from 1924–34 his nursery sold 44,000 plants of 'Lorraine Lee'. (One is tempted to draw parallels with 'Iceberg' today!) And not only is it prodigal of its blooms, but it is one of the most beautifully scented of all roses, and hardy to boot. Alister himself wrote in the *Rose Annual* of 1931: 'May I plead with those who grow "Lorraine Lee" not to overfeed or overprune it. I find it does wonderfully at Glenara if practically left alone.'

The *Annual* of 1938 speaks of a plebiscite held through the columns of the *Argus*, a now defunct Melbourne daily, which resulted in a triumph for Alister Clark, for his rose 'Lorraine Lee' headed the list. It was described as 'the most popular rose ever introduced in Australia'.

Much later I had a delightful letter from Wendy Langton, the proprietor of that invaluable antiquarian bookshop in Adelaide which specialises in garden books. She wrote:

> In 1941 my mother saved up nine shillings out of her housekeeping money and sent my brother, then aged nine, with his billy-cart around to the local nursery-man to bring home twelve 'Lorraine Lee' roses. These she planted as a hedge along the front fence and, as you can imagine, my memories of childhood homecomings are always fragrance-filled as a result.

Now none of this was known to me on the day of Tommy's visit. I had heard of 'Lorraine Lee' and of 'Blackboy', but the name of their breeder was unknown to me. However, I was ready for a new project and Tommy is persuasive, his enthusiasm infectious, so that when he said, 'I am writing about Alister's life. Why don't you collect the roses?' I agreed to do so.

Little did I appreciate the difficulties I would encounter. Nor did I realise that this would occupy a good deal of my time over the next ten years, and that the chances of finding more than a fraction of them were slim indeed.

In the first place, the people who knew him as adults are now mostly over eighty. In the second place, there are no real records. Alister's book was lost so the only sources of information, apart from sometimes unreliable memories, are early Australian rose books, the *Annuals* of the Rose Society and early nursery catalogues. Most of the descriptions are scanty in the extreme: ' "Bright Boy" — dazzling red blooms, tall vigorous grower' (Hazelwood's Catalogue, 1941). How many red roses would fit this description!

Photographs taken at the time are mostly of poor quality and nearly all black and white, so are of little help in identification. All but 'Lorraine Lee', 'Blackboy' and 'Nancy Hayward' had entirely vanished from nurserymen's lists. Nearly fifty years had elapsed since Alister's death. No one had any commercial interest in promoting his roses. Gardens change. Properties change hands. Old roses are rooted out and new ones planted.

I made a start, however, without delay. My first step was to invite Nancy Hayward to lunch. Fortunately, she is my husband's aunt, so when she visited Melbourne from Adelaide it was not difficult to persuade her to come to Bleak House. With the best of intentions I made a rushed trip to Atherstone, Ian Hargrave's nursery at Harcourt, and brought back a large bunch of 'Nancy Hayward' roses. These I arranged with care in a beautiful old vase which had belonged to my mother and put them on the lunch table.

Aunt Nan duly arrived and was ushered into the dining room. I waited expectantly for her cries of delight. Instead she exclaimed: 'I can't stand that rose! Alister never asked me if he could name it after me. It has too few petals, no scent, and is a perfectly horrible colour!' There was nothing for it but to remove them hastily to the kitchen. We were not off to a good start.

Sadly, she could tell me little of Alister. Her father, Sir William Irvine, had been Patron or Vice-Patron of the Rose Society every year from 1928, when the Australian *Rose Annual* was first published, until his death in 1943, so he must have known Alister well. But the family saw little of him and Aunt Nan's recollections were hazy.

My second step was to pay another visit to Eve Murray at Langley Vale. Tommy had told me that she and Alister had been good friends. The fact that they were both daffodil breeders had given them a great mutual interest.

It was a still, sunny March afternoon and as I pushed open the garden gate at Langley Vale I saw Eve in her wheelchair on the back verandah. With a large barrow of daffodil bulbs on one side of her chair and a barrow of pots and potting mix on the other side, she was potting up daffodils for sale at her next Open Day in aid of the Kyneton Hospital.

She was delighted to help and full of stories about Alister. Her eyes lit up as she talked of him and of the daffodil shows they had both attended and of old Hugh Dettman, Alister's friend and rival, who had lived in Kyneton.

Down at the bottom of the garden at the foot of a steep slope she had a collection of Alister's roses. With great skill and much laughter she manoeuvred her chair down the winding paths. She was only too happy for me to take cuttings, happy that the roses were not to be irretrievably lost. Here I found 'Ringlet', a fairly vigorous climber bearing great clusters of single pink and white blooms. Here also was 'Sunny South'. Much later, when I came to read the old *Rose Annuals*, I found that Alister himself had written of it: ' "Sunny South" is my favourite of all the seedlings and imported roses that I have tried out in the last sixty years or so'. W. H. Dunnallan thought it should have become Australia's national flower. He wrote in 1931:

> On a visit to a country town last week I came across 'Sunny South' growing in almost every garden, and in many places where there was no garden it flourishes amazingly without attention. I came upon a hedge of it a hundred yards

long and a mass of bloom … It can surely be said that Mr Clark has raised a universal Rose.

'Editor Stewart' was here, a splendid large vibrant cherry red Pillar rose with wavy petals and beautiful young red foliage. It was named after Alister's great friend who was for many years editor of the *Rose Annual*. Alister rejected a number of seedlings until he found one he thought worthy to carry his friend's name.

And here, too, was 'Fairlie Rede', a beautifully formed, fragrant, soft silvery pink. And 'Diana Allen', described in Hazelwood's Catalogue of 1941 as having blooms resembling small carnations. And 'Sunlit', which found its way to the USA. It produces in great profusion small blooms of softest apricot. It was illustrated in colour in the American *Rose Annual* of 1943 and described as being 'a rose worthy of a place in anyone's garden'.

Eve pointed out another tall bush covered in classic-shaped blooms of soft pink. 'He gave me that one to try out,' she said. 'He often gave seedlings to his friends. Sometimes he registered them later and sometimes he thought they weren't good enough. He died before the fate of that one was decided.' So I took cuttings of it, as well as of all the others, and when it grew and flowered we called it simply 'Mrs Murray's Seedling'.

There was a large, low bush, simply covered with clusters of the most cheerful bright pink flowers. 'That's "Cherub",' said Eve. 'Alister loved it.' From the cuttings of 'Cherub' I had a hundred percent strike and when it bloomed in the garden at Bleak House the following year everyone loved it. But by then I had gleaned more scraps of information about Alister's roses and 'Cherub' was described in 1923 by Brundrett, who marketed it, as 'a very vigorous climber with profuse, non-recurrent bloom'. Clearly this was not the low-growing, tireless performer I had got from Eve.

I put it on 'hold', pending more information. But in the meantime it was in constant demand since it flowered incessantly. Finally I persuaded John Nieuwesteeg to propagate it for me and we called it simply 'Not Cherub'!

Later on the afternoon of that visit as we sat on the verandah and drank tea, Eve reminisced about Alister, about the magic of the garden at Glenara, about his energy and drive, about the little dogs Edie, his wife, always kept, about the huge bowls of roses he took to every Rose Show, although he himself was not an exhibitor, and about his kindness to everyone he came in contact with. She told me how once, when she and Alister were driving together through Canterbury, he suddenly stopped the car and rushed into a house to ask directions. The woman who answered the door came out to show him the way and, inevitably, they walked around her garden discussing her roses. When he got back into the car Eve asked him why on earth he had asked directions when he knew perfectly well the way to go. 'Well,' he said, 'there was the most marvellous rose in the garden and I had to see it somehow!'

Little did I realise, as I drove home that evening, that this was the biggest collection of Alister Clark roses I was ever to find in one garden. Many subsequent searches ended in a blank, often after weeks of looking and many miles travelled. At most I might find one and that came to be cause of great rejoicing.

But with the institution of this search Bleak House had gained a purpose, something outside and larger than itself. If the garden was good enough and the search for the lost Alister Clark roses was successful enough, it might serve to reinstate in the minds and gardens of Australia this man who had devoted much of his life to the breeding of roses for Australian conditions, who won recognition and acclaim in America and in Europe and who had, to our shame, been forgotten here.

For Alister Clark was recognised not only in his own country. His roses were planted in the great rose garden at Bagatelle in Paris and at Sangerhausen in Germany. He was the first Australian to win the coveted Dean Hole Medal for service to the Rose (there has only ever been one other, the late Dr A. S. Thomas). He was awarded Honorary Life Membership of the American Rose Society in 1931; in Britain, he was elected Vice-President of the Royal Horticultural Society in 1944, an election which was described as a 'well-deserved recognition of a great horticulturist which is also a signal honour to Australia'. And when, on the death of T. A. Stewart, an award was instituted 'to be made at suitable intervals to those in Australia and New Zealand who have given outstanding service in the interests of the Rose' Alister Clark was the first recipient. To regain for this great Australian some measure of recognition in his own land was an objective worth striving for.

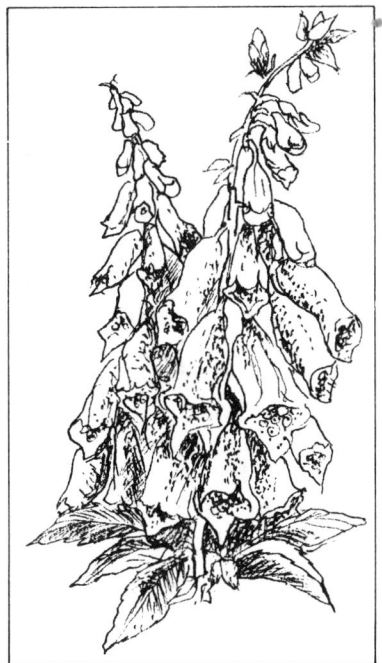

Foxgloves.

Glenara   *23*

On Alister Clark's death, such was the esteem in which he was held, it was decided to establish an Alister Clark Memorial Garden at the St Kilda Botanical Gardens in Blessington Street. The garden was to contain a percentage of his roses but also imported roses. Donations came from Rose Societies all over Australia, for his name had become almost synonymous with the Rose. The garden was opened (significantly, perhaps?) on a wet day in the presence of his widow, and it was felt to be a fitting tribute to a great horticulturist.

Having read of this, I set out one morning to visit the garden, sure that here I would find some more of the roses. I found the Blessington Street Gardens without difficulty, but it proved to be a bitter disappointment. Forty years had elapsed since Alister's death and the Memorial Garden was a tangle of dead and ailing rose bushes, broken trellis and weeds. The only identifiable roses (name tags were broken, misplaced or missing altogether) was 'Blackboy', struggling on manfully and, of course, the ubiquitous 'Lorraine Lee'. I could only assume that, when the Garden was established, no financial provision was made for its upkeep.

Disappointed, I returned home, filled with bitter thoughts about the shortness of people's memories, the transitory nature of all earthly things and other such profundities. Determined to rid myself of such unproductive ideas, I decided to make contact with Glenara itself.

On Alister's death an attempt had been made (in the absence of any children) to acquire Glenara for the nation. This came to nothing and the property had passed into private hands. The new owner cared nothing for all that Glenara stood for. Presumably his interest was in the acquisition of broad acres so close to the city of Melbourne. So oblivious was he of the garden and its place in Australia's history, that he even let stock in to eat part of it down. Fortunately, his tenure was short and Glenara passed then to a Melbourne solicitor and his wife, Eric and Ruth Rundle. Their main interest lay in horses rather than in gardens, and they took over where Alister left off at the Oaklands Hunt Club, one of their daughters being today the Master of the Hunt. But they were conscious of the beauty of the home and it has been meticulously preserved. So anxious is Ruth Rundle to retain the atmosphere of Glenara that some of Alister and Edie's curtains were hung again in the house this year and Alister's portrait hangs in the entrance hall.

I resolved to make contact with Ruth. Her husband had been killed not many months earlier in a hunting accident and she was living alone at Glenara. Tommy had recently been to see her about his book and experts from the Royal Botanic Gardens, Melbourne, had come to look at some of the rare trees that Alister's father, Walter, had planted in the garden. Now I came, wanting to look at the roses. After thirty-odd years of quiet possession of the property which had become their home, it must have been bewildering and sometimes more than a little annoying to have so much semi-public interest taken in it.

But Ruth Rundle was courteous and generous in the extreme. She listened to what I had to say, invited me to visit Glenara and to take what rose cuttings I wanted. Naturally she was worried about the state of the garden and apprehensive about people's reaction to it. When Alister lived there he had employed anything up to eight gardeners. Ruth Rundle had none – only a man to help with the mowing and someone who came in once a year to do a bit of pruning.

My sister from Queensland was holidaying with me and together we set out one still April afternoon for Glenara. It was with feelings of excitement and anticipation that I turned off the Bulla Road and into the gates of Glenara. There is nothing to be seen from the road. The gates are unremarkable and the drive leads through horse paddocks until it curves sharply and drops into the valley. Then through a gap in the hedge on the left-hand side of the drive the first roses come into view and one enters a magical world.

We parked on the gravel drive in front of the grand old home. The little red China rose, 'Cramoisi Supérieur', was in full flower on the verandah and in my imagination I saw it with the little yellow Banksia rose and the wisteria which were planted there also in flower. The gardens slope down from the house to Deep Creek and in Alister's day these slopes were thickly planted with roses. The stones outlining what were once beds are still in place and the surviving roses give some idea of what must once have been. Many of them were in the full flush of their autumn bloom on bushes the size of small fruit trees, climbing roses reaching up into the branches of trees, huge bushes of roses mounded together and supporting each other, filling the air with fragrance – and some poor little bushes ravaged by drought and wallabies and rabbits, but still putting on a brave show, such is the tenacity of the rose.

A picturesque wooden bridge leads across the creek, and the ground rises steeply on the other side, crisscrossed with winding paths which take one to the very romantic stone watchtower on the hill opposite the house. This was all once part of the garden. Now the only surviving plants are some cacti and a mass of seedling eucalypts. These slopes were once a carpet of daffodils, some of which still struggle through today.

Going down from the house to the right, winding paths lead through trees, a mass of smilax and periwinkle and a forest of agapanthus to great granite boulders overlooking the creek, and steps which had been cut in the rock leading down to the water. Here sweet peas still push their way up through the long grass and the daffodils are thicker.

In front of the winery and in the vegetable gardens where Alister had also put his untried seedlings are huge impenetrable mounds of roses, and everywhere stone edgings and carefully made steps speak of past glories.

Nostalgia was in the air, and romance — nothing of the atmosphere of depression and decay which had surrounded the garden at St Kilda. We both felt excited, and very privileged to be there and I found myself more determined with every moment to find again the roses bred in this beautiful place.

I had brought secateurs, a quantity of newspaper and a pile of plastic supermarket bags and we set to work. I took cuttings from sixty-four different bushes and, while I cut, Jennifer wrapped each bundle in wet newspaper and tied it in a plastic bag and numbered the bags Glenara 1-64.

How we were ever to identify them was a problem I did not want to contemplate. For the present my only thought was to preserve as many as possible before the rabbits or the wallabies or a future drought should do away with them altogether.

There were no garden records. There were no name tags or plans of the garden. Alister had grown roses other than his own so there was no certainty that the cuttings we took were even from his own roses. We put all these thoughts from our minds and worked steadily on till approaching darkness put an end to it.

It was quite dark when we got back to Bleak House, but the cuttings had to be potted up that night. Any delay decreases the chance of success.

My sister (who is not a gardener) was appalled at the prospect. While I searched in the shed (which had no light) for plastic pots and propagating mix (which fortunately I mixed in large quantities so that it would always be readily available) she slipped down to Malmsbury and came back with a cask of Lindeman's Claret.

'If we're going to be here until midnight,' she said firmly, 'we're going to enjoy ourselves.' So she stoked up the fire, put on a recording of Scot Joplin, got out the glasses and we set to work.

By midnight some two hundred and sixty little cuttings were safely in their pots. A good proportion of them struck. Many of the climbers did not. Those bred from *Rosa gigantea* stock are notoriously difficult to propagate. Some of them we were later able to identify. Some are still known simply as 'Alister Clark's Pink Floribunda', or 'Alister Clark's Cream' or 'Alister Clark, NOT Tonner's Fancy'.

Having got so far, I was at a loss as to how to proceed next. It was my husband (who has an encyclopaedic knowledge of all things Victorian) who suggested I go to see Tid Alston. Tid has a property at Oaklands Junction not far from Glenara, and her parents had been great friends of Alister and Edie. So this was the next step.

In her rambling, country garden, full of rare treasures, I did indeed find some of Alister's roses. Here was 'Glenara', called after his home, growing over two metres tall and covered, in late autumn, with semi-double vibrant pink blooms. Here was 'Restless', darkest red and wonderfully perfumed. It was one of the great survivors at Glenara but I had not known its name. Here was 'Princeps', a great red climber, and 'Mrs Harold Alston', a beautiful soft pink. Here, too, was the big rambler, 'Glad-some', and the little cherry-red Floribunda, 'Maud Alston' (named after Tid's mother). And here was the same little bright pink Floribunda which Mrs Murray had given me and called 'Cherub'.

Tid called it 'Suitor' and said Alister had given it to her mother who had been particularly fond of it. This posed another problem. According to available descriptions, Tid's mother had had all of the other names correct, but nowhere in old nursery catalogues or *Rose Annuals* or in lists of Alister's roses had I found any mention of a rose called 'Suitor'. Perhaps Tid's mother, like Eve Murray, had been wrong? It was not until seven years later that I found, in one of Alister's articles, a brief account of it. He spoke of a little Floribunda which pleased him greatly and which he planned to release next year under the name of 'The Little Visitor' 'and another, similar, which I plan to call "Suitor" '. So Tid's mother had been right, as she had been in every other case, but Alister had, in fact, never got round to releasing it. It has become one of my favourites. Cheerful and ever-blooming, it is just right in the front of a border.

And in Tid's front garden, growing to the very top of a great oak tree, was a rose which she described as a great cream single with a perfectly wonderful scent. Alister had given it to her mother but she, Tid, had never known its name. It bloomed only once, in the early spring and, though she had tried many times, she had never succeeded in striking it from a cutting. I tried too. Without success.

Some years later, Molly Dalrymple told me of a great cream climber she had had at a farm they had owned called Red Rock. It was one of Alister's and he had called it after her aunt, Mrs Richard Turnbull.

So I set out to look for Red Rock and found it near Riddells Creek. When I mentioned the rose, the present owner said, 'Oh yes. I thought it was a briar so we cut it right down.' My heart sank. Then she added cheerfully, 'But it didn't matter. It came up stronger than ever!'

We found it at the back of the house climbing over a tank-stand. I took cuttings — without much hope, for the leaves indicated that it was a gigantea hybrid. I got permission to come back in November and get some bud-wood if the cuttings failed.

Early in November that year I had a phone call from Tid. 'Come down today, if you can. The big cream rose is in flower.' I jumped into the car and set out for Oaklands Junction. It was indeed in flower and a breathtaking sight. Right from the top of the oak tree the cream blooms cascaded down and the whole garden was filled with the scent. I thought of Molly Dalrymple and her cream rose, which I had also never seen in flower, called 'Mrs Richard Turnbull'. If this was it, then the one at Red Rock should be in flower too. I drove hastily back to Riddells Creek. Sure enough, the rose was covered in blooms and they were identical. I took flowers and buds and foliage back to Tid. There was no doubt. Her big cream climber was 'Mrs Richard Turnbull'.

So the search went on. Other such leads ended in failure and frustration. Some-times — and these were exciting times — they were crowned with success.

As I became better acquainted with Alister's roses, with their scent and colour – often vivid colour, more at home under the Australian sunshine than under England's grey skies and soft mists – and their capacity to bloom again and again, I was increasingly puzzled to understand how Australian gardeners had allowed them to be lost – and in such a short space of time. Perhaps the War was partly responsible, when people's minds were turned to other things and there was little time for gardens. Perhaps it had happened because no one had any financial interest in promoting them. In his lifetime Alister had never wanted any remuneration for his roses – he gave them away, and garden clubs all over Australia were the recipients.

Even before Alister's death many of his roses were hard to come by, although he himself published in every *Rose Annual* a list of seedlings bred at Glenara. But he had no interest in exhibition roses. He bred for the garden not for the show bench and here, I think, is the reason for their becoming unobtainable. Alister himself and his friend T. A. Stewart provide the explanation in the *Rose Annual* of 1946, where Alister wrote:

> It is easy to see that we may lose Roses that are invaluable for breeding . . . I am glad to see *R. gigantea* (still) in good health. I hope younger men will now get to work on its pollen and seed-bearing properties, but alas! nurserymen are shy about propagating it, no doubt owing to the small demand for it and some difficulty in its propagation.

The 'small demand' is due to the huge size of most of these climbers. They are big roses for big gardens. Most of them bloom only in the spring and gardens with limited space cannot afford them. My first plant of 'Jessie Clark' came from a garden in Camberwell where she had virtually taken over the entire garden!

T. A. Stewart in the same *Rose Annual* wrote:

> We should aim in these countries of ours (he included New Zealand) that possess so many climatic advantages at having Rose blooms every day of the year, and I know it is possible because I have proved it in my own limited sized garden. It is here that Mr Alister Clark's roses are of such value because they have been bred largely for our conditions; but it is an appalling fact that many of these cannot now be obtained because our nurserymen cannot afford to grow them. The demand for the popular varieties that will be more effective on Show Day precludes the possibility of growing many of them as the lead given by the exhibitors is reflected in our lists of Recommended Roses and is followed by the public, who demand the same varieties.

Little has changed. At the 1991 Rose Show there was one small table for old-fashioned roses (and Alister Clark does not fit into this category either), but for the most part the thousands who pushed their way into the Town Hall were eagerly writing down the names of the roses which had won first prize.

I could not now plant a garden without 'Daydream' (which Alister himself likened to a waterlily) and 'Gwen Nash' ('the most beautiful thing in decorative pinks I can hope to produce'). It is hard to go past 'Sunlit' or 'Squatter's Dream'. And still there is nothing to compare with 'Lorraine Lee' for sheer length of blooming. You would look a long way to find better border roses than 'Borderer' and 'Suitor'.

24 *The Nursery*

As the boundaries of the garden were steadily extended, it became increasingly obvious that I would have to have more help. I still had Albert, but he came only one day a week. He was retired and had his own little garden and really didn't want to do any more.

In one day a week he could barely cope with the mowing. I had bought him a ride-on mower which he loved, but this is volcanic country and great mounds of stone rose up out of the lawn – 'floaters' they called them – and they made mowing a nightmare. The really big ones were not so bad – picturesque, even – but there was a multitude of smaller ones not so easily seen. Albert always assumed that if I was out of sight I was also out of earshot, and I would hear his deep resonant voice all over the garden as he shouted 'Y' bloody bastard!' when he hit yet another rock with the mower blades. No wonder he felt one day a week was enough.

It was at this point that the Fates, what my mother always referred to as 'the Boys Upstairs', sent a real treasure in the shape of Don Wild.

A couple of years earlier I had bought a dimunitive, century old weatherboard cottage on a quarter of an hectare of land in the neighbouring village of Taradale. To my practical, business-conscious friends I described it as an investment. Privately

I admitted it was bought on impulse because it was simply charming. It sat crookedly amidst gnarled old apple and plum trees, its steep roof descending low over the little front verandah, one multipaned window on each side of the front door, the whole thing dwarfed by a huge stone chimney — a cottage in a child's drawing or on an early sampler.

I renovated it with loving care — and much help from Albert — and we finished it off by planting a hedge of 'Cécile Brunner' roses right along the front fence, the tiny pink roses in scale with the cottage. We planted big, vigorous ramblers to cover an ugly, incongruous modern carport some previous owner had erected.

I couldn't bring myself to sell it, so decided to let it. The agent found a prospective tenant whose profession was described as 'artist'. This seemed in every respect appropriate, so, reluctantly, I signed the tenancy agreement. I visited him only once. He had covered the walls with larger-than-life oil paintings of grossly overweight nude women in purple, electric blue and lurid green, and in the spaces between the paintings he hung his guns, his idea of recreation being to shoot deer or wild duck.

In this alien atmosphere the 'Cécile Brunner' hedge wilted and slowly died, even the ramblers lacked vitality and the grass grew so high that the Country Fire Authority served a notice on me to clean it up as it was a fire hazard. At this point the tenant decided to move out. When the agent rang me a few weeks later to say he had a prospective purchaser I was feeling so discouraged by my sole experience as a landlady that I agreed to sell, albeit reluctantly.

Sickened by the cynicism of life in a big city and seeking tranquillity, Don Wild had decided to abandon his career and move to the country at any price. The week after he moved in, he came to see me. I had let the cottage furnished and Don wanted to buy the furniture. 'The only trouble is,' he said, 'I can't pay for it!' This proved to be not an insuperable problem. He suggested he should work at Bleak House in exchange for the furniture. 'You know,' he said, 'a day for a chair, and so on.' That seemed a perfectly reasonable arrangement and so began a long association which we both enjoyed.

Albert retired altogether soon after. I quite missed his presence in the garden — his little stiff military moustache and his shock of snow-white hair (which his wife said he rinsed regularly in lemon juice). Don took on the entire care of the lawns which, in his hands, were transformed. Edges were done with the whipper-snipper and the grass raked up and put into the huge compost bins we had built.

He scraped acquaintance with a horse-trainer in Kyneton and every week he collected a couple of trucks full of stable sweepings — straw and horse manure.

He developed a talent and a love for stonework, and drove our old truck down to the quarries, bringing it back loaded with flat, moss- and lichen-covered stone. He built low stone walls so that, with the help of the mulch, we gradually lifted the level of the beds and improved the drainage.

And the little cottage at Taradale was transformed. Gone were the guns and the purple nudes. It was filled with music and, as time went by, with the scents from the cottage garden which soon extended over the entire quarter hectare. A hedge of the Rugosa rose, 'Agnes', took the place of the defunct 'Cécile Brunner'. It is the only hedge of 'Agnes' I have seen. A soft, butter yellow, she sets no hips and flowers only in spring but must surely rank as one of the loveliest of all the Rugosas.

Of course, I wanted Don for more than one day a week. And equally 'of course', I couldn't afford it. Gardens, I had discovered, eat money. And so, after a good deal of thought, but with no real 'feasibility study', I decided to open a small nursery. I had never been involved in business, nor had I any business training, but somehow the garden had to be made to contribute to its own upkeep.

I started just by propagating my own roses and opening the 'nursery' at weekends. I could not keep up with the demand. Time spent in propagating plants is time not spent in the garden. The nursery went forward and the garden slipped back.

It became increasingly apparent that I would have to buy in rose stock, especially those roses — and there are many — which are difficult to propagate from cuttings. Budding has a much higher success rate, but I had no wish to plant up hundreds of multiflora to use as understocks. That would take even more time from the garden. Buying wholesale opened the door to a whole new world. I met the big growers for whom rose-growing was strictly a business affair. All of them were good to deal with and two, Walter Duncan in South Australia and John Nieuwesteeg at Coldstream, became real friends. John's family had been involved in growing roses in Holland, every generation of them, for over two hundred years. There was little he did not know about roses. Walter conducted his large wholesale operation from a two thousand eight hundred hectare sheep property and a grand old stone mansion north of Adelaide.

I came to look forward to June, when the big wooden crates crammed with bare-rooted roses arrived at Bleak House. Then followed a frantic few days for they all had to be sorted and labelled, orders separated from nursery stock, and all of them put into big pots filled with wet sawdust. These had then to be put in alphabetical order so that roses could be found quickly. And then, no matter what other pressing business there was, those roses had to be watered every single day. Sawdust dries out very quickly and if the rose roots are allowed to dry out there may be no evidence of trouble until the spring, when there will be no shoots. The difficulty of ensuring that this job is done reliably by often inexperienced, seasonal help must prove a real headache in big nurseries.

Often Nature takes a hand, for this is our wettest time of the year and we often had to work in sleety rain with driving winds and sometimes snow. We lived in gumboots, fur-lined caps and wet-weather gear.

Of course, things do not stay small. The demand was great and, to survive, I had to compete with other nurseries. Soon we were opening five days a week and, in the end, seven. No one wants to drive kilometres to a country nursery only to find that this is the day it is closed. If we wanted to compete with Melbourne nurseries we had to be open seven days a week. More help! More headaches! WorkCare, tax stamps, superannuation! The nursery must generate more cash flow (I was even learning the terminology!).

So I opened, in conjunction with Neil Robertson, who at that time owned the superlatively good Bookshop of Margareta Webber, a country branch dealing only in garden books. It was housed initially in Little Portion, but this rapidly became too small. When Neil sold his bookshop, and strangers took over, I decided to run mine independently. We built, with stone from the quarries, a beautiful room onto the back of Bleak House. Every care was taken to ensure that it would be in keeping with the original house. It had a high, cathedral ceiling, a huge open fireplace and every window overlooked the garden. It opened into a sunny courtyard. In no time it stocked not only books but ceramic pots, garden sculptures, cards, stationery, garden hats and aprons – anything connected with the garden.

Later the old barn was converted into tearooms. Home cooking (not mine!) and a big, cheerful, slow-combustion stove made it a welcoming place after a long drive – especially for customers picking up rose orders in the depths of winter. Its pine walls were ideal for hanging paintings. And so the Art Exhibitions started. These were a joy. They brought me into contact with fine local artists. Bleak House was ideally equipped for garden party openings on summer evenings. Molly Maddox's impressionist garden watercolours and Peggy Shaw's landscapes and paintings of the old buildings of the area were in the perfect setting.

When Jenny Phillips, that very gifted botanical artist who had drawn Little Portion some years earlier, produced her first four prints, we hung them in the tearooms. There was a pink hellebore, a green hellebore, a potato and a tomato. These are not only works of art but are botanically accurate, even the roots being depicted in finest detail. I thought again of Dean Hole who spoke of a painting of a bunch of grapes in his potting-shed as being 'so lifelike and luscious to look upon that they might have been the identical bunch which the American artist painted for his mother with such extraordinary power that the old lady was enabled to manufacture from it three bottles and a half of most delicious wine!'

Of course, we had many visitors. And nearly all of them I enjoyed. Gardening is such an all-consuming interest that gardeners quickly establish a rapport with each other. It was not so easy with some of the bus-loads from Melbourne. These were not always gardeners. Often they were bored or lonely people simply looking for a day out. These had little understanding of Bleak House and its aims, often making a beeline for the tearooms and sitting there over scones and jam and cream until it was time for the bus to go again. Or they made a beeline for the outdoor toilet, complaining vociferously of the distance they had to walk to reach it.

One morning, when we were expecting two bus-loads, I decorated the courtyard with pots of the Centifolia rose, 'de Meaux'. It is one of my favourites. Soft pink, many-petalled and compact, as all the Centifolias are, this one is diminutive, the tiny blooms measuring scarcely more than two centimetres in diameter. With the place teeming with visitors I came round the corner in time to hear a large, indignant old woman holding forth to a listening crowd: 'Call that a rose,' she was exclaiming, 'I've got them ten times that size. If they can't do better than that, they shouldn't be in business!'

We loved the visits of the Garden Clubs and the Heritage Rose Groups, who knew what they were looking for, and the visits of the elderly citizens groups. Bleak House, being so flat, was ideal for wheelchairs and for people who needed sticks. The pleasure they got from the garden was in itself sufficient justification for the time and care that were lavished on it. We had several handicapped groups who came regularly. It was hard to tell what they got out of it, but one day we potted up some of the little Johnny-jump-ups which seeded themselves everywhere in the gravel paths and gave them to them to take home. This they certainly enjoyed.

The dogs were something of a problem. Willy hated the visitors. He clearly thought they had no right to be in his garden, and he made his feelings very plain. In the end we built a proper doghouse and a large enclosed run for him. Cara, on the other hand, loved everyone but was often too exuberant. When they produced their first litter of puppies, we put them out on the lawn in a child's playpen one Sunday afternoon and sold them all.

Perennials were added to the nursery. As I paid more attention to underplanting in the garden and got more of the combinations right, we were often asked for plants. Most perennials multiply quickly and we started potting up the excess. A splendid new perennial nursery, Lambley Perennials, opened up in the Dandenongs and we steadily added more interesting plants to the garden.

But as with the roses, so with the perennials. If we spent too much time propagating the garden went backwards. The whole purpose of the nursery was to support the garden and that purpose would be defeated if we allowed the nursery to take precedence. Moreover, I am sure that many of our customers came just because of the garden. There are very many nurseries — too many, perhaps — and very few of them have any kind of garden, for the simple reason that the owners do not have time to manage both and the garden is abandoned as being commercially not viable.

For me, the nursery always came second to the garden. And while I enjoyed the challenge of running a business, and loved the contact with people, I grew more and more frustrated as the business left me increasingly little time for the garden.

A solution would have to be found, but for the present it eluded me.

Violets.

The Stockyard Garden 25

On the extreme south boundary of the property, between the boundary fence and the tearooms, was our work area. Every nursery must have one. Here were the compost bins, the old tanks for storing firewood used in the open fires, three glasshouses and a shadehouse, a potting shed, housing for the truck and bays for storing mulch and the sawdust which we stockpiled during the year in readiness for the bare-rooted roses in June. All of this had to be hidden from the garden.

So I planted a hedge of *Escallonia* 'Donard Seedling'. It grows to something over two metres high. I like its crisp, shiny, dark evergreen foliage, and the pale pink flowers are compatible with old roses. It is hardy and quick-growing.

My only regret was that, in doing this, I screened out 'Madame Grégoire Staechelin', surely one of the loveliest of all pink climbers. She completely covered a tank in the work area and made it a thing of glory in early spring. The blooms were followed by great pear-shaped hips which hung on for months. I had planted her there before I realised what an inestimable treasure she is. We picked great bunches of her to adorn the tearooms and bookshop. This invariably sold every plant we had.

With the work area screened off, we were left with an uncompromising rectangle which had been the stockyards. A century ago they had been hand-cobbled. The winters are so wet, the land so flat and the soil so heavy that the yards would otherwise have been a quagmire. But they posed a real problem for us. The cobbling was not even enough to be attractive, and every kind of noxious weed seemed to have established itself between the stones. For a brief moment I entertained the idea of a cobbled court with all kinds of rock plants growing where the weeds now grew. But sanity prevailed and I acknowledged the time and work involved and the unlikelihood of the rock plants ever finally vanquishing the weeds.

There was nothing else for it. The cobblestones had to go. We started digging them out by hand, but it was a mammoth task and in the end we had to get a bobcat to do the job. I pictured James Pennington a hundred years ago, without machinery and probably without much help, laboriously laying down the stones we were so recklessly pulling up.

This was the only part of the garden I designed on paper. Don and I drew countless diagrams before we finally decided what to do with this very uninteresting muddy rectangle.

We had proved the value of windbreaks on these open plains and the suitability of rambling roses for making them. So the next step was to erect a frame for a rambler hedge on the north side, parallel to the escallonia hedge. We used bush poles and wire again and planted the roses 'Apple Blossom', 'Sanders' White' and the creamy-yellow climber, 'Paul's Lemon Pillar'.

The west boundary was already sheltered with a large shadehouse for nursery plants. This was covered with the yellow Banksia rose, *Rosa eglanteria* with its scented foliage, *Rosa indica major,* used as a rootstock in the early days and found now in every old cemetery where the roses have reverted to the rootstock, with the rampant *Clematis montana* entwined through them all.

On the east side, so as not to block the view across to Mt Macedon and down to the wet-lands I decided on another Rugosa hedge. 'Sarah van Fleet' was my first choice. Sturdy and quick-growing, she bears her pink blooms in constant succession. She sets no hips but the prodigality of her flowering is more than adequate compensation. I always regretted that I did not plant the entire fence-line with 'Sarah van Fleet'. But the interests of the nursery dictated otherwise. It was desirable that people should see as many roses as possible in flower. And so I mixed Sarah with the soft mauve 'Delicata', the deeper pink 'Belle Poitevine' and the smaller, more delicate pink, red-stemmed 'Martin Frobisher'. 'Delicata' and 'Belle Poitevine' were fine but 'Martin Frobisher' was a mistake. He does not grow so robustly and, where he was, there always appeared to be gaps in the hedge. Here was the nursery once again to conflict with the garden.

We divided the rectangle roughly into two with a stone wall, made largely of the cobblestones, running north-south. We left two openings for rose arches to give more height to this flat area. On one of them I planted the rambler, 'Francis E. Lester', for its scent and its rapid growth. On the other arch I planted 'Madame de Sancy de Parabère' and 'Sombreuil'.

'Madame de Sancy de Parabère' was the only one of the little group of Boursault roses available at the time. She is a treasure. She flowers early on thornless, reddish-brown stems. The flowers are large, soft pink and they have a strangely ragged appearance which I find delightful. There seems to be some dispute about her date, but it would be safe to say that she came to England from France sometime in the second half of the nineteenth century.

'Sombreuil' is, to me, one of the loveliest of all roses. She is an early Tea rose, and she bears very full, flat, gloriously scented white roses which deepen to cream towards the centre. She was named for Mlle Marie de Sombreuil, a heroine of the French Revolution. Gordon Edwards has a rather lurid story of her having 'followed her old father, Governor of des Invalides into the Prison de l'Abbaye and avoided the massacres there by drinking a glass of blood'. The reason this enabled her to 'escape the massacres' has always eluded me.

On the east side of the dividing stone wall, the windbreak fence to the north was planted with the single, white, rampant-growing *Rosa longicuspis* mixed with honeysuckle. I tried the marvellous evergreen *Lonicera hildebrandiana*, but it succumbed to the harsh frosts and we were reduced to the much more plebian *Lonicera japonica*. We made an alcove here, roofed over, and open only to the south. In it we put an attractive old iron seat painted dark green and, on each side of it, as a gesture to formality, an old terracotta chimney pot, planted with box clipped to a ball shape.

There were three beds in this section and I planted two of them with Spinosissimas (syn. Pimpinellifolias), the little Scotch Burnet roses. 'Single Cherry' is entirely delightful, having tiny, single, cherry-red flowers like small rubies. 'William III' is semi-double and a rich, deep pink, verging on maroon. 'Andrewsii' is a softer pink and 'Irish Rich Marbled', my favourite, pink and cream and semi-double. They all have grey-green, ferny foliage which turns various shades of russet in the autumn and they set small black or chocolate-brown hips.

I never succeeded in finding a plant of 'Mary Queen of Scots', but I did include the species rose, *R. spinosissima altaica*, which has large, single white blooms with golden stamens. After much deliberation I included also *R. × harisonii*, which belongs to this group botanically but not aesthetically, its yellow colour, while sunny and cheerful, being out of place among all the pinks. I toyed with the idea of putting it in the Yellow Garden, but the nursery won again and I planted it where it belonged botanically.

As a ground cover in these beds I planted the little white prostrate rose, 'Snow Carpet'. Its tiny leaves matched those of the Spinosissimas as did the size of its little white double flowers, and it bloomed long after the others were finished.

In this area, too, I used one bed for the roses of the great contemporary English rosarian, Peter Beales, who has given us those two invaluable books, *Classic Roses* and *Twentieth Century Roses* – essential reading for any serious rosarian and for most keen gardeners.

I planted the few that were available at the time: 'Anna Pavlova', which everyone loved for its delicate pink, classic-shaped blooms and its perfectly heavenly scent. 'Norwich Castle' is too orange for my taste, but 'Royal Smile', creamy-white and strongly scented, was much admired. *Iris pumila*, pale blue, and white and rich plum colour formed an edging to this bed.

Along the east side of the dividing stone wall I planted a collection of Portland roses: 'Comte de Chambord', 'Jacques Cartier' and 'Rose du Roi à fleur pourpre' (the King in question was Louis XVIII). With their ability to flower recurrently they are ideal for small gardens. On the west side of the wall a narrow bed was filled with tulips with the creeping white thyme as a ground cover. It quickly made a dense mat and the tulips pushed through it each spring.

Two pillar roses were planted here on tripods, which I designed and got the local blacksmith to make. Painted dark green, they were unobtrusive and gave support to 'New Dawn' and 'Madame Abel Chatenay'. These gave height to this flat area and colour for months on end. *Iberis sempervirens* made an excellent ground cover. It flowers right through summer and autumn, is low-growing, so does not interfere with the roses, and is self-perpetuating as it sets seed so prolifically.

There was no lawn in this area, just rectangular beds and gravel paths and so, as another gesture to formality, I planted the little ground cover rose, 'Nozomi', from Japan as a weeping standard in a large wooden tub outside the back door of the tearooms.

And I discovered the virtues of Virginian stocks, the seeds of which can be scattered where they are to grow in autumn. By spring they have formed a mat of tiny flowers in pink, mauve and white, like the fine muslin gowns our great-grandmothers wore.

Barney Hutton came to see me and brought a plant of a white rambling rose, which, he said, ought to be in my garden. Barney is a great gardener with an extensive knowledge of plants, of early Australian nurseries and of garden history. He did not know the name of the rose he brought and, when it flowered next spring, neither did I. But it grew prodigiously. It rapidly covered the north wall of the old barn and bore each spring great clusters of enchanting little white roses with the faintest tinge of pink. It resembled 'Rambling Rector' but is not identical and I continued to call it 'Barney Hutton'.

I became increasingly worried, in fact, by people's passion for attaching names to plants, often without the knowledge or experience to do so. I thought often of a story Alister Clark told of how his heart sank when people came to see him bearing a basket of roses and asking him to identify them. Were they not aware, he asked, that to date (it was 1940) over 11,000 different roses had been imported into Australia and many of them he had never seen? And how many more, I wonder, have been imported since then? Add to this that roses are notoriously promiscuous and in every large garden little seedlings crop up which are chance hybrids and have never had a name, and the task becomes often impossible. If rosarians of the calibre of Graham Stuart Thomas and Peter Beales, the gurus of the rose world, sometimes require a chromosome count before they feel prepared to speak with certainty, how can we mere mortals claim to be able to identify strange roses at a glance? There are some which are unmistakable, but there are many more which, in the absence of proof, we would do better to call by the name of the donor or of the locality where it was found.

The Stockyard Garden, as we continued to call it, was probably the most protected part of the grounds, and the individual plants there thrived. But somehow it never really pleased me — I think because I had made too many compromises between the interests of the gardens and those of the nursery.

A primula.

The Alister Clark Garden 26

As the little cutting-grown Alister Clark roses in the shadehouse started to put on growth, and as their number continued to grow, I had to solve the problem of where they were to be planted.

Not only I, but also other people, had begun to be interested both in the man and in the roses he had bred. It would be a pity if they were dissipated throughout the garden. They really should be gathered together in a place of their own.

So I took another quarter hectare from the long-suffering farmer who was again leasing my land, and we started work on the Alister Clark Garden. It was situated to the north of the Yellow Garden and there was already a high fence there covered for the most part with the little pink rambler, 'Dorothy Perkins', who had for a time enjoyed great popularity in this country.

About this time I had a visit from two boys in their late teens who were looking for work. I asked them what skills they had and, to my surprise, they listed the building of stone walls among them. They had never actually built one, they admitted, but they had bought a book about it and would like to try.

So with Don's help a pile of rocks was brought up from the quarries and they set to work. I did not think for one moment that we would end up with a dry-stone wall. I expected they would just pile the stone up in random fashion. I was astounded when, at the end of the first day, two or three metres of dry-stone wall were in place. It took weeks to complete but we had, in the end, one of the best stone walls I have seen. It was a real feature of the garden.

The wall was splendid, but not high enough to serve as a windbreak, so we erected a lattice fence some two metres high behind it and extended this along both east and west sides so that the quarter-hectare was completely enclosed. It was the nearest I could get to my dream of a walled garden.

I planted the Alister Clark ramblers, 'Gladsome' and 'Milkmaid' on the south fence along with 'Dorothy Perkins'. On the east fence I put 'Nancy Hayward', 'Flying Colours', 'Cherub' and 'Milkmaid'. The latter is a wonderful rose — creamy-white flowers in clusters in spring and dense shiny green foliage. It grows very fast and had its part of the fence covered in no time. Fortunately I had weeded very thoroughly and mulched round it with thick newspaper covered with a thick layer of straw. This was fortunate indeed, for once it had grown weeding under it was an impossibility.

These were the only Clark ramblers I had ready to plant at the time so on the west fence I planted four of the superb rambler known in Victoria as 'The Edna Walling Rose'. What its real name is, I do not know, but the story is that, while Edna Walling did not breed it, she had used it in many gardens that she designed. It flowers late — into December — and bears great clusters of single, cupped blooms, white with the faintest pink flush. As it ages, the blooms take on a greenish tinge. It grows very rapidly to a great height and, while it was certainly not an Alister Clark rose, it was one with great significance for Australian gardeners. On the north fence, in front of the wall, I planted a couple of 'Félicité et Perpétue' and the ever-blooming 'Sea Foam' — no Australian connections here!

Alister Clark's great ramblers were a glory each spring and they made this probably the loveliest part of the entire garden. We put a gate in the west fence to link it to the main garden, and one in the south fence, opening from the Yellow Garden. Over each gateway we had an arch and a plaque reading 'The Alister Clark Garden'.

Many of Alister's roses are climbers, so I planned a path with three pergolas over it leading from the west gate to the north-east corner and terminating in a very pretty hexagonal-shaped summerhouse. A group of silver birches (*Betula pendula*) and some species lilac were planted behind this, and Alister's rambler, 'Jessie Clark', was planted to grow over it. I remembered the huge mound of her in front of the winery at Glenara and I do harbour some fears that the whole summerhouse will one day collapse beneath her weight. But she looks spectacular in early spring.

Wide beds were made on each side of the path and along the entire east and south fences. We bordered them with lavender, mostly *Lavandula angustifolia*, the 'Hidcote' lavender, cut into low hedges. Both Eve Murray and John Dettman, nephew of Alister's friend, Hugh Dettman, gave me some of Alister's daffodils and I was delighted to be able to plant them among his roses.

Gradually the collection grew. We had some notable visitors to the garden. From Eve I had got a vivid pink, single, bush rose which she had called 'Ella Guthrie'. One morning a delightful, white-haired, sprightly old lady of well over eighty visited us and, without any preamble, demanded to see the Alister Clark roses. I walked down with her and, as we came through the gate, she gave a cry of delight and started to run across the grass.

'Complicata' makes a large sprawling shrub.

Kordes' 'Frühlingsmorgen' (Spring Morning).

'Cymbeline' with the grey foliage of *Chrysanthemum haradjanii* and some yellow buds which should have been removed.

The cobblestones had to go to make the Stockyard Garden. The building in the background is Willie and Cara's house.

The entrance to the Alister Clark garden: 'American Pillar' on the left and 'The Edna Walling Rose' on the right. Through the archway a little grey artemisia was used as a groundcover.

Another Kordes rose, weeping 'Heidekönigin' (Queen of the Heath) with white lychnis, pink evening primrose, and one very persistent orange eschscholzia.

(*Top centre*) 'Maud Alston' blooms behind 'Hidcote' lavender in the Alister Clark garden. There is pink verbena in the left-hand corner.

David Austin's 'Hero'.

Alister Clark's 'Gladsome' on the fence with 'Maud Alston', iris and 'Hidcote' lavender forming a border.

(*Below centre*) 'Charles Austin' in front of the big pine near the gate into the Yellow Garden.

Bleak House from the bottom of the garden looking towards the Bookshop and the big pine.

The summerhouse in the Alister Clark garden with 'Jessie Clark'.

The rambling hedges are perhaps the chief glory of Bleak House. Looking towards the gateway from the Alister Clark garden. (Barbara Strange).

'That's me!' she cried. 'That's me!' Then, as she read the label saying 'Ella Guthrie' she turned to me in disgust.

'That's not Ella,' she said emphatically. 'She was my aunt and a poor, washed-out thing, like her rose. This is *me! Mary* Guthrie! Alister said it looked like a wild rose, so he called it after me, because I was always the wild one of the family.' Of course, I changed the label without delay. We had another rose correctly named and verified.

Cicely Lascelles came, also well into her eighties. She brought me a little plant of the rose named after her — a warm-pink, semi-single climber which flowers intermittently right through summer and autumn. Cicely Lascelles was a great golfer and Alister had been a foundation member of Royal Melbourne Golf Club, so it is very appropriate that this year, 1991, two plants of the 'Cicely Lascelles' rose have been planted in the gardens there.

A niece of Margaret Turnbull came, on a visit from New South Wales. On her return home she sent me cuttings of the rose 'Margaret Turnbull', a fragrant soft pink climber. Kitty Kininmonth's daughter came, and a niece of Jean Nicholl, who had been parlour maid at Glenara. She had many stories about Alister's kindness to all he met. In the Depression, she said, no one was ever turned away from Glenara. She had an old, faded photograph of him, taken in the garden, with a tiny bird on his wrist. I remembered an article of his I had read in the *Rose Annual* of 1945, written when he was an old man:

> One of the greatest charms in the garden is the presence of many of our native birds. I would willingly dig all day for the pleasure of having our blue wrens, scrub wrens and yellow robins watching at my feet for worms and insects. All three are great workers for our good. The yellow robin is bold and fearless and dives on anything that moves and will sit patiently within a few feet, and on a spade if laid aside for a few minutes. We have many other good workers among the native birds, with sweet notes which I cannot now hear. I leave the aphis to the birds, and they are able to keep them down ...

The photograph reminded me of a poem by the Queensland poet, David Rowbotham, writing of his father:

> You can not know the kindness of a man
> Till you see him in a garden with a spade
> And birds about his feet.

It could as well have been written of Alister. I was doubly glad that we had decided against the use of poisonous sprays.

There were memorable gardens visited in search of Alister Clark's roses. We went to the lovely garden at Delatite near Mansfield, home of the Ritchie family, one winter's day. In the rose garden — a formal rose garden with box hedges and gravel paths — was a little rose growing, not more than 30 cm tall. Sylvia Ritchie did not know its name. It had been in the garden for a very long time. It was a soft salmon-pink, she said, had a very unusual petal shape and bloomed continuously. I took cuttings and promised to let her know if, when I saw the flower, I was able to identify it. The cuttings all took and when the first little pink blooms appeared I was delighted with it, but had never seen it before.

Then one day in spring I was invited to tea by Mrs Florence Brooke, a legendary old lady of well over eighty who lives in a dark, rambling old mansion set in one of Victoria's truly historic gardens outside Daylesford — a garden famous for its fine and rare trees planted well over a century ago by Mrs Brooke's grandfather. She told me she had a whole bed of Alister Clark's rose, 'Marjory Palmer' which she thought one of his best — and another little one of his down in the vegetable garden.

On the day appointed it was pouring with rain. Jennifer was with me again and said it was sheer lunacy to go to look at a garden on such a day. It was her last day in Victoria and she was sure we could find something better to do.

So I rang Mrs Brooke and murmured something about its being so wet . . . not a day for a garden.

'Why not?' she demanded. 'Other people are coming. I shall expect you at three.'

It was a royal command. There was nothing for it. We put on raincoats, took gumboots and umbrellas and set out. When we arrived, we rang the bell several times before anyone came. Finally Mrs Brooke opened the door.

'I didn't think you'd come,' she said. 'It's so wet!'

We dared not look at each other but followed her down the long hall to the dining room where several other guests were assembled and the table set with a damask cloth and a fine old silver tea service and the log fire roaring in the open fireplace. We ate sandwiches and sponge cake and the rain poured down without intermission.

After tea the other guests departed but, having come all this way, I really did want to see 'Marjory Palmer' and the other little rose. Rain was no deterrent to Mrs Brooke so we all put on our wet-weather gear and set out.

It is a wonderful garden — undoubtedly one of the finest in Victoria. Giant trees form the basis of it. A tapestry hedge surrounds the circular drive with a towering oak in the centre. Aquilegias had naturalised under the trees. There were few flowers — this was not a garden for flowers — but we found the bed of 'Marjory Palmer' and I took cuttings. Then, with the rain still tumbling down, we visited the Kitchen Garden. And there was my little pink rose from Delatite in full flower.

'It's Alister Clark's "Borderer",' said Mrs Brooke. 'I've grown it for years.'

We walked down to a woodland area to see the bluebells which formed a dense carpet under the century-old trees. As we reached it the rain stopped, a mist descended and the sun came out through the mist. I do not know when I have seen anything so breathtaking.

On the way home, Jennifer, who is not given to poetic utterances, was very quiet until she said suddenly, 'Thank heavens we went. I could have gone down on my knees in that bluebell forest!'

We planted 'Borderer' in the Alister Clark Garden as a border round a circular bed with 'Marjory Palmer' and, in the centre, 'Margaret Turnbull' on a tripod.

It was not long after that, in the first days of November 1985, when the ramblers had been planted, the summerhouse and pergolas erected and the signs placed above the gates, that I was surprised one morning by a visit from Bruce Postle, one of the photographers for the *Age*. They were doing an article on Alister Clark in connection with the running of the Melbourne Cup the next Thursday. They had heard that an Alister Clark Garden had been established, and, since Alister had had such a great love for both roses and racing and his roses were planted at Flemington Racecourse, they were interested and had sent him up to get a photograph. His face fell when I explained that, though certainly a garden had been started, none of the roses was yet more than 30 centimetres high and there was, therefore, nothing to photograph.

But Bruce had had an hour and a half's journey from Melbourne and was not to be lightly discouraged. He insisted that we go down and look at it. Even his determination wavered when he saw the neatly laid out beds, the newly painted pergolas and summerhouse but not a rose in sight.

'Do you have any Alister Clark roses anywhere else in the garden?' he asked at last, looking with interest at the west gateway and the sign over it.

'Well,' I said, 'there's a huge bush of 'Lorraine Lee', but it's on the front drive.'

'Right!' he said. 'May I pick some?'

Since 'Lorraine Lee' is, at almost any time, covered in bloom I certainly had no objection, so together we picked a large bunch.

'Now, we need a ladder and some string or thin wire,' he said. The next hour was spent in painstakingly wiring the roses to the arch and trying to make them look as though they were growing there.

I remembered a story I had heard of how, one year, there had been no roses out at Flemington in time for the Melbourne Cup. In desperation the stewards had rung Alister who had picked great armloads and wired them to the fence. History seemed to be repeating itself – at least I felt that Alister would not have disapproved of our subterfuge.

The photographs taken, Bruce stayed to lunch. As he was leaving, he asked if I wanted a tip for the Cup.

'Of course,' I replied, but with some scepticism.

'Well,' he said, 'I woke up last night from a deep sleep and sat bolt upright in bed, quite certain that No 13 had won the Cup. I caught a No 13 tram to work. There were 13 of us in the office and 13 guests for lunch, I have a hunch it's right.'

Now the draw did not take place till the following day. When it did, What a Nuisance was in barrier 13 – 13 letters in his name. And the jockey was Pat Hyland – Patrick Hyland – 13 letters again. That settled it. I put the biggest bet I've ever had on What a Nuisance.

Jennifer rang me from Queensland to ask what she should back, she having no interest in racing except on this one day of the year.

'What a Nuisance!' I said emphatically. She had never put a bet on at a TAB so when she went in to put her $20 on, she asked an old fellow in a navy singlet and sandshoes (he being, she explained later, in her view the most likely type to be an habitual punter) to make out the betting slip for her. When she took it to the counter she found he had made it out for $20 each way – $40 not $20. One look at the queue behind her settled it. She was not going back to do it again. She put on $40!

Bill had backed two other horses but, with some misgivings, and murmurings about superstition, he put a 'saver' on What a Nuisance.

When the moment came, everyone at Bleak House gathered round the radio – we had no television up there – in a state of tense excitement. Something more than dollars was at stake, and a great shout went up from all of us when What a Nuisance came home! I was ecstatic. Jennifer won a packet. Neither of Bill's horses came anywhere, so What a Nuisance was truly a 'saver' for him. There was a spirit of elation. I wanted to write to Bruce Postle.

Then we read the sequel in the *Age*. He had withdrawn $200 from his Savings Account on the way to Flemington to cover the races for the *Age*, intending to put it all on What a Nuisance. When he reached the track it suddenly seemed too risky, too improbable a story, too crazy to risk all this on a dream — and he put the $200 back in his pocket. As What a Nuisance flashed past the winning post the stewards had to restrain him from jumping out of the tower.

I still have Bruce Postle's photograph of our embryo Alister Clark Garden, but the roses have grown apace and the arches and fences are genuinely covered now by Alister's ramblers. The bush roses in the beds there flower longer than any other roses in the garden and it is for me the loveliest corner of Bleak House. Now Bruce Postle would have something worth photographing!

Gradually Australian gardeners are coming to realise what has been lost and Alister Clark's roses are winning recognition again.

A bed of Alister Clark roses has been planted at Government House in Canberra. Moonee Valley Race Club has established a memorial garden to Alister Clark planted with his own roses. The memorial garden at St Kilda Botanical Gardens is being re-established. The Kyneton Botanic Gardens have planted a bed of Alister Clark roses, and they have been planted, too, at Royal Melbourne Golf Club as well as in many private gardens.

Some Kordes roses.
(Drawing by Anita Barley)

The Kordes Roses 27

The enthusiasm for old roses reached its peak in Australia in the early 1980s. There were, of course, a number of contributing factors, not the least of which was a widespread yearning for romance, which seems to have vanished from the daily lives of many people.

Australians are inveterate travellers. Sissinghurst had become the Mecca of Australians who had an interest in gardens. It is the very stuff of which romance is made — a poet, a castle, a moat, a priest's house, a study in a tower, mellow old brick walls — and old roses. The books of Anne Scott-James and Jane Brown became best-sellers.

Then to the overseas traveller's itinerary was added Mottisfont Abbey — a monastery, a grand old park, a walled garden — and old roses, old roses chosen by Graham Stuart Thomas himself.

We had a bad drought in the eastern states of Australia in 1982–3. Economically it was a grim time. We were in the midst of a recession. Unemployment was high. At such times many people turn to their gardens to find there peace and tranquillity and food for the spirit. The urge to create something beautiful is strong at all times, strongest, perhaps, in times of adversity.

The Heritage Rose Society was founded in Adelaide in 1978, due largely to the efforts of Trevor Nottle, who had attended the inaugural meeting of the American

Heritage Rose Society in 1972. He published, in 1983, his book *Growing Old-fashioned Roses in Australia and New Zealand*. In the same year Trevor Griffiths in New Zealand published *My World of Old Roses*. Australian gardeners began to be interested. Nursery men who had previously grown only modern roses added a few old-fashioned ones to their lists. Those who had grown a few, doubled the number.

Old roses conjured up pictures of monks in monastery gardens of the Middle Ages, of Redouté painting in Paris the roses which the Empress Josephine grew at Malmaison, of the old Flemish flower paintings, of castles and English country houses — all things very remote from Australia and yet very much part of our cultural heritage, of the books we read and the history we studied.

Technology was making inroads inexorably into every aspect of our lives. In revolt against it came a wave of nostalgia, a love of all things old. Victorian houses brought huge prices at auction, antique shops sprang up in every country town, samplers and old needlework pictures quadrupled in value. For those who couldn't afford Victorian mansions, there was a vogue for 'early settlers' cottages' (which still continues). Gables and attic windows and bull-nosed verandahs took the place of the square, flat-roofed, clinical structures of the previous generation.

And coincidental with all of this came the vogue for cottage gardens. Peter Cuffley published in 1983 *Cottage Gardens in Australia* and Trevor Nottle in 1984 *The Cottage Garden Revived*. Australian garden books are still few in number, so their individual impact is considerable. Instead of planting dinner-plate dahlias and the newest colour in gladioli, people were turning to the poppies and marigolds, lupins and foxgloves of the cottage garden. And with this came a demand for shrub roses, and for single roses as opposed to the ostentatious vulgarity of some of the newer Hybrid Teas.

Membership of the Heritage Rose Society increased. But the Gallicas and Damasks, the Albas and Moss roses flower only in the spring. Most Australians have small gardens and are reluctant to give space to something which is going to flower for only a few weeks in the year. The Hybrid Teas had spoilt us in this respect and most gardeners demand roses with a longer flowering period. By the mid-1980s even the heritage rose enthusiasts, while paying lip service to the species roses, the Gallicas and Damasks, were buying for their own gardens the Noisettes, the Hybrid Musks, the early Tea roses and the Bourbons, all of which still qualify as 'old roses' but are recurrent flowering.

The Bourbons, at least under our conditions, are very prone to black spot. With the new and increasing awareness of the need to preserve the environment, gardeners are less and less willing to use toxic sprays, so the Bourbons fell gradually into disfavour, though 'Souvenir de la Malmaison' still has her devotees. The Noisettes, the Hybrid Musks and the early Teas do exceptionally well here. They have enjoyed more than a passing popularity. They are ideal in mixed plantings, and they flower prolifically for many months of the year. They have in all probability come to stay.

Meanwhile the nostalgia for things of the past, the vogue for cottage gardens (and therefore for shrub roses) and the gardeners' leaning towards things romantic had not escaped the attention of the big rose breeders. Even the names indicate this. No more 'Jet Trail' and 'Super Star'. Now we had 'Heidekönigin' (Queen of the Heath), 'Rose Romantic' and 'Märchenkönigin' (Fairytale Queen). For some time breeders had been producing modern shrub roses. Ultimately it did not matter

to the home gardener whether the rose was old or new. What was of prime importance was whether it would fit in a mixed planting scheme, i.e. whether it could
be treated as a shrub or was more suited, as the traditional Hybrid Teas were, to
beds of roses only, and these were rapidly becoming, for many gardeners aware
of overseas trends and the great gardens of England, a thing of the past.

The big German firm of Kordes has released a steady stream of roses which have
found tremendous popularity here. They seem to do particularly well in our not
so very different although much warmer climate, and are very much at home growing
with other shrubs, perennials and ground covers. There are many single roses among
them.

One of the first of the Kordes roses to achieve popularity here was 'Sparrieshoop',
the rose I had planted over the tank at Little Portion. Pale pink, single blooms
with golden stamens are borne freely on a plant which grows to three metres. It
is not fussy about the soil it grows in and will even tolerate quite a bit of shade.

The 'Frühling' roses (Spring roses) rapidly became features in many of our gardens.
'Frühlingsgold' (Spring Gold) is truly the herald of the spring. One of the first
to flower, its soft, golden single blooms come with the iris at the end of October.
I love blue underplantings with yellow roses. *Penstemon heterophyllus* 'Blue Gem'
grows to about twenty-five centimetres and is a gem indeed. Blue violas — low-
growing and long-flowering — are ideal, as is *Veronica gentianoides*, which forms
a thick mat. Don brought seedlings of love-in-the-mist (so much prettier than its
botanical name, *Nigella*) from his garden in Taradale, and they quickly formed a
carpet of blue under 'Frühlingsgold', the nearby apricot 'Perle d'Or' and the creamy-
yellow 'Thisbe'. The seed-pods of love-in-the-mist are pretty in themselves, so I
could never bear to pull the plants out as soon as I should. In consequence, we
soon had a forest of blue which ultimately had to be thinned.

Quite carried away, I planted 'Frühlingsgold' and 'Frühlingsmorgen' (Spring
Morning) on the north side of the windbreak fence to the Stockyard Garden. They
grew to the height of the fence in a couple of years. A soft pink, single hollyhock
sowed itself — with wonderful good taste — just in front of 'Frühlingsmorgen'.
It would be hard to imagine a better combination.

In front of these two I planted two more recent arrivals from Kordes: 'Rose
Romantic' and 'Heidesommer'. 'Rose Romantic' is a softer pink and has a smaller
bloom than 'Frühlingsmorgen', but still single and much lower-growing. The flowers
are borne in huge clusters and right throughout the summer and autumn. It is
one of the last to stop. 'Heidesommer' is a treasure. Single, creamy-white roses in
clusters cover the plant for months, and the scent is the scent of gardenias, so that
weeding anywhere near it is a joy. I planted the pink and cream eschscholzia beneath
it, and a white penstemon nearby.

What a good investment penstemons are! Hardy and vigorous, they flower for
months on end, and when you cut them back at the end of the season, you find
that stems which had been lying on the ground have sent down little roots and
you have a whole collection of new ones. They come in a splendid range of colours.
We had a soft pink and a mauve which were wonderful with old roses, and a deep
wine red.

It was Kordes, of course, who, in 1958, sent out 'Iceberg', surely the greatest
triumph of any rose breeder for many a long year. And it was Kordes, too, who
gave us the warm apricot shrub-climber, 'Maigold', and that delightful little cherry-red

'Elmshorn' (named for their first rose nursery) which simply never knows when to stop flowering.

From Kordes, too, came 'Magenta', usually classed as a Hybrid Musk. I resisted buying it for years. Magenta is a colour I really dislike, redolent of tea-cosies, shapeless cardigans and old ladies' Sunday bonnets. But ultimately I succumbed. It is not, of course, magenta at all, but a wonderful soft, dusky mauve-pink with just a hint of brown. I planted it with 'Reine des Violettes', so aptly named Queen of the Violets, and the modern Floribunda 'Escapade', a mauve-pink and endlessly in flower.

It is, in the main, Kordes, too, that we have to thank for the ground cover roses, which are only now beginning to make a real impact on our gardens. One of the most vigorous is 'Immensee' (known here by its German name; in England it's called 'Grouse'). Quite prostrate, it bears little clusters of palest pink single flowers and, due to its capacity for rooting as it goes along, it covers a significant area with lightning speed. Definitely not for the small garden! It has a relative, almost indistinguishable from itself, called 'Weisse Immensee' (in England, 'Partridge').

The best of them, I think, is 'Heidekönigin' (Queen of the Heath — in England 'Pheasant'). A rich apricot-pink, semi-double and scented (and very thorny), it quickly forms a low mound. It flowers recurrently, but does not take root as it goes. It can be struck from cuttings, but not as easily as many others. It looks wonderful spilling over a wall. I planted it in this way at the front of the 'Frühlingsmorgen'-'Rose Romantic' bed. In eighteen months it had covered an area two and a half by one and a half metres and completely smothered two Tea roses in its path, so that where we had previously referred to this area as the 'raised bed', it now became the ' 'Heidekönigin' bed'. As long as you thoroughly eliminate any perennial weeds before planting it, and then mulch it very heavily to keep the weeds down while the rose grows, its dense, shiny green, disease-resistant foliage will ultimately make weeding unnecessary — fortunate, this, since its thorns make weeding a virtual impossibility!

There are many other Kordes roses which have attained tremendous popularity here — 'Orange Triumph', 'Bonn', 'Berlin', 'Fritz Nobis', to name only a few. Small wonder that the eminent Australian rosarian, the late Dr A. S. Thomas, described Wilhelm Kordes as 'one of the greatest rose men who has ever lived, possibly the greatest rose man of all time'.

It is chiefly to Roy Rumsey in Sydney that we are indebted for bringing these roses to Australia. Sometimes, as in the case of 'Heidekönigin' which was released in Germany in 1986, they come with remarkable speed. Some take much longer. The 'Frühling' roses were available in Europe as early as the 1940s and 1950s. They arrived here much later — perhaps fortunately, for their popularity was assured by the trend towards cottage gardens, for which they are so well suited.

And none of these, of course, though greeted warmly by the 'old rose' fraternity, are old roses — but they have the qualities we were looking for, the qualities we associate with old roses. They have the shrub form, as opposed to the stiff canes of the Hybrid Teas. They have soft colours. Many of them are single, reminding us of the little single species roses which go back to the beginning of time. And they have scent. Scent, which many of the Hybrid Teas lacked, as breeders concentrated on new colours. Scent, which to many gardeners is synonymous with the rose, and without which a rose is not a rose at all.

Poppies.

The English Roses of David Austin

S cent, too, is one of the great attributes of the David Austin roses. In fact, they have all the qualities Australian gardeners were looking for at the time when they reached our market. Varying in size from those suitable for growing in a shrubby border to those more suitable for growing in tubs, ranging in colour from cream and palest pink to deepest red and rich, glowing apricot, they are nearly all recurrent and, almost without exception, strongly scented. Add to this that David Austin gave to many of his roses names taken from Chaucer and Shakespeare, and it is not hard to see why David Austin's English roses have been such a resounding success. The names, of course, stamp them immediately as English, and therefore part of our heritage; they lend to them an aura of history and romance, evoking mental pictures of Stratford-on-Avon and Anne Hathaway's cottage, and of all that brave company who assembled together all those centuries ago to make their pilgrimage to Canterbury. So that, before we have even seen them in flower, we are ready to accept them as 'old roses in a new tradition'. Even the later names, such as 'Gertrude Jekyll' and 'Graham Thomas' link them with the greatest traditions in English gardening.

With all this in their favour, it is small wonder that they have had such an impact on Australian gardens. 'Constance Spry', one of Austin's earliest, bred in 1961, had established her position long before the others arrived, despite the fact that she blooms only in spring. Nicknamed 'The Tree Rose', she will grow to six metres, necessitating some form of support. In spring she is covered with large, deep pink, cupped blooms, wonderfully fragrant. I sometimes think I almost prefer the intoxication of such a dramatic performance once a year to the steady production of the recurrent bloomers. And 'Constance Spry' is tough. She will stand rough handling.

I was visiting a garden on one occasion with Walter Duncan, one of the great South Australian rose-growers, 'Constance Spry' was espaliered on a three metre high wall, but the owner of the garden complained that she flowered only sparsely. Without a moment's hesitation, Walter seized a pruning saw and cut her to within forty-five centimetres of the ground. I must admit, I watched with my heart in my mouth, but next spring there she was, at the top of the wall again, and literally covered in flowers.

Two of the other non-recurrent roses I would always find a place for are 'Shropshire Lass' and 'Chianti'. 'Shropshire Lass' (1968) grows to over two metres, so is ideal for the back of the border, where she will produce a wealth of almost single blooms of most delicate pink. 'Chianti' (1967) is truly the colour of old wine, deepest red and wonderfully fragrant. It grows to one and a half metres high and as much across. The old Gallica rose 'Tuscany' is one of its parents and 'Chianti' assumes the same deep, purplish tones as it ages. It will put up with poor soil and some shade. I always intended to plant a clematis to grow through these two and provide autumn colour — but this was one of those good intentions I never did put into practice.

There is a great number of David Austin roses now on our market, and more coming out each year. 'Hero' remains one of my favourites — a rich, glowing apricot-pink, a lovely cupped shape and constantly in flower. I waited anxiously for 'Leander' to grow beside it. But when it came it was one of the few to disappoint me — a medium-sized flower of a rather washed-out apricot. I decided not to give it garden room. 'Hero' would have to stand alone.

'Cymbeline' must be one of David Austin's outstanding successes. In form it is very like 'Souvenir de la Malmaison', but it has no propensity to ball in the bud. The colour is similar, too, but with the slightest touch of grey. It flowers for months on end and benefits from having the long canes bent down and attached to a low stake (link stakes are ideal) when it will flower all along the stem. I do love single roses, so would not be without 'Moth' (soft, fawn-pink is the closest I can get to its strange, muted colour) and the cream 'Windrush'.

'Chaucer' and 'The Yeoman' and 'The Wife of Bath' are all ideal for the small garden, or for growing in tubs, and 'Graham Thomas' must be one of the best deep yellows to have come out in recent times.

Initially I planted one large bed of David Austin roses near the maypole: 'Hero', 'The Miller', 'The Friar', 'The Squire', 'The Reeve', 'Chaucer', 'Cymbeline' and 'Chianti'. At the end of the bed was the lovely grey foliage of *Pyrus salicifolia*. As a border I used *Chrysanthemum haradjanii*. And, quite uninvited (perhaps they came with a load of mulch) came a mass of glorious poppies — softest pink, white, mauve and a deep wine colour, single and double, with the most appropriate grey-blue foliage. I could not have chosen better.

On an impulse, to demonstrate the miracles of cross-century breeding, I planted 'Tuscany' besides his offspring, 'Chianti', and then, in the corner of the bed, the pale mauve single rose, 'Lilac Charm', bred by Le Grice in 1952, and the vibrant reddish-purple 'News', the result of a cross (again by Le Grice in 1968) between 'Tuscany Superb' (1848) and 'Lilac Charm'. Roses tend to be promiscuous at the best of times, but what infinite possibilities are opened up if one can mate them across a time span of 120 years!

The David Austin roses achieved immediate popularity in Australia. It quickly became apparent to me that one bed of them at Bleak House would not suffice. So we mapped out a huge rectangular bed near the western entrance to the Alister Clark Garden in the middle of what I had once fondly hoped might be a stretch of lawn (a vain hope given our scorching January and February heat and restricted water). This bed was better prepared than any other at Bleak House. One does learn from one's mistakes. This time the perennial weeds were poisoned first. The bed was deeply dug. It had two truck-loads of manure and straw dumped on it and was left to lie fallow for two months. Then it had a top dressing of lime and blood and bone and was left for another month.

Here we planted a rich selection of David Austin roses graded in colour from the dark red of 'Prospero' and 'The Knight' through the whole range of pinks to the cream of 'Windrush' and the rich apricots and yellows of 'Abraham Derby', 'Tamora', 'Graham Thomas' and 'Yellow Button'.

And here we had room, too, to experiment with some new underplantings. We tried an assortment of cranesbills. *Geranium×oxonianum* 'Claridge Druce' with its pink flowers veined with magenta, did well, as did the pale pink *Geranium endressii* 'Wargrave Pink' whose foliage formed a good, dense mat. The lavender-blue *Geranium pratense*, growing to about seventy-five centremetres, was ideal under the larger, more robust roses such as 'Graham Thomas' but a bit tall for some of the smaller ones. My favourite was the low-growing *Geranium sanguineum* var. *striatum* whose flowers are palest pink. *Geranium sanguineum* itself, with its rather strident magenta flowers, I could not like, so, after a fair trial, it was banished.

We tried *Physostegia virginiana* 'Vivid'. It grew and flowered prodigiously, obviously revelling in the wonderful conditions. Soon it threatened to take over the whole bed so, reluctantly, because its spikes of lilac-pink flowers were very decorative, we removed it to a spot where it could ramp away to its heart's content. The white form, *Physostegia virginiana* 'Summer Snow' was much more manageable and bloomed for months on end, right through summer and autumn.

Under the yellow and apricot roses we tried *Euphorbia polychroma* syn. *E. epithymoides*, which formed a splendid yellow and green mound about forty centimetres tall. Its foliage is interesting in itself and we pronounced it an unqualified success.

Among the best of the campanulas we tried was *Campanula persicifolia*. Its mauve-blue flowers were perfect under pink roses such as 'The Reeve' and 'The Miller', and its foliage formed a good weed-suppresseing mat. The white form, *Campanula persicifolia alba*, was very effective under the deep red 'Prospero'.

We bordered this bed with a low hedge of green lavender (*Lavandula viridis*) which has a scent reminiscent of pine leaves, fresh, when you brush against it when weeding. It was interesting but not an unqualified success. It grew quickly, so needed cutting often and it seeded prodigiously so that we were endlessly digging up and potting the seedlings because I could not bear to throw them away. *Lavandula angustifolia* 'Rosea', which we had used elsewhere, might have been preferable, although the pink is very washed-out.

In this bed, too, we planted drifts of ixias. Many of the South African bulbs are ideal for our conditions, so long as they are in the sun and the bulbs get a chance to dry out during the summer.

The cherry-red one (*Ixia speciosa*) flowers very early, usually in September before any of the roses. I found a great patch of it growing on the roadside at Elphinstone near Castlemaine and brought a few bulbs home. They quickly formed quite a large clump. *Ixia maculata* with cream and yellow flowers was given me by a friend for the Yellow Garden. The most spectacular of them at Bleak House was *Ixia viridiflora* which grows taller — up to sixty centimetres and multiplies extraordinarily quickly and carries startling blue-green flowers which are wonderful companions for yellow or white roses.

I bought a couple of bulbs of the rare, palest blue one (it might be 'Elvira' but I am not sure) and planted it near the pale pink rose, 'Souvenir de St Anne's'. Behind them I put clary sage (*Salvia sclarea* var. *turkestanica*), an intriguing mixture of pale pink, white and mauve. Shortly after this combination had flowered for the first time I went to Tasmania on holidays. Motoring down from George Town where the River Tamar enters the sea, we rounded a bend in the road and came across a whole paddock of pale blue ixias. There was no garden, not even a house, yet here they were in full and glorious flower with the sea as a background. I had read that they do best in Tasmania and here was proof. While some of my others had multiplied rapidly I had really struggled with my few bulbs of this pale blue one, and still had only a modest clump to show for it.

Because it was so big, we watered this garden with sprinklers. It was a mistake. The bulbs do need to dry out and the roses are certainly less subject to black spot if the leaves stay dry. And for those with a restricted water supply, sprinklers are very wasteful.

The David Austin roses flourished. I struggled with one or two, but the fault was probably mine. They seem to cope well under Australian conditions, some growing considerably larger than the estimated sizes given in English books. Most gardeners have welcomed them with enthusiasm — some, in fact, are interested in little else. Some of the 'old rose' devotees are less convinced and tend to treat them with some reserve. Certainly, in most cases, although it is hard to pinpoint the reason, you would not mistake them for old roses. Paradoxically, though, the Heritage Rose people have welcomed the Kordes shrub roses and are now taking part zealously in the search for Alister Clark's roses, which make no claim to be 'old'.

Cyclamen.

Vale Bleak House 29

Bill and I were married in late 1985. He had bought a cottage in South Yarra, not far from the Melbourne Botanic Gardens, and for a time we tried to keep Bleak House going. It meant that we were too often apart. His business commitments kept him in Melbourne and, although we had help at Bleak House, it did not really function unless I spent most of my time there. Something had to go. And it became increasingly clear that that 'something' would have to be Bleak House.

We took careful stock of what we wanted. Although Bill's whole life is centred round the city, he did not want to live there. The years when he had owned a property deep in the forests of Dandongadale in Victoria's mountainous north-east had given him a love of fresh air and open spaces. He found life in the city claustrophobic. I could not live without a garden. We reached the conclusion that we would have to live on the outskirts of Melbourne so that he could commute to the city daily, without spending too many hours in the car, and we could have a few hectares. So we drew a circle round Melbourne with a radius which we considered to be commuting distance. The choice fell on Gisborne – forty-five minutes from Melbourne on a freeway.

So we sold the cottage in South Yarra – without regrets on either side. It had been merely a place to spend a few days when convenient. And we bought in Gisborne a delightful century-old house on just over one hectare of land, overlooking the town and dropping down to Jacksons Creek.

For a time I tried to run Bleak House from Gisborne. It did not work. I was constantly on the road, constantly tired, and had insufficient time either to set about making a new garden at Gisborne or to maintain the garden at Bleak House in the way I knew it should be done. Neither place was giving us any satisfaction.

The years at Bleak House had convinced me that making a garden is one of life's richest experiences, that it brings with it an inner peace which is not found anywhere else. But it must be done without haste. There must be time to enjoy what one is creating — time to sit on the terrace and watch the glow of the sinking sun on a summer evening; time to walk in the autumn mists; time to kneel to examine the delicate tracery on a cyclamen leaf, or watch the opening of a crocus, or a mother bird feeding her young on a spring morning. There must be time, too, for friendships with other gardeners, for visiting gardens, for exchanging plants, for enjoying the camaraderie which exists everywhere among gardeners.

The decision had to be taken. Bleak House had to go. I could not bring myself to sell it. I had a deep love for the old bluestone cottage with its sloping ceilings, massive stone walls and open fireplaces, and the atmosphere it evoked of early days in Victoria. I loved the quarries, busy once, but deserted now except for the rabbits and the birds who made their nests there — I had never made my quarry garden. I loved the wet-lands with the black swans and wild duck and happy memories of rowing there on Sunday evenings as the sun went down. So we decided to lease it.

I thought of the prophetic words of the old German saying on the plaque in the courtyard:

> Ich geh' hinaus
> Ein andrer kommt herein . . .
> I shall go
> Another will come . . .

They had proved to be prophetic indeed. I hoped that that 'other' might come to have a love of Bleak House and some understanding of the work and planning, the love and care, that had gone into the making of it, and that the garden might have, at least for a time, some degree of permanence.

Leaving it was hard. Very hard. But Bleak House will be with me always for I took with me all that it had taught me in the last ten years. It had given me practical lessons: how to prepare a bed, the need for windbreaks and shelters, the role of established trees, the importance of drainage and of mulch and compost, how and when and what to prune, what plants were suitable as ground covers under roses. I left behind me a lot of mistakes. I am sure I will make more in my new garden, but they will be different ones.

All that I have learnt about roses will always be linked in my mind with Bleak House. I had developed an impatience with the long-running and sometimes vociferous antagonism between the lovers of old roses and the protagonists of the new. What is important is not whether the rose is old or new, but whether it can fill the role you have cast it for in your garden. There is a place for them all.

I would always grow old roses for their sheer spring beauty, and plant summer and autumn flowering perennials with them to give colour when they are gone. There is nothing to equal the Rugosas and the Spinosissimas for hedges, or the rampant old once-flowering ramblers for climbing into trees. The delicacy of colour and richness of scent of the early Teas will always assure them of a place. For prodigality of bloom it is hard to beat the Hybrid Musks, and the Noisettes will always be in demand where recurrent flowering climbers are needed, on pergolas and summerhouses. The species roses have a special role to play at the very back of a border or where Australian native plants are grown. As shrubs in a border, the Kordes roses are unsurpassed, and the David Austin roses, with their rich literary and historical associations, their strange scents and unusual colours, are certain of a place for many a long day.

The Australian roses of Alister Clark will eventually be accorded their proper place in our gardens for their rich colours and incredible length of flowering. For me, they will always have a special significance both because of the pleasure they had given me during the search for them and because I felt I had come to know, through his diaries and letters, this gentle, fine, kindly man who bequeathed such riches to the Australian gardener.

As I turned my mind to the planning of my new garden, one thing was certain. Although I was deeply grateful for the framework of established trees there, this garden, too, would be, above all, a rose garden. No other flower has, for me, the same combination of sheer beauty with history and romance. With the rose you bring into your garden the scents and the hues and the glory of past and present centuries, of near and distant lands. They would be the very fabric of my new garden.

With the experience gleaned at Bleak House I would plant them on fences and up trees, as hedges and over arbours and summerhouses, looped along chains, prostrate as ground covers, as shrubs in a border, as weeping standards, in tubs on a terrace. And I know that I will be rewarded each year with an exuberance of blossom, a variety of foliage, an intoxication of perfume and a wealth of colour ranging from purest white to richest purple, which makes of a garden a magic place and gives to its owner a tranquillity of spirit, a renewal of hope and a deep sense of joy.

A Hillside
of Roses

Preface

A Hillside of Roses is the sequel to *Garden of a Thousand Roses*. It describes the garden my husband and I have made following our move from Bleak House (the garden described in *Garden of a Thousand Roses*) to Gisborne.

The two gardens are very different, and roses described in the first book are not discussed again in this one, although they may be mentioned.

This second garden benefited greatly by the experience gained from the first. Far more attention has been paid here to plantings other than roses — trees, perennials, bulbs, etc. — and to certain basic problems and principles of design.

This second garden houses the collection of Alister Clark roses formerly held at Bleak House and a small collection of other roses bred in Australia, both registered with the Ornamental Plant Collections Association.

The Alister Clark Collection has recently attracted a generous sponsorship from Burns Philp & Co to enable a breeding programme to be carried out at the Victorian College of Agriculture and Horticulture, Burnley, using the roses of Alister Clark and crossing them with other carefully selected roses. The aim is to continue the work of Alister Clark in breeding a rose which will bloom for twelve months of the year. The programme is under the guidance of Dr James Will, Senior Lecturer at Burnley.

My grateful thanks are due to *Your Garden* and to Lynette Cooke for the use of some of their photographs taken in the garden; to Peggy Shaw for all the black-and-white drawings in the book; to Rosemary Manion for her map of the garden which forms the endpapers of the book; to Vida Horn for her painstaking work in checking plant names and compiling the index; and to Hyland House for their sympathetic treatment of both book and author, and for many fine lunches enjoyed along the way.

Dedicated to Rachel and Tony, Molly and Emily, in the hope that they may one day experience the joy of making a garden.

The Finding of Erinvale *1*

As the agent's car drew up at the gate, hope and anticipation once more gave way to disappointment and despair. For here we were at yet another neat, almost new, faithfully constructed, completely unimaginative and characterless brick veneer. It was, as all the others had been, complete with low brick fence, concrete driveway, rotary clothes hoist and a random scattering of natives and shrubs.

I hardly heard the agent as he went once more into his spiel about cathedral ceilings, bench-top stoves, en suite, and that latest, and apparently in the agent's eyes indispensable absurdity, the "parents' retreat". Somewhere in this area which we had selected with so much thought there must be a house with something of the personality and atmosphere of Bleak House, the little century-old bluestone cottage which I had restored with such loving care over the past ten years and which, I was almost beginning to think, would prove to be irreplaceable.

We had chosen this area both for its scenic attractions and for its proximity to Melbourne. Neither of us had any wish to live in the city, but Bill must be able to commute daily with a maximum of one hour's driving. We had decided finally on Gisborne, forty-five minutes drive from Melbourne on a freeway.

Gisborne lies in a valley at the foot of Mount Macedon. Settled early in Victoria's history and being on the route to the goldfields, it was already a flourishing township by the end of the 1850s. Wide streets, lined with substantial buildings, were planted with English trees. The park in the centre of the town has still very much the atmosphere of the English village green. Jacksons Creek, its banks lined with willows and silver poplars, flows in leisurely fashion through the park and under the highway.

A steep winding road leads down from the busy freeway into the town. At the foot of the hill stands Macedon House, classified by the National Trust, a solid imposing monument to Gisborne's history. Across from it, recently carefully restored and now used by the Macedon Historical Society, is the fine old Court House.

Surely in a town such as this it was not unreasonable to hope we might find a house with some air of the past about it and surrounded by at least a hectare of ground. Yet here we were, for at least the twentieth time, standing at the gate of something I knew before I had set foot in it was certainly not for us.

With a sigh I started to explain all over again to the agent that this was not what we were looking for. With an equally profound sigh and an exaggerated air of patience he once more suggested Mount Macedon. That was where the older homes were, splendid old places having what he reverently described as "established English gardens". If only we would inspect some of those, he felt sure we might be satisfied.

It was tempting. Undoubtedly some of the finest gardens in Australia are there — gardens established in Melbourne's boom time with English trees, carpets of bluebells and primroses in the spring and cyclamen in autumn, rhododendrons twelve metres high and little creeks rippling over pebbles. But roses need sun. They will grow, but do not flourish, in that high misty atmosphere in the shade of the great trees. And it was still, above all, roses that I wanted to grow.

With a sinking heart I got back into the car. On the return journey to Woodend the agent suddenly slapped his knee and cried that he knew the very place. He couldn't imagine why it had not occurred to him before. Of course, it was not really on the market as yet, but the owner had called in to discuss it with him, and it was only a matter of time. So he rang on the car phone and arranged to take us there without delay, certain that he had a sure sale.

All the way he enlarged upon the virtues of "this magnificent property" — a garden which would fill any gardener's heart with joy, established trees, an old home, carefully renovated, of course, and everything in tiptop order. I began to feel convinced and, despite all our previous disappointments, I felt hope reviving once more.

We turned in at neat picket gates in a rough stone wall and drove up a tree-lined drive, the agent drawing my attention to each splendid specimen as we passed. I said nothing. How could I explain that here was a gardener's nightmare? For the long drive was planted with one oak, one elm, one beech, one sorbus, one silver birch and so on all the way from the gate to the house. I pictured the owner going through his nursery catalogues and ticking one of everything there. They had been planted meticulously four metres apart. I felt sure that they had been carefully nourished and fertilised so that each one was, in itself, fine and healthy, but the total effect was ludicrous. It was the sort of thing I had done myself when, at the tender age of twenty and in total ignorance, I had acquired my first home and planted my first garden.

The gravel drive was raked to perfection. Not a weed in sight. Concrete edges surrounded all the beds, fixed sprinklers ensured adequate watering. But the beds were like the drive, one of this and one of that, with no thought given to foliage or colour or design so that one was left with an impression of total chaos. The only solution would be to cut down most of the trees and to replan and replant the whole.

Any attempt to explain this to a non-gardener was futile. I tried not to sound disparaging as we went through the myriad dark poky rooms of the stuccoed house and I was quite silent as we drove back to Woodend. The agent ushered us into his office and left us for a moment to collect his files.

And there on the wall was the house I had been looking for. Long and low, weatherboard, painted green and white, with chimneys and iron lace and French doors opening onto a wide verandah. And trees. All around were trees.

It was with tremendous excitement that I greeted him as he came back into the office.

"That's it," I said. "That's what I want!"

He looked pained, disbelieving.

"That!" he said, his voice betraying his contempt and incredulity. "You wouldn't want that. It's over a hundred years old. There's no en suite, no family room, no dishwasher, no clothes hoist . . ."

"No parents' retreat?" I couldn't help interjecting.

He looked at me suspiciously. Then he continued with his catalogue of defects.

"The wallpaper is hideous. The carpets are old. The stove has had it. It needs renovating from top to bottom. And, what's more, there's not a flat piece of land in the whole place."

It took a lot of talking to convince him that he would not be wasting his time if he took us to see it.

Finally, resigned, and in no good temper, he drove us back through the Black Forest to Gisborne. Erinvale was almost in the town, one of the early homes on the banks of Jacksons Creek just behind Macedon House.

As we drove in through the iron gates on that hot January afternoon and I looked up at the century-old Portugese oak, flanked by two equally old walnuts, which dominated the entire garden, I knew that we had found what we were looking for.

Someone, apparently hoping for a visit from a prospective buyer, was making a futile attempt at sweeping the overgrown gravel drive. We went past two tumble-down wooden garages, through a battered wooden gate in a solid wall of ivy, past a broken-down patio surrounded by bamboo, to the back door. The front door was apparently inaccessible.

The house was all that the agent said it was. An attempt had obviously been made to renovate it in "period" style — maroon flock wallpaper, brown velvet curtains and, incredibly — it must have been at a sale — an orange shagpile carpet. The bathroom — there was only one — was black and yellow, black tiles and yellow fittings and a black and yellow wallpaper with a pattern of voluptuous naked ladies. The agent could be forgiven for thinking it out of the question.

But through it all, the old house had somehow retained its dignity. The high ceilings, the fireplaces, the deep skirting boards, the ceiling roses and arched hallway spoke of better times — times which might conceivably return. Through the windows of a back room I caught sight of a grotto built into a stone wall with a little pond, all overgrown with ornamental grape and ivy.

We left the house and went out into the garden. Here, too, all that the agent had said was correct. There was not a flat piece of land in the whole place. We slipped and scrambled up the steep bank behind the house through a positive forest of young seedling oaks and steadily encroaching blackberry. I caught the agent casting an anxious glance at his two-tone shoes.

But on the south side of the house was an open paddock rising up to two magnificent elms, and an old horse contentedly munching away in a jungle of thistles. From the vantage point at the top of the hill you could look down over the whole town.

Somehow we forged a passageway through to the north side and slipped and slid down the slope again. At the bottom, overhung by a giant weeping willow and a thicket of plum trees, was a deep, irregularly shaped pond. At the head of it was a weatherworn statue of a boy holding a flat platter, and at the narrowest point a little arched stone bridge.

Before we arrived back at Woodend I had mentally repapered, recarpeted, replumbed, pulled down the sheds, torn out the ivy and bamboo and blackberry, and Erinvale was ready to be lived in once more.

R. pimpinellifolia 'Single Cherry' forms a hedge around the circular drive.

Set among the trees, Willy's house is often taken to be one of the original farm buildings. The rose in the foreground is 'Raubritter'.

The dry stone walls are a feature of the garden. This one is in the Centifolia Garden with *Dianthus* 'Beatrix' growing along the top.

'Madame Grégoire Staechelin',
also known as 'Spanish Beauty'.

Winding steps lead up from the
circular drive to the house.
Spilling over the wall in the
foreground is 'Raubritter'.

Seven plants of 'Madame Grégoire Staechelin' growing round three sides of the house are a feature of the spring. The
little hedge rose is *R. pimpinellifolia* 'William III'.

Making a Start 2

We took possession in April, possibly the loveliest month of the year in Victoria. The first trees were just starting to turn, and the great golden ash in the front garden was a glory to behold, an omen, I thought, of joys to come in this new garden.

I got up very early on our first morning, averted my eyes resolutely from the mess left by the removalists and climbed to the highest point of the land between the two great elms on the south side. With the horse gone, the grass was waist-high. The blackberries seemed thicker and more impenetrable than I remembered them and the thicket of elm suckers denser.

I was out of breath when I reached the top and sat down on an old tree stump to survey our new domain. The land sloped down to the south, towards the creek, and to the west, towards the road. The sun was just coming up behind me. A kookaburra sitting on the railing of the old wooden bridge over Jacksons Creek burst into great gales of laughter. When I thought of the garden we had left behind and compared it to the task that now faced us I was not sure whether I wanted to join him or to burst into tears.

The kookaburra won, and then and there I set about the practical business of planning how to tame this wilderness. The stump I was sitting on was midway between the two elms and here, I decided, was the perfect place for a little rose arbour — with a seat where exhausted visitors intrepid enough to climb to these heights could rest their weary legs and enjoy the view down over Gisborne. The row of poplars screening the old Court House was just starting to turn gold.

I thought of garden design lectures I had attended where the emphasis seemed always to have been on the desirability, if not the actual necessity, of having a central axis. I wondered what these gurus of the gardening world would have advised if confronted with our rugged irregular site.

It was obvious that the first step must be to engage the services of a bull-dozer driver. Until the land was terraced nothing could be done. Three or four terraces sweeping round the side of the hill, following the natural contours of the land, were what was needed. Forget about axes, I told myself firmly. They were out of the question here.

But before we could start work at all, before anything could be done to either house or garden, we had to erect a fence — a two-metre high fence round the entire property — for Willy, our dear blue heeler who had come down with us from Bleak House, while being devoted to us and normally the very soul of good humour, exhibited a marked antipathy towards motorbikes and all human beings under the age of fifteen. So the first essential was to fence him in.

Colin Phillips, who had done several miles of fencing for us at Bleak House, came down to discuss the job. We decided on treated pine posts and cyclone wire. That would enable me to have the same great banks of rambling roses which had, for me, been the chief glory of the garden at Bleak House.

But we were not in the country now. The local Council had to grant approval before we could erect any kind of fence. When I described what I wanted to the Planning Officer I was met with a pained incredulity. Did I not realise that the property was in the part of town marked Residential A? It was a pity to erect fences at all, but a fence such as this would be an eyesore. Treated pine and cyclone wire! After much discussion he decreed that such a momentous decision as this would have to be referred to the whole Council. The Planning Officer could not take it upon himself to approve something so out of keeping with this picturesque part of town.

The next Council meeting was set down for the following Tuesday evening. I rushed home, pulled out all my photographs of Bleak House and took the very best ones showing the rambling hedges to the Kodak shop to be enlarged. I took them round to the Council chambers late on Tuesday afternoon.

The following Thursday I had my permit, together with a letter regretting any inconvenience that had been caused.

So Colin set to work, and before many days were past our property was safely enclosed and Willy, who had to his great indignation spent long hours shut in the laundry, could run free again.

And then came Peter Cochrane — not with a bulldozer but with a bobcat, which he said was easier to manoeuvre on the steep slopes. For four days he worked on the south side, and at the end of that time we had four banks and five terraces. Right at the bottom he left space for a pond. We would get run-off and seepage from the hill, so it was the logical place for it. And in this at least I would gain the approval of the gurus, who have decreed that ponds should always be at the lowest point if they are not to look incongruous.

Huge boulders had been thrown up by the bobcat and Peter had placed these with great skill in the two less steep banks. With careful planting we would probably get away without retaining walls here.

Having done this, he departed cheerily, leaving us with a raw and ravaged hillside, bare save for the two giant elms towering over a scene of devastation, and an appealing old wizened, misshapen apple tree which still bears each year a generous crop of delicious crisp little apples.

I lived with this chaos for a week or two, becoming more and more frustrated as my efforts to reduce it to some sort of order seemed increasingly ineffectual. It was clear that I needed help — retaining walls had to be built and paths laid before any planting could begin.

An advertisement in the local paper might produce someone, but he would be an unknown quantity. Then one morning, in an inspired moment, I took myself up Mount Macedon and consulted Stephen Ryan at Dicksonia Rare Plants. If anyone knew the district's gardeners it would be Stephen. I had been a customer for years and had been met always with cheerful good sense, practical advice and a real knowledge and deep-seated love of plants.

Stephen knew that we had moved. He knew Erinvale and the type of problems we were likely to encounter. He listened to my tale of woe, nodded his head and said promptly: "You need the Flens boys."

The very next afternoon, while I was slashing away at the blackberries, Nick Flens turned up. He stayed for five years.

Born in Holland, Nick came to Australia aged ten. Thin and wiry, with great physical strength and infinite resourcefulness, Nick had no knowledge of plants — nor any interest in acquiring any — but an understanding of tools and machinery, unfailing good humour and, most importantly at that time, a real flair for stonework.

He surveyed the devastation wrought by the bobcat and summed the situation up with the comment: "What we need is stone, lots of stone, then I could build retaining walls."

Now stone was something of which we had almost unlimited quantities. We had leased the house and garden at Bleak House, but not the broad acres and the old stone quarries — those quarries in which I had once dreamed of making a garden, a garden of daffodils and tulips, iris and snowflakes and mellow stone walls. We had used the stone at Bleak House, for building and for the garden, but the supply seemed inexhaustible. What I had not expected was that I would have the infinite good fortune to find someone who was able and willing to work with it.

So right through that first winter Nick came three or four days a week, drove our battered old truck up to Malmsbury and came back with load after load of stone. This he converted into skilfully constructed dry stone walls. He has

134

a wonderful eye for a curve and a line. It was never necessary to tell him where the wall should go. He knew it better than I.

And while Nick built, Bill and I demolished. The derelict old garages came down and were replaced by a brick paved terrace. The ramshackle old pergola outside the back door was ruthlessly pulled to pieces. In its place stands a pretty back porch and a conservatory — a wonderful place for growing geraniums and for having lunch on sunny winter days.

The old pergola and the original pond were thickly edged with bamboo. If I had ever harboured any thought of planting it, this would have cured me. It had encroached more and more on the garden and its roots had been largely responsible for breaking the concrete walls of the pond. For weeks Bill mattocked and hoed and crowbarred until finally every root had been removed.

Ivy was the next task. The tumbledown wooden fence which totally enclosed the back courtyard, hiding a beautiful weeping elm from sight, was covered in a dense wall of ivy. Bill claims not to be a gardener, but I know no-one with such a faculty for destruction. Before too many weekends had passed not a trace of ivy remained.

The blackberry took longer. The entire property was infested with it. I decided that, much as I hate to use it, poison was the only answer. It was just as I was about to discharge the first bucket of Roundup that, underneath the great mounds of blackberry, I caught sight of rhododendron leaves. They turned out to be nothing special — most of them were the uninspiring mauve *R. ponticum* which I had seen growing wild on the hills of Scotland and Ireland, or a singularly unattractive deep pink. But apart from the trees (which were magnificent) they were all we had. So poison was out. Once again we set to work with fork and hoe, mattock and crowbar and secateurs. Removing blackberry roots became first priority for many long weeks.

By the beginning of September the first walls had been built, the bulk of the blackberry was gone and we were able to think about our first plantings.

Of Barton Vale 3

It was at Barton Vale, an old house in Tasmania, that my love of gardens had first been awakened. We had bought, in unfashionable West Hobart, at the end of a gully running back into the hills and bearing the romantic name of Salvator Rosa Glen, an old stone convict-built house on over a hectare of what had once been a garden. The house was approached by a long, tree-lined drive — in my ignorance I could name none of the trees except the two great weeping silver lindens (*Tilia petiolaris*) which stood at the gate, and a holly which overhung the front verandah.

All the romance of old Hobart was there: a heavy front door with an intricately wrought semicircular fanlight, an imposing wide entrance hall, a fine staircase, attic rooms with sloping ceilings, cellars with barred windows, stone flags in the kitchen and scullery where a steep ladder led up to the tiny, irregularly-shaped maid's bedroom (the ladder was taken away at night to prevent her from taking flight), rich cedar architraves and skirting boards, and cedar shutters which closed over the windows inside. I loved every aspect of this neglected old house, so redolent of Tasmania's early history. An old conservatory at the end of the front verandah became a dolls' house for my youngest daughter, and steps led up to a roof garden complete with flagpole and a view down over the harbour, where we could watch the ships sailing up the Derwent.

And the garden! It was divided, as English gardens are, by high stone walls into a front garden, a rose garden, a kitchen garden and an orchard. At the end of one of the walls a derelict summerhouse supported, with difficulty, a huge climbing Cécile Brunner rose, one of the very few I could have named at that time. The ancient apple, pear and plum trees still bore abundant fruit. Thousands of bulbs appeared each spring – daffodils, narcissi and snowflakes and, under the old linden trees, a carpet of bluebells and the South African *Scilla peruviana.*

And there were paeonies – great voluptuous blooms which came up in their dozens in the rockeries outside the scullery door. And in the orchard was a stone ruin which had once been a tiny two-storied cottage (for a gardener perhaps?) clothed in wisteria and ornamental grape.

I was young, and had young children and a full-time job, and little time to spend acquiring even a smattering of the vast body of knowledge there is to absorb about plants and gardens. But it was here that I first formulated the desire – more than a desire, the resolution – that I would, at some time in my life, make a garden.

And as I wandered now through the garden at Erinvale, stood under the giant oak and looked up at the tree-house in its branches, stooped to walk beneath the overhanging boughs of the walnuts, and crossed the little stone bridge, the memories of Barton Vale kept flooding back. Here was the same air of romance, of times long gone, the almost tangible presence of the people who had made this garden, who had planned and planted and laboured to create something beautiful.

Despite the obviously long periods of neglect, there was still much remaining, much on which we could build.

In front of the house were three shallow terraces, covered now with couch and blackberry, clover and nettles. They must once have been gardens, for in the centre of the first one was an ancient metal structure designed to support a weeping rose. I decided to leave it there, to remake the beds around it, and to plant a weeping 'Lamarque' as the central feature of the front garden. 'Lamarque' has all the virtues one could possibly want in a weeper – a mass of creamy–white double blooms, not just once a year but repeatedly, a delicious slightly lemony perfume, very pretty pale green foliage and a naturally lax habit of growth.

But before there could be any planting, some practical matters had to be resolved. There was no toolshed and no place to put one, for there was no back garden, no place where such things as toolsheds could be tidily hidden away. The house stood close to the back of the block with a steep hill rising straight up behind it to the back fence. Peter Cochrane, at risk of life and limb, put in a path two-thirds of the way up. This permitted us to work the slope and also to pass from the south side of the garden to the north without first descending to the level of the house. I watched him with my heart in my mouth, expecting that at any moment Peter and the bobcat would land in the living room.

While Peter's path made working the garden easier, it did nothing to solve the problem of the toolshed. Bill remarked helpfully (several times) that you could buy ready-made galvanised iron sheds at McEwans. No doubt we could have. But wherever we had sited it, it would have quite destroyed the atmosphere I was hoping to create.

In the end I designed, aided by memories of the ruin in the orchard at Barton Vale, a picturesque little two-storied building with a high gabled roof, which serves as toolshed and storage and a bedroom for Willy. Guests usually take it to be part of the original stables, dating from the days when Erinvale was a farm. It holds all the tools, the mowers and brushcutters and chainsaws, all that mechanical paraphernalia which seems to have become an essential part of gardening — and over Willy's lambswool bed I hung a splendid old print of St Francis in rich reds and golds, the work of Meister Bertram, the first German painter of animals.

A double carport was constructed nearby and behind it, out of sight, two huge compost bins. Over on the newly bulldozed south side we built three more — for wheeling heavy barrows up and down the slopes would be impossible. These three we hid behind a lattice fence with an arched entrance. On the back and sides I planted that vigorous old creamy rambler, 'Albéric Barbier', and in front on each side of the arch, 'Adam', an interesting old rose which first made its appearance in British gardens in 1833 and is said to be the first of the Tea roses. It bears blooms of a subtle amber colour with just a hint of apricot.

And now, with the problems connected with cars, tools and garden rubbish disposed of, I could turn to the far more interesting matter of planning the garden.

Here the sloping site was a great asset. The ground at Bleak House had been perfectly flat and a good deal of thought and ingenuity had gone into making it more interesting and trying to prevent the visitor from seeing the whole thing at once. On this site there was no possibility of doing that and, just as the contours of the ground determined where the terraces should go, so the positioning of the house and the big trees really dictated where beds should be.

I started from the premise that this should be, as Bleak House had been, first and foremost a rose garden. I wanted as many roses as I could grow — in beds, on arches and pergolas, up trees, trailing down walls, as groundcovers, as hedges. And I wanted all kinds of roses — species roses, old European roses, Tea roses, modern shrub roses, Rugosas, Hybrid Musks, Floribundas, climbers and ramblers and the English roses of David Austin.

In front of the house, where the three terraces had once been, flagged steps led down to a circular drive. These terraces were quite overgrown with weeds and blackberry. On the right of the steps the top terrace was given over almost entirely — apart from the sea of weeds — to an ancient white camellia, a towering holly, a gigantic old poplar reaching for the heavens and a sad old plum. I resolved to leave them all. I cut back the holly so that it was possible to walk up the steps again. The ancient camellia was treated fairly drastically and has since shot again and flowered well last year. The poplar is a glory in both spring and autumn so I left it well alone. The old plum posed a real problem. In the end I planted 'The Edna Walling Rose' on one side and 'Tea Rambler' on the other. Both have reached the top of the tree. The plum flowers in spring and the roses in early summer. I don't know which is the lovelier.

On the left of the steps, sharing the terrace with the weeping rose and not two metres from the front verandah, was an enormous contorted willow. Even I, although I have no taste for destruction, had no difficulty in deciding that he must go. Not only would nothing grow near him, but his roots would, in time, undoubtedly undermine the foundations.

So the next step was to call in the tree surgeon — not Paddy McGuinness, who had done such a very thorough job with our old willow at Bleak House, but a cheerful, active fellow by the name of Charlie. If he had a second name, I never heard it. He set to work with a will whistling as he went and, in less than half a day, to the constantly reiterated tune of 'Click go the shears, boys', the grand old willow was reduced to a sad mess of broken branches which Charlie carted off to the tip.

That very night there was a most violent storm. The wind howled round the house and the branches of the holly kept up a constant drumming on the iron roof. At the very height of the storm there was a report like a pistol shot followed by a dull thud which indicated clearly that something was seriously amiss. My mind flew immediately to the big oak and I rushed out in the rain with a torch, fearing the worst. But there he stood, quite unmoved by the violence around him, as he had been for well over a hundred years.

The next morning we discovered two large branches of another old willow on the front lawn. It was decided, without too much difficulty, that he must share the fate of his brother. So Charlie was recalled, and we were left with an open space on the lawn and very much more light and sunshine for everything else.

Some Trees that Belong 4
to the Rose Family

I was busy already with rose catalogues, thumbing through them night after night looking for old friends and for roses that I had not previously grown. But the very first consideration − even before roses − was trees. The old part of the garden was richly provided, but the south side was crying out for trees, for here there was nothing but the two big elms and the old apple tree.

I wanted rambling roses all along the fence − old favourites such as 'Albéric Barbier', 'Albertine', 'Francis E. Lester' and 'Tea Rambler'. To these I added 'Blairi No. 2' − a strange name for a rose. Apparently 'Blairi No. 1' wasn't up to much. But 'No. 2', bred in the UK in 1845 of uncertain parentage, is quite splendid. It can reach considerable heights − estimates vary from four metres to eight − and bears, in early summer, large flat very double blooms of soft pink, shading darker towards the centre. Towards the bottom of the slope, where water tends to lie during wet winters, I planted 'Sympathy'. This must be one of the best reds in the garden and, what's more, it stands wet feet far better than any other rose I know. Bred by Kordes in 1964 it bears a constant succession of dark red double very fragrant blooms right through summer and autumn.

On this fence, too, I planted an unknown beauty which we call simply 'Zdralkas Rose', as it came to me from Bob and Trish Zdralka who own a beautiful garden at the foot of Mount Macedon called Raintree Cottage. The rose is a vigorous rambler. Its flowers, a pleasing soft pink, are single, slightly ragged in appearance and borne in great profusion. It has created considerable interest among Heritage Rose enthusiasts, many of whom have wanted to attribute it to Alister Clark. There is really no evidence for this, so we shall continue to call it simply 'Zdralkas Rose' – and enjoy it.

Inside the rambling roses I wanted a row of trees. This would form a visual barrier and also provide protection from the cold winds from the south. If planted at the same time, the roots of the ramblers would establish a firm hold before the trees were big enough to be any real competition. And ultimately the ramblers would find their way up into the branches of the trees.

At Bleak House we had had more success with crab apples than with any of the other trees I had planted, and this climate was not dissimilar. It was almost by chance that I had planted them there, spurred on by my first visit to Bolobek, that most English of all Australian gardens.

It was in the early 1980s and I was mourning the death of three lemon-scented gums (*Eucalyptus citriodora*) given me by a dear friend and killed ruthlessly by the first harsh frost. Helen Vellacott, a friend from Castlemaine, rang and told me that the garden at Bolobek was to be open in aid of the National Trust. We arranged to go together. We would take a picnic lunch, for this was the sort of garden that demanded time.

The month was October, one of the loveliest months of the year in Victoria, so I could not believe our misfortune when I woke that morning to find it was snowing. We rarely had snow at Bleak House but, if it was snowing there, it certainly would be at Macedon.

I rang Helen to put off our trip. But she was adamant. Of course we must go. It probably wouldn't last in any case. We did put off the picnic, however, and agreed to have lunch at Bleak House before we set out.

All through lunch, as the snow continued to fall, I waited for Helen to broach the subject again. But I waited in vain. As she swallowed her last mouthful of tea, she rose to her feet and announced in a tone that brooked no argument that it was time we were on our way.

Over six hundred dedicated and enthusiastic gardeners were at Bolobek that day. Small wonder, for I cannot recall a lovelier sight than this great garden under snow. We could well have been in England, for the century-old trees lend it an air of continuity not often found in Australian gardens. They contribute, too, to the atmosphere of tranquillity that reigns here at all times – doubly so under a blanket of soft snow. Even the hordes of people and the sea of umbrellas could not detract from it.

Of all the glories of the garden on that day, it was the crab apple walk which remained most vividly in my mind. Twelve trees of *Malus* 'Golden Hornet' in full flower and arching overhead to form a tunnel, at the end of which at a meeting place of paths stood the most exquisite little statue. Many of the tiny treasures under the trees, the English primroses, the mottled leaves of the cyclamen, the *Alchemilla mollis* and tiny wood anemones, seen on many subsequent visits, were covered by snow, but the candelabra primroses on either side of the path still held their heads proudly erect.

I had no camera with me, but I have no need of a picture to call up again the sight of those crab apples flowering in the snow.

So I had planted crab apples at Bleak House to replace my lost lemon-scented gums. Not 'Golden Hornet' but *Malus floribunda*, 'Veitch's Scarlet' and *Malus ioensis* 'Plena'. They did better than any other trees I planted, seeming not to mind either the cold winds and wet feet of winter or the drought conditions of summer. And they are beautiful, not only in spring, but again in summer as the little apples ripen, and in autumn when the leaves of many of them turn a glorious scarlet.

So when I came seriously to consider which trees to plant inside my rambling hedge, it was crab apples which first came to mind.

It was an exciting day when I brought the first trees home. There were two of *Malus floribunda* because it is probably my favourite. It makes a fine spreading shade tree and is one of the first to flower in spring, when from scarlet buds come pink to ivory-coloured flowers in profusion. I had to have one 'Golden Hornet' in memory of Bolobek — white flowers and a heavy crop of golden fruit. There are two of *ioensis* 'Plena' for its spreading habit and its great flat heads of fragrant, double, pink and rose-tinted blooms. Then one 'Lemoinei' for contrast. It has bronze-coloured leaves and claret-red flowers. 'Parkmanii' is recommended for small gardens. We don't quite qualify but I bought one anyway for its rose-pink flowers and plum-coloured fruit. One *Malus spectabilis*, for its name and its mass of soft pink blooms. Then two primarily for their fruit: 'John Downie' with white flowers and large orange to red fruit which are very pleasantly flavoured, and a 'Jack Humm' from New Zealand with large crimson fruits which hang in big clusters like cherries and are so thick skinned that even the most persistent of birds tend to leave them alone.

These were planted with great ceremony a few metres inside the south-west fence and I felt I had really made a beginning.

Then came a holiday in Tasmania and a visit to Olive Room's garden, Tamarleigh, on the outskirts of Launceston. It was a lovely still day and I found Olive clad in a voluminous green apron, her snow-white hair hidden under an old felt hat, watering pots of tulips in a little enclosed courtyard at the side of the old two-storied house. The rose 'Paul's Scarlet' grew right up to the second-storey windows and was just coming into bud. On the opposite side of the courtyard were two little low rooms with green wooden shutters on the windows, once the dairy and the meat house. And arched right across, from one side of the courtyard to the other, was that vivid exuberant tireless performer, 'Nancy Hayward'. Then and there I fell in love with Olive Room and Tamarleigh.

There are many times, when one is looking at Tasmanian gardens, that one is reminded of England. It was certainly so here where hedges are such a feature of the garden and give it form. The land belonging to Tamarleigh runs right down to the River Tamar and the paddocks are surrounded by hawthorn hedges. A pergola, ending in a stile and a view to the river, is covered in wisteria. The white and the blue, planted together, were intermingled now and climbed right to the top of a tall, slender silver birch. On the other side of the stile an old brown cow munched contentedly in the sunshine.

A hedge of *Lonicera nitida* (shades of Margery Fish) divides the orchard from the garden. Compact and thick, it is cut twice a year. We passed through a gap in the hedge to the orchard.

At one time in its long history Tamarleigh had been run as a commercial orchard and the old trees are still there — huge old almonds, apricots, peaches, plums, redcurrants and black, gooseberries, mulberries and cherries. And underneath them now was a positive army of tall bearded iris. For all the overflow from this extensive garden finished up in the orchard, and later in the summer cornflowers, love-in-the-mist, penstemons, poppies and verbenas would form a rich carpet.

And dominating the whole was a huge and venerable Manchurian pear (*Pyrus ussuriensis*) in full and glorious bloom, a cloud of white.

"Yes," said Olive. "I treasure that tree, for it was the thing that reconciled me to Tamarleigh."

The old stone house had been built in 1882 for five thousand pounds (a huge sum in those days) as a wedding present for the young bride of a Presbyterian minister. It had twenty hectares of land and was run as a small farm.

But it, like many an old home, fell on evil days. It changed hands many times. It suffered decay and neglect.

Then, some forty years ago, Olive Room's husband came home one evening to their pretty, comfortable home in Launceston, with its neat well-kept garden, and announced that, as she had always wanted a farm, he had bought one.

Olive saw it first in spring at just this time of year, but on a cold wet blustery day. She was overcome by misery as she stood at the head of the stairs and looked at the damp stained wallpapers, the bare boards and broken windows. The top storey had been uninhabited for years and used as storage for sugar and flour by a grocer owner who cared nothing for the beauty of the old house.

Trying to swallow her disappointment, and choking back tears, she walked out onto the front verandah and looked down at the tangled overgrown garden.

And there, in the corner, rising out of a sea of neglect and crowned in glory, was the Manchurian pear, and at its feet a carpet of blue hyacinths. And suddenly she had a vision of what the garden might become, and from that moment, and increasingly as her family grew up, Tamarleigh became her life.

When I got home from Tasmania the first thing I did in the garden was to plant a pair of *Pyrus ussuriensis*, surely one of the loveliest of all the members of that very extensive Rosaceae family. I never see them in flower or in their glorious autumn colour without thinking of Olive Room and her garden. A little climbing rose has seeded itself under one of them. I shall leave it there for a year or so till it produces its first good crop of flowers and I can judge whether it is worth preserving. This year I scattered a mass of pink and white poppy seed beneath it.

And of the trees that belong to the family of the rose it was not only the Manchurian pear which first came to my notice in Tasmania.

Years earlier, when my children were very young, we moved to Hobart from Brisbane. I knew nothing of gardens, but the romance which was Willowdene, a little weatherboard cottage on over a hectare of land in South Hobart, which was our first Tasmanian house, could not leave anyone untouched who had the slightest eye for beauty. It nestled in the side of a hill sloping down to a winding creek. It, too, had been an orchard, and I delighted not only in the spring blossom and subsequent generous crops of every sort of fruit, but also in the thousands of daffodils which clothed the slope down to the creek and which we picked by the armful so that they filled the old house with sunshine.

At the gate, like a pair of sentinels, stood a pair of *Sorbus aucuparia* (the mountain ash). I did not know their name but loved them for their froth of white flowers in the spring and even more for their summer crop of bright red berries, which brought the birds in great flocks to the garden, and for the fiery scarlet of their autumn leaves.

Sorbus aucuparia already had a place in our new garden. There was one in a corner near the gate, past its prime perhaps, but still showing a brave face to the world.

So, without having planned or intended it, I was well on the way to making a small collection of trees that might illustrate to some degree the extent and complexity of the vast Rosaceae family.

5 *Less than One Hectare*

While at the outset nearly a hectare had sounded quite a lot, it was rapidly being borne in upon me that I was going to be short of space. Having enjoyed the luxury of a country garden, where an extra bit of land could readily be appropriated from the adjoining sheep paddocks should the need arise, I was beginning to find the fixed boundaries of a town garden intolerably restrictive.

Half a hectare was taken up by the house and outbuildings and the huge old trees which had first attracted us to Erinvale. Roses would not do well here. They need sunshine.

This left only the half-hectare on the south side. The two grand old elms with their far-reaching arms and roots took up a good deal of space. Nothing would grow under them. And I had already planted up the south border with crab apples. Any other trees I wanted would have to be carefully placed if they were not to block sun from the roses that I wanted to plant in wide beds along the terraces.

There was still the steep bank leading down to the pond. Roses would not grow there as water seeped through the bank, keeping it moist for most of the year.

So for this spot I decided on the willow-leaved pear (*Pyrus salicifolia* 'Pendula'), also known as the weeping silver pear — not one, but four, two on each side of the southernmost steps leading down to the pond.

This graceful little tree enjoyed an enormous popularity in this country when the enthusiasm for white gardens, influenced by Vita Sackville-West's exquisite white garden at Sissinghurst, was at its peak, leading to a spate of imitations. The willow-leaved pear will forever be associated in the minds of visitors to Sissinghurst with the gentle figure of the Vestal Virgin which stands beneath it. When one reads Vita's lines about her one cannot help feeling that she was, perhaps, the impetus to the creation of this lovely garden. She is the personification of the gentleness, the beauty and the touch of mystery which pervades it:

> How tender, simple, shy, divinely chaste,
> She wilting stood,
> Her suppleness at pause, by leisure graced,
> In robes archaic by the chisel woo'd
> That smoothly flowed around her waist
> And all her figure traced,
> And at her feet in fluid ripples broke.

Who could come in contact with all this represents and not fall in love with *Pyrus salicifolia*? So many people did so that Robin Lane Fox was moved to describe it, some years ago, as "a status symbol". And so, in consequence of its becoming too well-loved and thus too commonly seen, it fell into disfavour among the gardening elite, too often intent upon cultivating only the rare.

Irritated by this attitude, I planted four. And, also on this bank, two *Amelanchier canadensis* (the shadbush), another member of the rose family. A cloud of white blossom appears early in spring, followed closely by the young foliage in a delightful and distinctive shade of pinkish-bronze. This turns to green, and then to a fiery scarlet in autumn.

It is not only the *Pyrus salicifolia* in this part of the garden which will, for me, always be associated with Sissinghurst, for I planted also two *Sorbus cashmeriana*, which grows in the rose garden there. This medium-sized spreading tree, the mountain ash from Kashmir, has blush-pink spring flowers, which pale as they age and are followed by clusters of white berries. I planted two at the outset, but one succumbed later to the perpetual dampness.

And that was all I had room for. An intolerable thought! For if I was serious about establishing a small representative selection from the vast body that makes up the Rosaceae family, I must include at least the quince, the medlar and more of the crab apples and *Sorbus*, together with some of the *Prunus* and *Crataegus*. And, leaving the Rose family aside, I wanted dogwoods, lilacs and magnolias.

To the north of Erinvale was a bare paddock, extending to the next corner and bounded by Mill Road to the north and Erinvale Close to the east. Steeply sloping and covered in rank grasses and blackberries, it was the epitome of neglect. Its only trees were a row of stunted cypress along part of the south boundary, and a few poor old fruit trees. Obviously it had once been part of Erinvale and this had been the orchard.

From the local Council I found out the name of the owner and wrote to him, asking whether he might be interested in selling. The answer was a firm, uncompromising "No". He had owned the block for five years and planned to build his dream home there.

My heart sank. Not only would that put paid to any thought of extending the garden, but I had visions of a large brick veneer, two-storied in all probability, with arches and a four-car garage looming up on our boundary and overlooking the entire garden — not to mention blocking out the northern sun. There could even be a swimming pool with weekend parties and barbecues and loud music.

It was of no help to tell myself that we should have foreseen this. No use either to try to persuade myself that at our (rapidly advancing) age a hectare of garden was all that we could properly look after.

And, after all, Penelope Hobhouse at Tintinhull had made a garden people crossed the world to see. And it was only one hectare. Margery Fish, at East Lambrook Manor, had inspired thousands of gardeners with the jewel of a garden she had created on the same small area in the middle of a village. And she had not started gardening until she was well into her fifties at the end of a busy professional life in London. It was all a question of discipline, I told myself; of resolutely selecting only the best and excluding anything that did not measure up.

I went back to my catalogues and lists. But I am not good at excluding.

I decided to start with those terraces in front of the house — three on the left-hand side of the path which wound down to the circular drive, and two wider ones on the right.

On the right were not only the old trees (the camellia, holly and poplar), but a stunted magnolia of unknown name and four big old rhododendrons. It was obvious that, if I wanted to plant roses here, they would have to be the strongest and hardiest. I wanted them to flower in succession, so I chose, for early spring, the Kordes roses 'Frühlingsgold' and 'Frühlingsmorgen' (both now 2.5 metres high) and to follow them *R.* 'Dupontii'. This is thought to have been, perhaps, a cross between *R. gallica* and *R. moschata* but there is no certainty about it. It grows into a large shrub and its pure white single flowers with golden–brown stamens are one of the real joys of the spring. It is sweetly scented and sometimes bears decorative hips. To these I added *R. alba* 'Maxima' and *R. alba* 'Semiplena'.

At the bottom of the second terrace is a one-metre high retaining wall dropping down to the drive. Here I decided to plant nine or ten 'Raubritter' (Robber Baron). It is the best rose I know for trailing down over a wall. It is another Kordes rose, bred in 1936, the result of a cross between the old garden rose × *macrantha* and a rambler not available in Australia called 'Solarium'. It produces long lax canes which tend naturally downwards, although it can be trained up trees or stumps and mine shows a marked inclination to climb up the magnolia. It produces in early summer a myriad of small cupped roses, silvery–pink on the outside, deeper within. They remind me of the flowers of 'La Reine Victoria', except that they are smaller and far more numerous.

'Sombreuil' — a modest climber and one of the best of all the white roses, has a heavenly scent.

R. pimpinellifolia 'Irish Rich Marbled' forms one of my favourite hedges.

'Souvenir de St Anne's', a sport from 'Souvenir de la Malmaison', deserves a place in every garden.

Tanacetum ptarmiciflorum with tall bearded iris and a clump of *Gladiolus* × *colvillei* on the bank leading down to the pond.

'Devoniensis', also known as 'The Magnolia Rose', looks down from the top of the pergola leading into the Old Rose Garden.

The eastern boundary fence is covered with 'Kew Rambler' and Alister Clark's 'Gladsome'.

'Madame Grégoire Staechelin' adorns the pillars of the front verandah.

Graham Stuart Thomas has given 'Raubritter' pride of place in the wonderful garden at Mottisfont Abbey. It is trained along the wall of a pond, which is a meeting place of paths, a focal point in the garden.

Ideally I suppose it should be deadheaded after flowering — it only does it once a year — but this is a mammoth task. I set myself the objective of doing so many a day for a few weeks.

All of the roses chosen for this bank flower only once, in spring or early summer, but they have the vigour to contend with the existing shrubs. Edging the path I decided to plant a few recurrent roses for constant colour — 'Souvenir de St Anne's', that exquisite sport of 'Souvenir de la Malmaison' and without the latter's capricious habits, and 'Marie van Houtte', and perhaps the cream 'Gruss an Aachen'.

A wide verandah runs across the front of the house and along the south side. Here I would plant seven of the climber 'Madame Grégoire Staechelin', popularly known, with every justification, as 'Spanish Beauty'. Years ago, I had persuaded my friend, the artist Peggy Shaw who is responsible for all the delightful drawings in this book, to do just this on her verandah at Castlemaine. The result was breathtaking and has become one of the sights of the town at the time of the Castlemaine Festival. 'Madame Grégoire' flowers early in unbelievable profusion, her great pink semi-double blooms scenting the garden. I would eventually paint the weatherboards the very palest pink, with the roof, iron lace and shutters deepest green.

So far, so good.

On the left-hand side of the path were those three terraces infested with blackberry and couch, clover and nettles, and with the old iron weeping rose support in the middle of the top one. For this prime position I had already chosen the lovely creamy Noisette rose, 'Lamarque'. For the rest, because I wanted permanent colour when I opened the front door, I settled for Hybrid Musks and David Austin roses. I would plant two or three each of 'Pax' and 'Penelope', 'Felicia' and 'Cornelia' — not 'Buff Beauty'. It grows too exuberantly and is the wrong colour in any case — two of little 'Menja' and two each of David Austin's 'Hero' and 'Canterbury', 'The Prioress', 'Charmian' and 'Lucetta'. And then, since the colour was right, two of the Australian rose 'Carabella' which is hardly ever out of flower, and two standard 'Escapade' to lend height and to balance the weeping 'Lamarque'.

This was all fine. But my lists still grew and, despite the exercise of the most rigid discipline, there were more and more, both roses and trees, which I could not bring myself to cross out.

I found myself walking day after day to the top of the garden and, instead of concentrating on the splendid view over Gisborne, casting covetous eyes on the unkempt block next door.

And then, one morning, I drove Bill to the station as I often did when he did not want to drive. Instead of taking the usual route through the town I came back past the top of the garden and there on the fence of the coveted paddock was a huge red and blue sign saying "For Sale".

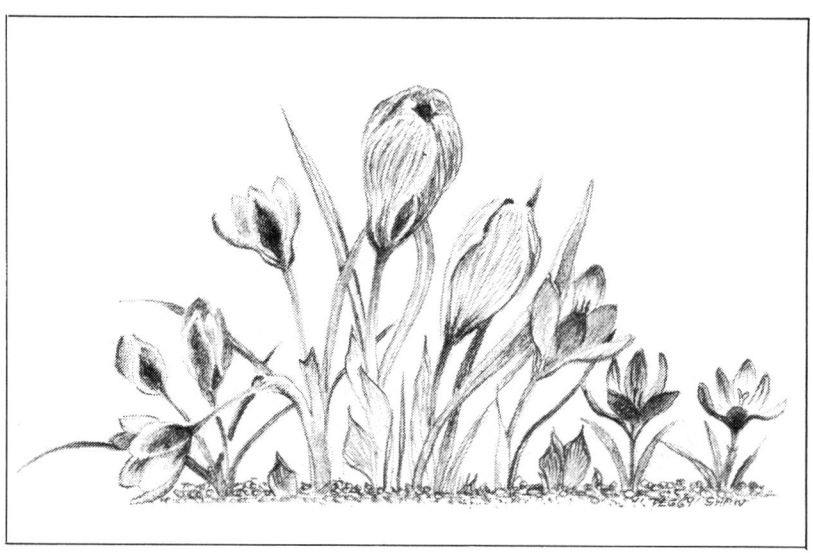

6 *Covering the Banks*

Of course we bought it. And equally "of course" there was no haggling and no indecision. Never has an agent earned his commission with so little effort.

By any standards it is a beautiful block of land, what the advertisements call "a prime piece of real estate". For us, it was more than that.

Bounded on three sides by roads, it has a breathtaking view down over the town — a view of trees, resplendent then in their autumn finery, and surrounding hills and a picture postcard little white church in the middle distance. We could easily have been in one of the UK's home counties.

On the opposite side of Kilmore Road, across from Erinvale's front gates and stretching from the creek right up past the new block, is a grand row of oak trees, planted over a hundred years ago by the founding fathers of Gisborne to whom we should be everlastingly grateful. This steep hillside is inhabited only by nine or ten horses, thoroughbreds, who make a valuable contribution to the picture postcard scene created by the little white church.

On the day our purchase was concluded, I walked many times round the boundaries of the block, had my lunch on the highest point and gathered a bucketful of windfall apples from the old neglected trees to give to the horses. Willy took part in all of this with enthusiasm, beside himself with joy at having all this extra space to run in.

On the "nature strip" – absurd name – someone had planted golden elms and, just inside the western fence line, silver birches and aspens (unfortunately alternately). These must stay, but a couple of contorted old wattles could go, and a massive old misshapen cotoneaster, even though it did have the merit of belonging to the Rose family.

The row of cypresses was four metres inside the southern boundary. This would leave just sufficient room for a back drive, invaluable for deliveries of sand, gravel or the indispensable mulch.

Nick arrived early on the following Thursday. I think he shared my joy in the new acquisition – or else he gave a very good imitation of doing so – though it would appreciably increase the area to be mown (by now he was doing all our mowing as well as building the dry stone walls). Mowing, however, was for the time being out of the question.

The high fence having been extended to include the new block, we had a slasher in to cut the long rank waist-high grass. This had the effect of making the block seem even steeper and Nick, who is seldom defeated by any difficulty, declared the task of putting a ride-on mower over it to be "mission impossible".

Back came Peter Cochrane with his bobcat and we ended up with four terraces on this side of the garden. They are neither uniform in depth nor straight, for I wanted at all costs to preserve the old orchard trees. So the bobcat had to wind its way in and out between four or five old apples, a couple of pears and three or four plums, all well past their prime. A sad old almond which had looked on point of death has now, with water and a modicum of care, turned into a fine specimen clothed each spring with the starry blooms of *Clematis montana*.

With four irregular terraces completed, the lowest slope merging into the old part of the garden with its wealth of fine trees was still too steep to work on, so Peter suggested making a path along it, as he had done behind the house. But a straight path would have been out of place, so we decided to follow the winding track made by Willy in his daily pursuit of the postman – a pursuit doomed, of course, to perpetual disappointment by the existence of the high fence. But dogs have a genius for finding the best and quickest way.

Now the ride-on mower could be used and the grass kept under control, but we had three more banks to cope with. Two of them were too high for the construction of retaining walls to be feasible. One was over two metres high, the other closer to three. There was no alternative. We would have to clothe them with plants.

Bill was filled with consternation when this was mooted. "No more garden," he said. "You can't possibly cope with more garden."

I was almost inclined to agree with him. But somehow those banks had to be covered – and retained. So we would plant just groundcover roses on the banks, and lots more trees on the rest of the block. They would require no work once they were established.

The banks were prepared. Stones were set aside for future use, the soil roughly smoothed over and sprayed with Roundup. After this they were left for a month, then a second dose of Roundup was applied to do away with the next crop of weeds. I am well aware of the existence of pre-emergent weedkillers but I have an uneasy feeling, which refuses to be dispelled, that we do not yet know enough about the long-term effects on the soil of some of the poisons we use so freely. With the second crop of weeds done away with, the groundcover roses were planted.

Rosa wichuraiana, the most vigorous of them all and the parent of many of the others, I rejected out of hand. I had planted it at Bleak House and found it uncontrollable — fit only for dam walls on country properties.

'Heidekönigin' was then, and is still, my first choice. I had grown it and 'Repandia' at Bleak House with considerable success. But not so much had been demanded of them. 'Heidekönigin' lies quite flat, has attractive dark green glossy foliage (important in a groundcover plant) and produces throughout the summer medium-sized mid-pink scented blooms. It doesn't put down roots as it goes, so is quite easy to control. But whether it would have sufficient spread and density to cover this daunting expanse remained to be seen. It seemed rather like entering a sprinter for the Melbourne Cup.

'Repandia' next. It had been rather overwhelmed by 'Heidekönigin' at Bleak House, but I decided to give it another chance. It covers itself in early summer with tiny shell-pink flowers which are followed by diminutive scarlet hips, themselves very decorative. I need not have worried about it. It tore down the slopes, putting down roots wherever it touched the ground, and needing to be ruthlessly chopped off at the bottom with shears to prevent it from taking over the entire block. Not one for the small garden, despite its deceptively delicate appearance.

Then Alister Clark's 'Milkmaid'. Bred from the lovely apricot Noisette rose, 'Crépuscule', this is a rich creamy colour, not unlike 'Albéric Barbier' and just as robust.

For good measure I put in a couple each of 'New Dawn' and 'Sea Foam'. These are superb in flower but do need to be pegged down if they are to succeed in such a situation as this, for they are not by nature prostrate.

'Snow Carpet' and 'Nozomi' I discarded. They could not cope with an operation of this size, nor with the competition they would be exposed to. I would find a place for them elsewhere. At the north–east corner where the bank is highest and steepest I planted a really rampant fellow which we call 'Neil Robertson' for the simple reason that it was a gift from Neil's garden. I suspect that it is a chance seedling from *R. brunonii* which grows there. It has long narrow leaves, delightful medium-sized white flowers slightly flushed with pink (not unlike the flowers of *R.* 'Dupontii') and cheery little red hips which last into the winter. It has stretched its rapacious arms in all directions, and has needed severe discipline to encourage it to confine its attentions to the bank. With constant vigilance on my part I think it may be a success.

Then I was fortunate enough to acquire just one plant of 'Madame Alice Garnier'. A treasure this one! Bred in France in 1906 from the irrepressible

R. wichuraiana, she has small shiny green leaves on a plant which will climb, if required, but can equally easily be trained downwards, and bears in summer clusters of salmon–pink medium-sized sweetly perfumed blooms with strangely quilled petals.

I gave virtually a whole bank on the south side to the indefatigable *Rosa bracteata* – the exquisite simplicity of those flat purest white single flowers with their great boss of golden stamens more than compensates for the wicked thorns and grasping habits.

Another offspring of the very fertile *R. wichuraiana* is the Rugosa hybrid, 'Max Graf', bred in the USA in 1919. It has the disease-free foliage we expect of Rugosas and bears single flowers of a bright lipstick-pink – but, alas, no hips. A relation, 'Red Max Graf' was bred by Kordes in 1980. Its striking scarlet single blooms are wonderfully set off by the dark leathery foliage.

I tried also 'Pink Bells', bred by Poulsen in Denmark in 1983. It is charming, bearing tiny double bright pink flowers in great profusion on a low dense spreading plant armed with tiny, but very vicious, thorns. It is a delight but I have put it in the wrong place. It is no match for 'Heidekönigin' and 'Milkmaid', who are threatening to smother it. Next winter I shall move it to a lower bank where there is less competition.

It was marvellous to have all these banks to experiment with. The ground-cover roses are for the most part of fairly recent origin and many of them I had not seen growing. I decided to try some of Meilland's landscaping roses, much advertised as being hardy, disease-free and requiring little pruning, suitable on this account for parks and public places. 'White Meidiland' has to rank high among white roses. The flowers are pure white and born in great clusters. They hold on for days and are ideal for picking. The plant is low-growing and spreading but not really a groundcover as it does not lie flat. The only fault I have found with it is that the flowers die in a most unattractive fashion which, unless you regularly remove the spent blooms, spoils the total effect.

'Scarlet Meidiland' with bright cherry-red blooms is also a joy. I planted it on the edge of a low stone wall and here it is ideal.

This winter I have put in three of another of this group, 'Candy Rose', along the edge of a path. It is described as having semi-double deep pink flowers on a low spreading plant. Since it has 'Frühlingsmorgen' somewhere in its complicated ancestry I am expecting great things of it.

I have not planted 'Flower Carpet' although its aggressively pink blooms have stared up at me from the pages of every gardening magazine and from every nursery bench over the past twelve months. I am not sure whether it is the colour or the over-insistent promotion which most puts me off. When I was starting to cover these banks, I did plant the much more attractive 'Rosy Carpet' bred in the Netherlands as long ago as 1983. I have been told, but cannot personally vouch for it, that it has the same parents as 'Flower Carpet'. But even it is too strident to be planted among the old roses and has had to be moved to the Australian garden where its bright colour does not jar.

On one small relatively isolated piece of bank, I decided to plant 'Immensee', known in England as 'Grouse'. I chose it partly because it will tolerate semishade and the bank I intended it for is shaded by two ancient apple trees and two plums. It was not faintly discouraged by this! I realised early in the piece that it would have to be kept under strict control, so started clipping it off with the shears at the top and bottom of the bank. Not in the least deterred, it has climbed instead up one of the plum trees in company with a striking rich claret-coloured clematis.

'Immensee' was bred by Kordes in 1982 from a *R. wichuraiana* seedling and 'The Fairy'. The *R. wichuraiana* seedling was, without a shadow of a doubt, the dominant parent. I see little of 'The Fairy' in 'Immensee'.

It is essential with all these groundcover roses to be scrupulous in ridding the ground entirely of all weed growth before planting, and to mulch very heavily with thick newspaper and straw in the first year to smother any subsequent growth and give the roses a chance to establish themselves. Once they get going, weeding is difficult, if not impossible, but after a year or two it also becomes unnecessary.

Four years on, I can say that, without doubt, the banks of groundcover roses are as much a feature of Erinvale as are the early-summer-flowering rambling fences.

Some More Trees 7

On the north side the top terrace is the deepest. This was the place, then, for an extension of my small collection of the trees belonging to the Rosaceae family.

As always, I was greatly influenced by fine specimens I had seen in other people's gardens, and by associations with fine gardeners. I think this is true of most gardeners. I seldom visit a garden where I do not learn something or find something to admire, a plant I have never seen before or a combination I have never thought of, something I would like to try for myself.

And this must not be thought of as slavish imitation. Every garden imposes its own rules and conditions. We each compose our own "song of praise" and, as the garden matures, it gradually becomes a living tapestry of people we have known and places we have loved – a gallery of memories.

In choosing from the vast number and variety of *Prunus* available, my mind turned immediately to Margery Fish's well-loved garden at East Lambrook in the south of England. This garden is unique – and I use the word advisedly for, despite the fact that it is little over one hectare in extent, it is one of the truly great gardens of our time. I was immediately drawn to Margery Fish by the fact that she, like myself, did not start gardening until middle age.

Over the years I have bought nearly all her books and refer to them constantly. *We Made a Garden* remains my favourite and I find myself dipping into it in search of information and then reading on and on, unable to put it down. So much so that visiting her garden was like coming back to a place one has known well.

Here were the many varieties of geranium she had written about with such love; here the variegated Solomon's seal (*Polygonatum*) and the variegated honesty (*Lunaria*) she used to light up deep shade. Here were the great heads of paeonies ("a garden couldn't be contemplated without paeonies", she said) and here were her "pudding trees". There were, thank goodness, no dinner-plate dahlias. These had been her husband's great love and abiding passion. Margery described them as being "only fit for the circus".

So almost tangible was her presence in the garden she had made that I half expected to come round a bend in the path and find her there on her hands and knees, weeding. For Margery Fish was a hands-on gardener. Only by working long and closely with plants do you acquire the intimate knowledge she had of their wants and needs, their strengths and their weaknesses.

She was certainly one of the great gardeners and plantswomen of our time. Informality and profusion (all the beds are mixed plantings) are the keynotes but, when you look past these, you see the rarity of much of the planting and realise that this garden has been created by a connoisseur.

It was in Margery Fish's garden that I first became aware of the extraordinary beauty of *Viburnum plicatum* 'Mariesii', its spreading branches laden with great umbels of upward-facing white blooms. Later I planted two at Erinvale and never walk past them without living again the delight of that morning spent at East Lambrook Manor.

And it was there that I saw *Prunus padus* 'Watereri'. It was in full flower on the edge of the lawn which slopes down to the house. I used up half a film and still did not capture the essence of this graceful little tree with its racemes of cream flowers hanging like wisteria blooms from every branch. I searched Melbourne and rang interstate nurseries but did not succeed in finding it. I did find *Prunus padus* (the bird cherry) but not the variety 'Watereri', so I settled in the end for *Prunus padus* and have been delighted with the multitude of tiny white blooms. The popular name is deceptive, however. Its little black fruits are extremely bitter and any resemblance to cherries is purely visual.

Prunus serrula has been a great success. Hardy and drought-tolerant, its chief glory is its bark, which is the rich colour of polished mahogany.

Prunus subhirtella 'Autumnalis' was another good choice. I planted two, one on each side of the wide steps Nick made leading from the middle terrace to the upper one. They bear a profusion of tiny white or pale pink blooms during autumn and winter when so many other trees and shrubs, and all the roses, are dormant. Hugh Johnson, to whose *Encyclopaedia of Trees* I constantly refer, tells me that they will ultimately reach a height of ten metres. Fortunately they are taking their time about it.

From among the hundreds of species of *Crataegus* it was difficult to make a choice. Hawthorns (*Crataegus oxyacantha*) were already here in abundance.

If we are not constantly on the lookout for the myriad of tiny seedlings which come up each year, it would rapidly become a superabundance.

I left the three or four on the boundaries and planted rambling roses to grow through them – 'Rambling Rector', as delightful as its name, grows with astounding rapidity and weaves its way in and out through the hawthorn branches to cascade down from the top in early summer in a shower of little white semi-double roses with bright golden stamens. Its origins are lost in time, but it bears a close resemblance to one of Gertrude Jekyll's favourites, 'The Garland'. Here, too, was a home for one or two of those little cutting-grown 'Albertines' which I can't resist striking each year. And here, too, I planted one of Alister Clark's *R. gigantea* hybrids, 'Golden Vision'. Its other parent was the well-loved Noisette rose, 'Maréchal Niel', and its semi-double flowers are just the same shade of pale creamy-yellow. On opening they fade to nearly white. Like all the *R. gigantea* hybrids it grows rapidly.

Another *Crataegus*, which I bought on impulse on a visit to Tristania Park Nursery at the foot of Mount Macedon, is *Crataegus lavallei* var. Carrierei – I don't think it has a simpler name! I saw it in a crisp, cold autumn, its branches laden with oval shining vermilion berries the size of crab apples, and its leaves already turning red–bronze. I bought two and have not regretted it.

The last of this variety which I permitted myself was *Crataegus tanacetifolia* (tansy-leaved thorn). And this is another which has, for me, personal associations. I saw it first in a rambling old country garden outside Harcourt in central Victoria. The Springs is owned and worked and loved by Joan Wilkins, who is one of those people who give the impression of having been born in a garden. Probably she has read widely, but I felt that she had, in fact, learned from the plants themselves. I am quite certain that gardening fashions and the edicts of landscape designers would be quite foreign to her. This is a garden which, like Topsy, just grows, plants climbing into and over each other, the odd weed tolerated, or more probably never even noticed. Narrow dirt paths wind in and out among this profusion but Joan knows where each tiny treasure is and can go unerringly to it.

I saw *Crataegus tanacetifolia* across an unexpected clearing. I am short-sighted and at a distance I took it to be an exceptionally well-grown plant of *Rosa glauca* (syn. *R. rubrifolia*), for it has the same deep blue–green foliage, and the little orange berries are easily mistaken for rose hips. This striking resemblance alone would justify its inclusion in a rose garden. But it needs no justification. Its own merits earn it a place. The small white flowers with red anthers are a joy in the spring – and it has, moreover, in contrast to the common hawthorn, no thorns.

All of the *Crataegus* are drought-resistant and ask very little attention. An ancient hoary Washington thorn (*C. phaenopyrum*) in the old part of the garden must have survived years of total neglect but its five-pointed leaves still turn brilliant orange and red in autumn and it is festooned in winter with tiny scarlet berries.

"It is eccentric to eat medlars or to grow quinces today," writes Hugh Johnson. In this case I must admit to being an eccentric for I would not have a garden without both of them. The medlar (*Mespilus germanica*) is a short crooked quaint little tree whose rough dark leaves turn a fiery russet in autumn. The single white flowers could easily pass for the blooms of some of the species roses, and are followed by brown fruits like outsized rose hips. They are said to be edible if left on the tree to go soft preferably having survived a frost, but, having tried them once, I advise strongly against it.

The quince I associate with derelict houses and vacant allotments. In all the now almost deserted gold towns in central Victoria there are sad dilapidated cottages, tumbling down and overgrown, often reduced to nothing more than a lone chimney or a pile of rubble. And very often there is a quince tree or, indeed, a whole copse of them. But their origins are anything but gloomy. They are found naturally in such exotic places as Northern Persia and Turkestan.

Quinces must be among the very hardiest of trees, though looking at their pale green leaves, white-felted on the underside, and their wealth of Dresden china blossoms in spring, this is hard to believe. Country cooks (and I do not qualify) use quinces to add a tang to apple pies and make jelly from the great golden fruits − a jelly which is the clearest rich pink.

I planted three medlars in a little group, and two quinces. The effect of two of anything always seems to give much more than twice the effect of one. Later I found a gem of a tree called *Pseudocydonia sinensis*, which has all the virtues of its relative, the common quince, but is, in addition, semi-evergreen and blessed with very decorative flaky brown bark. But by the time I found it, I had room for only one.

Of Hedges 8

I had planted hedges at Bleak House largely as a matter of necessity. Without them, gardening on those windswept plains would have been nearly impossible. Even with them it was difficult enough.

But I am sure I did not realise then the importance of hedges to the structure of a garden. At Bleak House hedges were planted for practical, utilitarian reasons. At Erinvale it is largely a matter of aesthetics.

One of the oft-quoted principles of landscape gardening — and one which few of us would dispute — is that it should not be possible to see all of the garden at once.

But this must be modified to some extent in the case of a garden on a hillside. Here I wanted to be able to stand at the highest point and get an overview, a bird's-eye view, of the whole garden. I wanted to be able to see roses on four levels, roses climbing up trees, tumbling down banks, spreading out as groundcovers and standing, disciplined and sedate, in beds.

And yet, when on the lower levels, I did not want to be able to see any more than the section I was in, with only an occasional glimpse of glories above. I wanted paths that rambled and beckoned, steps that curved, only hinting at a destination beyond. I wanted hidden gardens, secret places. I think that every gardener brought up as a child on *The Secret Garden* longs privately for just such a place.

And this is where hedges come in. They divide each level of the garden into sections, sometimes very private and secluded sections. At the same time, when seen from above they lend the garden shape, and pattern, and definition. They impose on all its rosy exuberance form and structure and prevent it from seeming a shapeless mass. With such an important role to play, the choice of hedge plants is of vital importance to the success of the garden as a whole.

Yew and box and hornbeam, used with such discernment in English gardens, did not seem appropriate to an Australian country garden. Besides which, they are very slow.

I wanted my hedges not too tall. I did not want to exclude the sun, so essential to good rose growing. A row of young cypress had been planted by the previous owner ten metres in from the short south fence line on the new block. These I had resolved to leave.

But I wanted no more cypress hedges. Although later I planted a semicircle of *torulosas* (*Cupressus torulosa*) behind the summerhouse Nick built at the highest point looking down over Gisborne.

All Erinvale's land, except for the Kilmore Road frontage, was on the way to being enclosed by hedges of ramblers. These had been the outstanding feature of the Bleak House garden. They were what I missed most when I came to start a new one.

The frontage along Kilmore Road was too shady for roses. So here, between the existing trees and the old mauve rhododendrons, I planted camellias, mostly sasanquas, and all in shades of pink. Heavily fertilised each autumn and then mulched with oak leaves put through the muncher, they have done reasonably well. With more frequent watering they would undoubtedly do better.

Then to the rose hedges. Unless you have a small garden or a large staff, I think it is a mistake to plant recurrent flowering roses as hedges. They need regular deadheading if they are to look their best, and most of us have not the time for that.

Among the most effective roses for hedges are those descended from *R. pimpinellifolia* (syn. *R. spinosissima*), the Scotch Burnet roses. Their fine ferny foliage is attractive at all times. They don't need deadheading for their blooms fall cleanly and are succeeded by unusual little black or brown hips. They are tough and hardy. They stand wind and tolerate poor and sandy soil. They need no pruning except for the occasional removal of dead wood. After they have flowered I give them a quick cut with the shears to put them into shape again.

Erinvale has two gates on to Kilmore Road with a semicircular drive leading from one to the other. Round this semicircle I put in forty-nine plants of *R. pimpinellifolia* 'Single Cherry'. Its glowing jewel-like single cherry-red flowers with prominent cream stamens are a delight every spring. Even the ones in semishade under the big trees flower tolerably well.

The south and west verandahs form an L, and I enclosed this on one side with a hedge of *R. pimpinellifolia* 'William III', and on the other with a hedge of *R. pimpinellifolia* 'Irish Rich Marbled'. It might have been preferable to have used the same rose on both sides but nowhere could I obtain a sufficient number of either. I had tried at Bleak House planting several members of the one family to make a hedge, but I had never been happy with the experiment. To be an effective hedge they really need to be all of one kind.

R. pimpinellifolia 'Irish Rich Marbled' is indisputably my favourite member of this group – tiny soft pink-and-white double blooms absolutely cover the bushes each spring. But in the autumn 'William III' steals the show. In spring his small, magenta-coloured double flowers play second fiddle to 'Irish Rich Marbled'. But in the autumn 'William III's' ferny foliage turns to a myriad subtle shades ranging from dull gold to russet red.

The only recurrent member of the group – and even this does not need dead-heading as the blooms fall so cleanly – is the deservedly popular 'Stanwell Perpetual'. This I planted as a short hedge along a terrace on the sheltered north side of the house which Bill christened the gin and tonic terrace.

The word "*spinosissima*" means "closely beset with thorns". This they certainly are, but they are tiny spiny thorns, not great vicious ones. Their approved name "*pimpinellifolia*" translates as "having leaves like a pimpernel" (I don't think I have ever seen one, except as illustrations in my childhood favourite *The Scarlet Pimpernel*). The popular name is Scotch Burnet, although in point of fact they are found in the wild from Siberia to the Caucasus. Certain it is that the Scots have a very proprietary attitude towards them, as evidenced by a recent visitor to Erinvale. I found him, an elderly white-haired Scotsman, a long-time exile in Australia, standing quite alone in front of a bush of *R. pimpinellifolia* 'Altaica', a small white single member of this very extensive family and, as he turned to me, his face wreathed in smiles, he murmured softly:

> The rose of all the world is not for me
> Give to me the little white rose of Scotland
> That smells so sweet and fills
> The heart with longing.

How could I possibly tell him that this particular variety was introduced into gardens in the British Isles in 1820 from its home in the Altai mountains in Siberia?

I presume that 'the rose of all the world' referred to is the charming old bright pink-and-white-striped Gallica rose, 'Rosa Mundi'. It is not my favourite among the old striped roses. 'Camaieux' is more subtle, and *Centifolia variegata* more gentle. But 'Rosa Mundi' has an irresistible fascination, a fatal attraction, due in part perhaps to the romantic tale of its being named after the beautiful mistress of Henry II and in part to the fact that it is a sport of *Rosa gallica* 'Officinalis', grown by the monks in monastery gardens all those years ago.

There is a hedge of 'Rosa Mundi' enclosing the kitchen garden at Hidcote and this, too, is pruned unceremoniously with the shears after flowering is over for the year.

I resolved to have a hedge of it along the west side of the area I had reserved for my old roses. But again I could not find a sufficient number of plants. I recalled that I had read in that truly inspirational book, *The Education of a*

Gardener by Russell Page, that he had once made a hedge of the Rugosa roses 'F. J. Grootendorst' and its sport 'Pink Grootendorst' planted alternately. What is good enough for Russell Page is good enough for any gardener so, being far too impatient to order the plants and wait until next year to put them in, I decided to use 'Rosa Mundi' and *R. gallica* 'Officinalis' alternately. This, I think, has worked. Their colours are in perfect harmony and their foliage and habit of growth very similar.

In another part of the garden I used 'Pink Grootendorst' to line a path leading from one section to another. All the Rugosas make good hedges, dense and thick, and 'Pink Grootendorst', nicknamed 'The Carnation Rose' because of its little frilled petals, blooms happily for months on end. One of the six bushes threw one branch which sported back to the parent rose 'F. J. Grootendorst', a rich red. I am sure I should remove it or the whole bush may revert and this would rather spoil the hedge. But I find the rose's ability to do this so fascinating that up till now I have left it.

'Nozomi', the little Memorial Rose from Japan, makes a low-growing, attractive hedge on top of a stone wall. I am resolved to prune it hard each winter or it will become straggly.

But all our hedges are not rose hedges. We have a splendid lavender hedge at the top of a bank of Rugosa roses. I sought the advice of Rosemary Holmes at the Yuulong Lavender Estate. She recommended the French lavender (*Lavandula dentata*), which blooms almost all year round. It needs pruning only once, in January. The scent is wonderful as you brush against the bushes when walking along the path.

To enclose the Kitchen Garden we used *Escallonia* 'Iveyi' with dark glossy green foliage and pure white flowers. It grows quickly and we need to cut it three or four times a year because we want to keep it at a height of about one metre.

In the garden we had a big bush of *Teucrium fruticans* (shrubby germander). I love its pale blue flowers as well as its grey foliage, so I tried striking it. This was such a success that I ended up with twenty or so little plants which I used to make a hedge at the end of a blue and yellow bank.

I could not resist planting a hedge of *Lonicera nitida*. I thought of the role it played so successfully in Olive Room's garden and I re-read Margery Fish's delightful *We Made a Garden* – but how *did* she ever put up with Walter and his overbearing ways? I followed her advice and put the little cuttings straight into the ground where they were to grow, at the top of the steepest bank in the whole garden. I watered them in, but from that day to this they have received no further attention and yet we have a neat compact little hedge which we intend to keep at a height of no more than thirty centimetres. If it got more water and an occasional feed we would have to cut it very frequently to keep it at this height. As it is, on a starvation diet, we cut it only a few times a year.

Somewhere in the garden I shall find room for a plant of *Lonicera nitida* 'Baggesen's Gold', although I don't think I want a whole hedge of it. If given its head it can reach a height of three metres and the arching branches, clad in eye-catching gold foliage, bear small white scented flowers and, as if this were not enough, they are followed by deep purple berries. It was bred by Niels Baggesen who moved to England from Denmark and set up a nursery in Kent. It was he, too, who bred the beautiful blue–green Lawson cypress known as 'Pembury Blue' (*Chamaecyparis lawsoniana* 'Pembury Blue'). I have planted a pair of these towards the bottom of the garden to help hide the very ugly concrete bridge which was built over Jacksons Creek six months after our arrival. It replaces a slightly leaning rustic wooden one deemed inadequate to carry the ever-increasing traffic up Kilmore Road as Melbourne moves inexorably closer to Gisborne.

9   The Old Rose Garden

The shape of the terraces on the north side of the garden had been governed entirely by the position of the old fruit trees. The bobcat had weaved its way in and out between them and we had been left with a very large top terrace, moderately large second and third terraces and a shallow fourth one.

It was the third terrace which was ultimately to become the Old Rose Garden. Facing north, it was bounded on the northern fence line by young aspens (*Populus tremuloides*) which had now formed a little thicket. Between the trees I planted the Alister Clark ramblers, 'Jessie Clark', 'Doris Downes' and 'Mrs Richard Turnbull' and, because it is evergreen and would continue to give some cover in winter, three *Rosa laevigata*. In time there will be an impenetrable barrier along this, as along so many of our fences.

On the south side of the terrace a spreading, healthy old apple tree, in spring one of the sights of the garden, and an untidy old plum tree formed a natural dividing line between this section of the garden and the next. Between them, again with the aim of creating an evergreen barrier, I planted two *Escallonia* 'Apple Blossom' and one *Choisya ternata* – I suppose it is the scent as well as the small white flowers which earned it the nickname 'Mexican orange

162

blossom'. Up the plum tree, a sturdy old fellow with a mass of tangled branches, I planted another of the appropriately rampant climber 'Rambling Rector'.

The east side of the Old Rose Garden was cut off by the steep bank — varying from three to four metres in height — left by the bobcat. This I had already clothed with groundcover roses.

On the west side, at the top of the much shallower bank dropping down to the lowest level, I had planted my hedge of 'Rosa Mundi' and *R. gallica* 'Officinalis'.

So here was the framework of what was to become the Old Rose Garden. I did not have in mind anything so trendy as 'garden rooms'. I had seen and loved both Sissinghurst and Hidcote and been filled with admiration bordering on awe for the creative genius behind each one. But every garden makes its own demands, dictates its own conditions, governed by soil and climate, by the lie of the land and the nature of the surroundings, so that any attempt at slavish imitation of the creation of another is doomed from the outset to disappointment.

Nor can plans copied from a book, or designs commissioned from a landscape architect, ever give the intense satisfaction gained from working out for ourselves, often by trial and error, what best suits the particular corner of the universe which we regard, for the time being, as our own.

I had planted mixed borders on the south side of the garden choosing my roses for their colour or foliage or habit of growth, and mixing the old with the new.

Here, on this more lately acquired north side, I saw the opportunity to create a little garden devoted entirely to that historically fascinating romantic evocative collection which we term "old roses". And, since most of them bloom only in the spring, I would pay particular attention to the underplanting so that there would be interest for much of the year.

At the base of the tall bank I laid out a wide, sweeping bed running from the north–west corner to the south–east. Between this and the rose hedge on the west would be an open, restful expanse of lawn.

Because it is traditional, and I am a firm believer in benefiting from the wisdom and experience of earlier generations, and because I wanted to introduce a note of formality, I decided to edge this bed with box, which I would keep at a height of twenty centimetres. Box is expensive, but I had two or three well-grown box plants in pots. From these I took literally dozens of cuttings and waited, more or less patiently, until they had struck. Box cuttings tend to be reliable, but slow.

Meanwhile, at the north–west corner, Nick constructed a wide pergola, using treated pine posts and lattice, and another at the south–west corner. Since these are the points of entrance and departure, the roses planted on these pergolas are of prime importance. They must be recurrent and, above all, they must be perfumed so that, as one enters and leaves the garden, the scent lingers. For the one pergola I chose 'Devoniensis' ('The Magnolia Rose'), with whom I have had a long love affair going back to my Bleak House days. Its rich creamy flowers, which it produces in abundance from spring to autumn, look down through the lattice as one passes beneath. For the other I selected another great favourite. The flat quartered seductively perfumed blooms of the Tea rose, 'Sombreuil', are just as lovely, though the plant is less vigorous and certainly more easily controlled.

Of course, there was not room here for anything like the vast number of old roses I wanted to plant. I decided to choose my very favourites from Bleak House – although it was surprising, when the list was completed, how many came into this category – and some which I had not grown before.

So room was found for 'Charles de Mills' and 'Cardinal de Richelieu', for the heavenly 'Complicata' and the subtle rosy-mauves 'Jenny Duval', 'Anaïs Ségales', and 'Belle de Crécy'. No old rose garden would be complete without the Damasks, the incomparable 'Madame Hardy', the early-flowering 'Quatre Saisons', 'Ispahan' and 'Celsiana'. From the great range of Alba roses I chose *R. alba* 'Maxima', *R. alba* 'Semiplena', 'Félicité Parmentier' and 'Königin von Dänemarck'. From the Mosses I selected 'Chapeau de Napoléon', 'Général Kléber', the brilliant 'Henri Martin', little 'James Mitchell' and the deepest purple 'William Lobb'. What a masculine bunch they are!

The Centifolias, those most subtle and seductive old French roses, were to have a private garden all to themselves. And somewhere else, on the south side perhaps, room would have to be found for the species roses, the Rugosas and the Hybrid Musks.

Meanwhile I had a nucleus, enough to make a start. Now to choose some which were new to me.

I had planted that little gem of a rose, 'Gruss an Aachen', at Bleak House, but it had never thrived. Perhaps it resented a certain lack of attention. My most vivid memory of the White Garden at Hidcote is of 'Gruss an Aachen'. It is not quite white, rather a warm ivory colour with just a hint of softest apricot. Nor is it quite an old rose, having been bred in Germany in 1909 from that old favourite, 'Frau Karl Druschki'. But it looks the part, so I decided to include it. I planted it beside the pergola destined for 'Devoniensis'. It has flourished, although it gets entangled from time to time with the long arms of the pale mauve–blue clematis 'Sir Garnet Wolseley', which was planted to climb the pergola in company with 'Devoniensis'.

Of the very small group known as the Boursault roses, few are available. I had grown and loved the climber, 'Madame de Sancy de Parabère', and now suddenly 'Morletii' appeared in one or two catalogues. Bred in France in 1883, it sends up great arching reddish canes which bear ragged medium-sized deep pink blooms over a long period in late spring and early summer. In autumn the greyish–green leaves turn wonderful shades of orange–red. It was known for a long time as 'Inermis Morletii', Morlet's thornless.

Having recently visited Hidcote, I had become interested in the Lindsays, mother and daughter, and in the role they had played in the development and subsequent history of that famous garden – Norah, so elegant, so sophisticated and beautiful, with such charm and such a flair for design; and Nancy, reclusive and difficult and fascinated by plants. Lawrence Johnston encouraged this passion and Nancy undertook plant-hunting trips to Turkestan, Iran and the remoter parts of the Near East.

It was Nancy Lindsay who brought to England in 1949 the beautiful pink Damask rose, 'Gloire de Guilan', used in Persia for the making of attar of roses. Probably of considerable antiquity, it makes a sprawling shrub, perhaps one metre high. Walter Duncan sent me two plants from South Australia when I told him of my interest. Nancy left no description of 'Gloire de Guilan', so I did not know quite what to expect. Had she done so, I thought, on reading her description of 'Kazanlik', I would have been little the wiser. She describes that rose, which I must confess I regard as a somewhat insignificant little flower, as having "cascades of ambrosial, pellucid rose pink flowers with lambent coral hearts over jungles of mint green"! She apparently had all the linguistic talents required for writing a passionate Gothic novel!

It was Nancy Lindsay, too, who gave to Graham Stuart Thomas that exquisite rose, 'Belle Amour'. This she had found in an old convent at Elboeuf on the Seine. He suspected it had Alba or Damask parentage, but in colour it is a delicate salmon pink, a shade not found in Albas or Damasks. The scent is quite delicious, and it makes a sturdy bush over 1.5 metres high.

These two, I decided I must plant − for their associations as well as for their beauty.

Then a couple of Portland roses for their recurrent flowering. I chose 'Arthur de Sansal' whose deep, maroon−purple flat quartered blooms, which fade later to the colour of Parma violets, are produced over a long period in summer. It is low-growing and good in the front of a bed. And I found a plant of 'Pergolèse', whose small bright cerise flowers also fade to purple. If regularly dead-headed its flowering period is considerably prolonged.

I cannot account for my undeniable love of the old striped roses, for I positively dislike many of the modern two-toned ones. Probably it is the more subtle colouring of the older ones that makes the difference. Whatever the reason, I could not resist either 'Georges Vibert' or 'Camaieux', both bred by the great rose breeder Jean-Paul Vibert in France. The flowers of both are pale pink, striped deeper crimson−pink, and those of 'Camaieux' take on a mauve−violet tinge as they age. Both bushes are low-growing, barely reaching one metre, so I put them both in the front of the bed.

Also from Vibert came the rich old Gallica rose, 'D'Aguesseau' − an arresting splash of vivid crimson − and by contrast another of Vibert's, 'Petite Lisette' − miniature blooms of rose−pink against greyish foliage. I am delighted with all four so feel I owe an apology to Vibert for the unkind words I have sometimes said about his Noisette rose, 'Aimée Vibert', named after his daughter. Although it does turn an unfortunate shade of brown as it ages, it compensates by generous repeat-flowering.

He was an interesting character was Vibert, nothing of the gentle dreamer one might picture from looking at his roses. He grew up in Paris during the turbulent days of the French Revolution and became a soldier in Napoleon's army. He was compelled to leave the army because of his many wounds, and it was then that he became a gardener and devoted the rest of his life to roses.

It is said that some days before Vibert's death at the age of eighty-nine, while he was arranging his daily vase of roses he said to his grandson: "See, my child, a man knows truly what he has loved best on earth only when in his last days he finds it still in his heart. Like the rest of the world I have thought that I adored and detested many men and many things. In reality I have loved only Napoleon and roses." (*The Old Rose Advisor*, page 18.)

Because Graham Stuart Thomas, who early on became my bible for all matters relating to the rose, described the rose 'Violacea' as "a glorious burst of colour", I resolved to include it in my new planting. Its single flowers are a deep purplish–red which, try as I might in respect to Mr Thomas, I cannot like. In fact, I dislike it almost as much as I dislike 'Roger Lambelin'. Thank goodness it is at the back of the bed and now almost obscured by 'Henri Martin' and 'Belle Amour'. I trust it will not be interpreted as a sexist remark if I draw attention to the large number of men who rank deep red roses among their favourites, and the very small number of women who do.

To complete the bed I planted three more Moss roses: 'Louis Gimard' (rich lilac–pink with muddled centres), 'A longues pédoncules' (lilac–pink again, with softest grey–green foliage) and 'Salet' (quartered delicate pink with just a hint of mauve).

With these, I considered my planting finished. And then I came upon a plant of 'Rose de Rescht', a charming little rose whose origins are unknown. I found room for it when I discovered that it, too, had been brought back to England by Nancy Lindsay after one of her plant-hunting expeditions. It is a rich dark red in colour and fades as it ages to magenta. I feel sure she would have found far more poetic words for it.

Underplanting in the Old Rose Garden *10*

Because most of the old roses bloom only in spring and I had given them a garden to themselves, underplanting was of paramount importance. Unless I chose with care, this part of the garden would be very dull for a large part of the year.

For no better reason than that I love it, and in any case I needed height at the back of a very wide border, I planted in the south–east corner a *Magnolia grandiflora*. It flowered this year for the first time, two glorious ivory-coloured chalices with a perfume unmistakable and unforgettable.

Like many gardeners, I habitually overplant. I know that I have planted other things too close to my magnolia and that, in time, they will not flourish — but what pleasure I shall have from them in the meantime. And when the time comes that they have to be moved, I feel sure that a spot will be found for them.

Many of the old roses grow into tall shrubs — the Albas, in particular, are already very big bushes. So at the back, too, I planted a little group of the deceptively delicate looking *Tamarix pentandra* (syn. *Tamarix ramosissima*).

In late summer and autumn, when the roses are finished, the tamarisks lift their arching branches high above them — great plumes of frothy, long-lasting pale pink flowers. Round their feet I planted clumps of the very tall-growing mauve–pink *Aster cordifolius* 'Silver Spray', which flowers at the same time. Both need little attention and we don't water them.

At the base of the bank I planted several roots of the great white poppy, *Romneya coulteri*. It was chosen for its grey–blue foliage, as well as for its tissue-paper flowers with their prominent golden stamens. I made a conscious decision to disregard the tales I had heard of their becoming invasive. In the event, for me, they did the opposite. There is seepage through the bank at the spot I chose for them, so they do not have the dry conditions they need. In consequence they look permanently unhappy, they sulk and decline to flower. They will have to be moved — with great care as they resent interference.

Much more successful was the grey-leaved *Salvia argentea*. It is planted near the flamboyant pink rose, 'Complicata', for which its spectacular grey felted leaves are the perfect foil. Its flowers are unexciting. It would not matter to me if it did not flower at all.

Another salvia, which would be worth growing for its foliage alone, is *Salvia forskaohlei*. It has great broad grey–green leaves which lie quite flat to the ground. But from them it sends up one hundred-centimetre high spires of purple–blue flowers. If you cut the dead heads off, the plant will send up more. It flowered this year with the pink rose 'Belle Amour' in the very early summer and looked splendid. It did it again in company with *Tamarix pentandra* and the ground-cover rose 'Heidekönigin' in late summer and looked just as good. Then in autumn it put on another grand display — a solo performance this time — and I was grateful for it. It does seed rather prolifically if you allow it, but any excess is easily removed — or given away to gardeners unfortunate enough not yet to have made its acquaintance.

Another newcomer to my garden last year was *Francoa appendiculata* 'Bridal Wreath'. It is quite lovely enough for any bride, sending up from clumps of crinkled bright green leaves racemes of small pink flowers shaped like tiny bells. It is frost hardy and, if given a place in the sun, will bloom all through summer and into autumn.

Here, too, I planted *Filipendula palmata*, which also goes by the much prettier name of meadowsweet. In summer its tall feathery heads of shell-pink flowers tower high above the lower growing Gallica roses. From its appearance I would never have guessed that it, too, is a member of the very extensive Rosaceae family. The books tell me that it needs a moist spot, but ours, the roots shaded no doubt by the roses, seem to do well on a very restricted water diet.

Potentilla nepalensis 'Miss Willmott' was chosen for several reasons, and she has paid dividends. She produces her charming deep-pink flowers all through summer and autumn and even into June. She is planted towards the front of the bed and is rather taller than I wanted — about forty-five centimetres — but the old roses, now sturdy bushes, cope with this, so she has kept her place. And what rosarian could resist a plant with the name of Ellen Willmott attached to it? I have only once held in my hands a copy of her life's great work, *The*

Genus Rosa, but Graham Stuart Thomas in his beautiful book, *A Garden of Roses*, has made accessible to us again many of Alfred Parson's exquisite rose paintings commissioned by Miss Willmott for this work. I never tend my cheerful little potentilla without thinking of the colourful, tempestuous, passionate woman after whom it is named — a gardener all her life, the owner of three world-famed gardens and the employer at one time of over one hundred gardeners, her name will be associated always with the history of the rose.

Then the sedums. With *Sedum* 'Vera Jameson' I have had little luck. But I mean to try again. The purple-tinted foliage is attractive in its own right — even without the dusky pink flowers which it bears in autumn.

But I have extensive patches of *Sedum spectabile* 'Brilliant' which bears flat heads of mauve–pink flowers in late summer. I even like it when the flowers turn brown, and delay cutting them until the early spring when the rosettes of blue–grey leaves are a delight in themselves. These little rosettes form round the base of the old stems and I have moved them and divided them with unfailing success. Indeed it has reproduced itself so irresponsibly that I even moved it recently to another part of the garden — the dry exposed bank under the great elms where the species roses grow. Being so drought-tolerant and needing so little care, it is thriving even here.

I have never been quite convinced by those garden designers (some of them, I suspect, pure theoreticians) who state categorically that a plant should not be used in more than one spot in a garden. On the day I decided to move some of my young sedums to the species bank I had been reading that compelling writer, Elizabeth Jolley, and her words stuck in my mind: "I know now that an image can be repeated often, as a phrase of music can be repeated, perhaps with slight changes of rhythm or key . . ." She was, of course, speaking of writing. But so it is with the garden. A certain happy combination of plants can be repeated in another part of the garden, perhaps with a change of accompanying textures or slight variations in colour combinations. As with music, the impact becomes stronger with repetition, the pleasure increased by familiarity. So I was delighted to find my sedum, which gives me such pleasure in my garden of old roses, growing in a thick border in Neil Robertson's garden in company with a host of blue agapanthus. The effect was quite different and decidedly stunning.

Achilleas are indispensable — not the invasive white one which is so prominent on stalls in country markets and which is so tough and indestructible that we had planted it to cover an island in the middle of a large dam at Bleak House. When last seen, it was making remarkable progress.

The newer ones come in a range of subtle colours, require little attention save for the removal of deadheads, and flower long and joyously. 'Apple Blossom', a mauve–pink, is perfect in the Old Rose Garden. And I would not be without the creamy-yellow *Achillea* 'Taygetea' with its grey foliage — and what vitality a touch of soft yellow lends to any planting.

With them I planted *Allium giganteum* — one precious bulb, an expensive gift from a dear friend. It is the prima donna among alliums, growing to a height of two metres and bearing dense umbels of fifty or more star-shaped purple flowers. It is impossible to ignore it when it is in flower, and all eyes turn to it. I trust that it will take a leaf out of the sedum's book, and breed and multiply prolifically.

And here, too, are the Formosan lilies which flaunt their bold white trumpets above narrow pointed blue–green leaves almost head-high in later summer.

In ever-increasing clumps, which will soon need dividing, is *Stachys officinalis* 'Rosea Superba', a sophisticated form of bishop's wort imported by Lambley Nursery from the nursery of that world-famed plantswoman, Beth Chatto. Its crinkled dark green foliage makes a good weed-smothering groundcover, and the pink flowers are borne for months on end.

I made the mistake, a few years ago when this garden was first being planted, of including *Physostegia virginiana* 'Rose Bouquet' — it sounded so suitable. It adapted itself enthusiastically to its new home, and in no time reached a height of eighty centimetres, quite overpowering everything within reach. It was relegated to the compost heap and its place taken by the white form, 'Snow Crown', which is much more amenable and grows happily side by side with the roses. Although even it has a tendency to seed rather too prolifically.

This spring I shall promote the beautiful blue-foliaged *Ruta graveolens* 'Jackman's Blue' from the kitchen garden to the Old Rose Garden. The aromatic foliage will be a wonderful foil for the mauve–pinks and purples of the old roses. But the acidic yellow flowers have no place here and must be cut off before they open.

Poppies sow themselves. I never know where they come from or where they go. I have never sowed the seed or bought the plants. Perhaps they came in soil with plants brought from Bleak House, but they come — not in ones and twos, but a great army of them — as certainly as summer sunshine, all colours from white to pale pink to mauve to deepest claret colour, single and double. I love them at every stage, from the first appearance of the blue–grey leaves, to the glory of their blooming, to their perfectly formed and frilled apparently ceramic seed pods.

And every autumn I buy punnets of violas — pink, mainly, and some pale blue (I think they go by the name of 'Blue Angel') — and I plant them wherever there are gaps between the perennials. They perform splendidly for months on end, sow seed, and often come back again next year.

The Monet Bank with *R. banksiae* 'Lutea' in the background and sisyrinchium, the scarlet *Geum* 'Mrs Bradshaw' and a blue-green ixia in the foreground.

The white Rugosa rose 'Schneezwerg' with *Kniphofia* 'Maid of Orleans'.

A clump of early-flowering *Gladiolus × colvillei* at the foot of 'Madame Grégoire Staechelin'.

The little groundcover rose 'Pink Bells' with *Nepeta × faassenii*.

The Centifolia Garden in spring with 'Fantin-Latour' in the foreground.

The Old Rose Garden. Standardised bay trees and box edgings give a touch of formality.

Early flowering *Iris xiphium* push up through a bed of blue violas

'Heidekönigin' spills down a steep bank in the Old Rose Garden. *Iberis sempervirens* seeds itself through the garden.

Iris pumila form a dense carpet long before the tall bearded iris come into flower.

Set against a dark wall of box this little sculpture marks the beginning of a long flight of steps.

Tall bearded iris and lupins flower before the roses. *Tanacetum haradjanii* makes a low growing edging.

The Centifolia Garden 11

This is a tiny very special garden, a garden of treasures, bordered at the north end where 'Sombreuil' nods down over the pergola leading from the Old Rose Garden, by the old apple tree, the escallonias and the choisya. On the south corner is another old plum tree which bears, each year, huge crops of glowing purplish–blue plums that taste so good I never can resist reaching up and pulling down another one to eat while I am working nearby. Beside this tree Nick built another pergola and on it I planted that unassuming little thorn-less rose 'Renae', which flowers untiringly all summer long.

On the west side I planted a short hedge of *R. centifolia variegata* and 'Reine des Centfeuilles' alternating. This is more or less a continuation of the 'Rosa Mundi' hedge on the other side of the pergola in the Old Rose Garden. *R. centifolia variegata*, aptly nicknamed 'Village Maid', I had grown and loved at Bleak House. It must be the gentlest of all the striped roses, with palest pink stripes on a cream ground. 'Reine des Centfeuilles' is almost equally vigorous and Peter Beales remarks accurately that it is "disorderly in habit"! Disorderly or not, its clear pink flowers, quartered and button-eyed and almost flat in shape, more than compensate for any lack of discipline the bush may exhibit. This whole little hedge, in fact, might be termed disorderly. The Centifolias do tend to send out such long, waving canes. Thorny, too! I shorten them somewhat after flowering and peg them down when they become too straggly.

A statuesque old pear tree overhangs the hedge from the path below, and a huge bush of David Austin's 'Dapple Dawn', planted on the same path, raises its enchanting head well above the hedge and peeps over into this very private garden.

The bank on the east side had been planted up with the irrepressible ground-cover rose, 'Immensee'. It needs regular trimming but its dense green foliage and pure white single flowers form a fitting background to the garden. Below the wide bed which runs along at the foot of the bank, Nick built a retaining wall of the old moss and lichen-covered bluestone.

Along the top of the wall the salmon-pink *Dianthus* 'Beatrix' blooms almost without ceasing. I planted precious bulbs here, too, the sort of things that are easily lost in a big garden — fritillarias and trilliums and erythroniums. And under the spreading apple tree is a steadily growing patch of *Cyclamen hederifolium*.

At the base of the blue plum tree I planted the pale pink climbing rose 'Narrow Water'. Bred in Ireland in 1883, it is winding its way steadily into the tree and bears its clusters of palest pink roses late into the autumn, long, long after the Centifolias have stopped. Beneath it I have planted several roots of the clear blue *Tweedia caerulea*. Its long, fat seed pods are full of promise for the future.

In this garden there is a small, curved stone seat — it is a place for sitting, warm and protected and private. And in the centre of the lawn is a pretty, old, weathered stone urn with the figure of a child and, around the edge of the pot, a tiny box hedge 7 to 8 centimetres high.

The undisputed queen of the Centifolia Garden is the incomparable 'Fantin-Latour', associated for ever with the glorious old gardens of France. Here, too, is 'Petite de Hollande' and the rich and mysterious 'Tour de Malakoff'. Also 'The Bishop', deepest purple with overtones of magenta and grey, upright and richly scented; and the glowing pink 'Paul Ricault', classed sometimes as a Centifolia and sometimes as a Hybrid Perpetual, but well worthy of garden room however you choose to class him.

Sadly, so small is this garden, I found no place for the delightful little 'de Meaux' with its miniature blooms of typical Centifolia shape. It would do well in a large pot, so surely room will be found for it eventually.

It was in this garden of treasures that I made my first attempt to grow the enchanting blue poppy, *Meconopsis betonicifolia*. It is one of those priceless plants for which we have to thank the intrepid plant-hunter and explorer, Frank Kingdon-Ward. He found it growing in Tibet in woodland conditions and wrote that "the flowers flutter out among the sea-green leaves like blue and gold butterflies; each is borne singly on a pedicle, the plant carrying half a dozen nodding, incredibly blue four-petalled flowers with a wad of golden anthers in the centre."

I had seen isolated plants, but I saw it first growing in profusion in that amazing indescribably beautiful garden, Inverewe. It is situated on the wild north–west coast of Scotland, where the wind gusts in from the sea, and there is nothing between it and Labrador. The bare surrounding mountains were a deep navy blue. It was midsummer, but the heather was not yet in bloom on the moors. There were few signs of habitation on those barren mountains save for the black-faced Highland sheep, huddled into ledges and crannies for protection against the wind.

And in this wild windswept place, on this bare peninsula of pink sandstone jutting out into the sea, Osgood Mackenzie had made his garden. It is a garden like none other. And the miracle is not so much the legendary wealth of plant material which the garden contains and which brings botanists and plantsmen from all over the world, but the fact that there is a garden here at all.

Fittingly, it is a wild garden, a magic place. It would be easy to get lost in the maze of winding paths. *Rhododendron ponticum*, which we had seen growing wild all over the Highlands, was used here to make hedges. There are no garden beds, save in the vicinity of the house, and no landscaper has imposed on this wild and seemingly untouched place his textbook vistas and axes. One is left with the feeling that no human hand has been involved, that the grand and majestic trees, the towering tree rhododendrons, the myriad vines and creepers aspiring towards the heavens have planted themselves.

And in these wooded glades were great sheets of *Meconopsis betonicifolia*, their petals the blue of the sky on a spring morning, the blue of Mary's robe in a Renaissance painting. I thought I could imagine something of Frank Kingdon-Ward's pure delight as he saw them first growing in the fields in Tibet. And now here was this seemingly fragile flower, its petals tissue thin, far from its mountain homeland and withstanding all the gales which lash this part of Scotland's coast and douse the garden ceaselessly in sea spray.

Looking back on that day, I ask myself repeatedly what perversity it is that makes these poppies not only survive in such conditions, but positively thrive in them and yet, given the choicest corner of my garden, treated with greater consideration than any other plant, fed on compost and leaf-mould, given dappled sunshine and protection from wind, they droop, pine and ultimately vanish quite away. For vanish away they did. Not once, but several times.

The determination to try yet again has nothing to do with the challenge of growing difficult plants. It is their sheer beauty that impels one not to give up. So I planted them again this year, two plants. They came up and they had buds which I resolutely cut off, according to instructions. They should not be permitted to flower in their first year. The leaves lived on. I have marked the place and will watch next spring for the very first sign of life.

12 *Some Early Tea Roses*

T he little square garden which we call the Gallery Garden is a special place. Bounded on two sides by the verandahs and on the other two by rose hedges, it is sheltered and warm, despite the fact that it faces south–west — an aspect no rose grower would choose.

Because it is overlooked by the long dining room windows, by French doors opening out from the living room and by the glass-walled gallery that runs along the bedroom wing, it was obvious from the outset that this part of the garden would need special care. There would be no once-flowering roses here. I wanted colour for as much of the year as possible, long-flowering roses, selected underplanting and, almost as importantly, scent.

Early Tea roses were the obvious choice. Not the high-centred, stiff-limbed, ubiquitous Hybrid Teas, but the early Teas which preceded them and are noted for their soft, subtle colours, small bushes and heavenly perfume.

Pink was to be the dominant colour — pink, because it is the colour of so many of the early Teas; pink, because the rose on the verandah posts is the glorious 'Madame Grégoire Staechelin'; pink, because the house is now painted the very softest pink, the palest echo of the colour in the roses, so faint that in hot sunshine the colour is difficult to discern, and only when the house is in deep shade can you say with certainty that it is painted pink – the shutters and the roof are dark blue–green.

Beds were dug and carefully prepared round all four sides of the square. An archway on the west side opens to a long flight of steps which leads down to the front garden. Over this arch I planted the cheerful little Noisette rose, 'Champney's Pink Cluster'. I had grown it on a similar arch at Bleak House and it had taken some three or four years to reach the top of the arch. So when I chose it for this prime position I was confident it would not get out of hand. My confidence was somewhat shaken when I saw it recently at Lismore Castle in Ireland, where it was more than halfway up the towering old grey stone castle walls. I can only hope it took a very long time to get there.

On the south side a copse of aspens (*Populus tremuloides*) forms a natural arch which leads out to the south terraces, and on the north–west corner two steps lead up to the verandah.

As a centrepiece I chose a small weeping cherry (*Prunus subhirtella*), which is covered with purest white double blooms in spring. Under it I placed Hans Knorr's graceful little statue of the Madonna which I had brought with me from Bleak House. Remote and ethereal, she sets the tone for whatever part of the garden she is in. Round her feet I planted tiny white daisies and a brilliant blue star-shaped allium (*Allium cyaneum*). This was found on limestone ledges in the Lotus Mountains in the Chinese province of Gansu and brought to England in 1875. It grows usually to 10 to 15 centimetres and bears its flowers in summer. I was frightened of losing it in the garden, but felt sure I would not if I planted it at the Madonna's feet.

This little circular bed is surrounded by the nearest approach we have to a lawn, though even this, when compared with the velvety swards which are such a feature of English gardens, would have to be termed simply grass rather than dignified by the name of lawn.

Of the Tea roses selected after a lot of thought, the leading role was given to the gentle hauntingly scented 'Duchesse de Brabant', which is said to have been President Theodore Roosevelt's favourite buttonhole rose. It had done wonderfully well for me at Bleak House under far less favourable conditions, so I felt it could be relied upon here. It is, of course, far more effective to plant in threes or fours rather than singly. Here I went to extremes and planted seven. With unity thus established, I could afford to plant some of the others singly.

Next came 'Dr Grill'. I cannot understand how he has not enjoyed a better press. Bred in France (as very many of the early Teas were) in 1886, he is an exquisite shade of palest pink with faint coppery overtones. He has the fragrance we expect of all his breed and flowers long and joyously.

With him I planted 'Lady Mary Fitzwilliam'. She was bred in England in 1882 (one parent was the superb 'Devoniensis' to which I had given such a prominent position in the Old Rose Garden). 'Lady Mary' is something of a mystery. She was initially not a great success, and then for a considerable period was thought to have been lost altogether. Indeed a fear is sometimes expressed that even now the rose sold under this name is an imposter. However that may be, she certainly warrants a place in a garden of Tea roses, both on her own account and because she became historically of considerable importance. As Peter Beales expressed it in his *Twentieth Century Roses* "when put to stud – unlike her counterpart 'La France' who was virtually sterile – she proved very fertile and was used extensively by both French and British breeders". One United States researcher puts the number of her offspring as high as 1300.

In the corner shaded by the aspens is a deceptively delicate-looking pale pink fuchsia. It survives the winter frosts and, if cut back hard each year, bears masses of minute, tubular flowers for months on end. Underneath it is the lavender–blue *Campanula poscharskyana* which is proving an excellent groundcover. *Colchicum byzantinum* push through unfailingly in the autumn.

With them is the pink constant flowering *Dianthus* 'Beatrix'. I propagate some more each spring – almost every cutting takes – and pull out the old plants as they get woody.

The rich mauve–blue *Geranium himalayense* provides contrast, and late each autumn I plant punnets of white primulas which are still in flower when the pink tulips burst into bloom in October, to be followed in due course by white lilies.

When I was a child in Queensland we regarded ageratum as a weed. But it is just the blue I wanted in this garden. Unfortunately it is an annual and frost tender. I solve this problem by buying punnets in early spring, potting the tiny plants up singly as I do with tomatoes and capsicums, and putting them into the glasshouse until all danger of frost is past. Then on Melbourne Cup Day I have a grand planting out. The ageratum treated in this way last spring flowered steadily until the next winter's first frost.

There was room for one more rose and the choice fell on 'Dame Edith Helen' – a clear pink classically shaped Tea rose without the tendency of many Teas to drop their heads. Each summer she bears, on a bush not much more than one metre high, a crop of deliciously scented blooms.

I had sought information about her, but discovered little. Her parentage, it appeared, was unknown, but she had been bred by the British firm of Dickson in 1926. And so I continued to enjoy her wealth of blooms and thought little more about the origin of the name. Until I visited Mount Stewart outside Belfast.

It was a fleeting visit, little more than a courtesy call, paid between breakfast in Belfast and a plane to Leeds in the early afternoon. By no stretch of the imagination was it sufficient to do justice to the beauty and complexity, the ironies and idiosyncrasies, that make up Mount Stewart. Here, in 1921, Edith Helen, Marchioness of Londonderry, having inherited what she saw as a most dismal and depressing pile surrounded by gloomy and oppressive shrubbery, set about making a garden.

On this first visit, time forced us to restrict ourselves to the formal gardens near the house. First to the sunken garden, based on a design by Gertrude Jekyll with a colour scheme of blue, yellow and orange. On a surrounding walkway grew Noisette roses as I have seldom seen them – 'Alister Stella Gray' in glorious profusion and 'Maréchal Niel' looking down from above, a mass of rich creamy-gold.

Through an archway in a dense hedge to the Shamrock Garden — here was topiary that made us laugh out aloud: the Irish Harp and real and imaginary creatures. And in the midst of it the Red Hand of Ulster, a bed of closely planted red begonias shaped like a human hand. This peaceful garden was a far cry from the gory tale of the two adventurous Scots who were told that the first to land on Ireland's shore should be the owner of Ulster. The McDonnell (or was it the O'Neill?), fearing to lose the race, cut off his left hand, threw it upon the sands and claimed Ulster for his own.

On to the gentleness of the Mairi Garden, where the present owner, Lady Mairi Bury, had been put to sleep in her pram as a baby — a quaint summer-house, old roses, soft blues and pinks and creamy yellows and a whimsical sculpture of a child.

Then to the Italian Garden — glowing pinks and yellows, *Rosa chinensis* 'Mutabilis', standard white wisterias, stately iris. Round the whole was a balustrade and on it the creatures of the ark and the ark itself, exquisitely sculpted. There were rabbits and cats, monsters, a fox with a red rose encircling his neck . . . all of this a perpetual reminder of a group of friends brought together in London by the vicissitudes of war and giving to each other the names of the creatures gathered into the ark.

From there to the Spanish Garden with huge pots, the creations of local crafts-men, a hedge of close-clipped Leyland cypress (× *Cupressocyparis leylandii*) cut into arches, paved paths, a tiled summerhouse and palm trees.

A moment only in the Wild Garden — a lasting impression of sheets of the heavenly blue *Meconopsis betonicifolia* to rival those of Inverewe, and with them the even rarer *Meconopsis napaulensis*, a delicious pink.

A brisk walk through the Lily Wood, a carpet of Chatham Island forget-me-nots (*Myosotidium hortensia*), at the foot of semicircular stairs a *Tamarix tetrandra* trained as a standard, through wrought-iron gates crafted to a design by Kate Greenaway, and we were back at our starting place.

The car whisked us round the lake at high speed. At a distance we saw the imposing iron gate leading into Tir Nan Og, the Land of the Ever Young, the burial ground for the family. We did not see the walk planted with the Mount Stewart rose (thought to be, perhaps, a seedling from *R. moschata*), nor the Rhododendron Wood, nor the Silver Jubilee Avenue planted in 1936 to honour the Silver Jubilee of George V and Queen Mary, in red, white and blue.

When we arrived home in late June, one of the first things I did in the garden was to prune 'Dame Edith Helen'. I did it with particular care, and will never look at my rose again without thinking of this most remarkable woman, a woman whose vitality, creativity and wonderful sense of sheer fun are so brilliantly reflected in her garden. When the time was ripe, early last spring, I gave 'Dame Edith Helen' an extra-large handful of my precious stock of Hoof and Horn.

On this same visit to Mount Stewart I first saw 'Mrs Oakley Fisher' — single flowers of pale apricot–buff with amber stamens are borne in clusters through-out the season. I don't know what gave rise to the singularly persistent myth that single roses have no scent. 'Mrs Oakley Fisher', among many others, gives positive proof that this is false — she has the most delicious scent. Her colour made her unsuitable for the Gallery Garden with its predominantly pink and white planting, but I found a place for her later on in a bed on a south terrace. Here she grows happily in company with the arresting 'Golden Wings', a modern shrub rose. This, too, is single, with brownish stamens. It is a Pimpinellifolia hybrid (as are 'Frühlingsmorgen' and 'Frühlingsgold') and will reach 1.5 metres. So I put 'Mrs Oakley Fisher' in front – she attains barely .8 metre – and at the back a couple of plants of *Mimulus aurantiacus*, a charming shrub which bears apricot tubular flowers from late spring to autumn. It tends to be brittle and Willy has broken it a couple of times in his sorties after the postman, but it strikes very easily from cuttings, so is easily replaced.

Also in this bed on that south terrace is 'Fortune's Double Yellow'. Robert Fortune was sent to China by the Royal Horticultural Society in 1842 to search for new plants. He found the rose in an old Chinese garden at Ningpo and sent it back to England in 1845, for which we should all be profoundly thankful. It grows into a large rather untidy shrub and in spring it bears a profusion of ragged creamy–buff flowers, just touched with apricot. I think it has the dubious honour of being the thorniest most recalcitrant rose in the whole garden. I hate working anywhere in its vicinity, for I swear it reaches out and grabs me, my pullover or my hair or whatever is nearest. Despite this regrettable tendency I would not be without it. It should be remembered that it blooms on last year's wood so should be tidied up – if you feel sufficiently strong and courageous – straight after flowering.

In this bed, too, is 'Irish Elegance', bred by Dickson in 1905 at Newtownards, only a few miles from Mount Stewart. Its large single golden–apricot blooms make it the perfect companion for 'Mrs Oakley Fisher'. It distinguished itself by winning a Gold Medal from the National Rose Society despite the fact that single roses were not highly thought of at the time when it was released.

I was inspired to plant it after a trip to a little country town in far north–west Victoria. I had a phone call from an elderly rose enthusiast with the delightful name of Maureen Maloney who was quite sure that she had found another of the lost Alister Clark roses in the grounds of her local church. It was single, as many of his are, constantly in flower, and the glowing colour, too, suggested Alister Clark. She was sure that I would want to add it to my collection.

I have to confess that a long car trip was something I could very well have done without at that time. So many of such trips end in disappointment. However, it seemed churlish to show no interest. And it just might be an Alister Clark rose. So next weekend, in no very positive frame of mind, I set out.

Two hours driving brought me to my destination – a dusty deserted little country town, typical of so many, with one long straggling main street, a pub, a service station and a general store. And surely that had to be Maureen Maloney, standing in the middle of the road, one hand shading her eyes as she gazed anxiously up and down the street, the other hand on her hip.

She welcomed me effusively. On the kitchen table was spread a very substantial morning tea. Afterwards we walked round her garden. This had been her mother's house. She had been a keen gardener, "lived for her garden, she did", as had Auntie Irene. It was quite a tiny garden, but the tour took a disproportionately long time as each plant had to be examined and its history told. I began to fear that we would never get to the church at all. However, eventually we set out.

Long before we reached it, I could see the flowers of 'Irish Elegance' hanging over the fence. The bush measured 1.5 metres by 1.5 and it was in full and glowing flower. I had never imagined it could put on such a display. My only acquaintance with it hitherto had been a poor under-nourished plant in a friend's garden. Growing in the shade of a giant eucalypt and competing with its greedy roots for what nourishment it could scrounge, it had always had only a tenuous hold on life.

True, I had not found an Alister Clark rose, but I went home filled with gratitude to Maureen Maloney. All the way home I debated where I should plant it, should I be fortunate enough to find a plant, for it is stocked by very few nurseries. Of course, the perfect place was with 'Mrs Oakley Fisher', so the bed was enlarged to receive it. It has a long way to go before it attains the proportions of the bush in Maureen Maloney's churchyard, but it gives me great joy nonetheless. My only regret is that I have not room in that bed for the old Chinese rose, *Rosa chinensis* 'Mutabilis'.

13 *The Monet Bank*

Directly behind the house the ground rises up sharply to form the steepest bank in the whole steep garden. At the top of it, looking down at Erinvale, is our only neighbour.

It was this bank which Peter Cochrane on his bobcat had been determined to traverse, at imminent risk of life and limb, to make an access path from the south side of the garden to the north. It had, without doubt, been one of the most nerve-racking mornings I had experienced. I think I have some concept of how it must have been for Peter.

Ultimately his efforts were crowned with success — and that without any mishaps — and now a fine wide gravelled path cuts the slope in two. The upper half, culminating in our boundary fence, I decided to plant entirely in blue, white and yellow, the colours of the spring.

Early on, it was christened the Monet Bank. How it came by this name I am rather at a loss to explain. For Monet's garden when I visited it in early summer was anything but yellow and blue. Tall bearded iris had dominated the scene in this most entrancing garden, and great clumps of paeonies, jewel-like in rich pinks and reds. And 'Albertine' had just been opening its first buds on the pink walls of the house. The whole vital garden was a celebration of colour.

Perhaps it was simply that the classic blue and white of his kitchen and that sunniest of sunny yellow dining rooms had made such an indelible impression. In any case, the 'Monet Bank' it remained.

The high fence at the top of the bank was planted with twenty or so banksia roses – the yellow (*R. banksiae* 'Lutea'), the single white form (*R. banksiae* var. *normalis*), which I love for its absolute simplicity, and the double white form (*R. banksiae* var. *banksiae*). They were chosen because they have the reputation of being evergreen. And certainly in warmer climates they live up to this reputation. But unfortunately in cold frosty Gisborne they do lose most of their leaves and the flowers, alas, coming so early in the spring, are frequently turned black in the bud by a late frost. I regret, in many ways, that I did not choose the infinitely charming 'Félicité et Perpétue' or the glossy-leaved *R. laevigata* for this important position.

For the rest, I chose initially some of the little single yellow species and near species roses. My intention was to let them grow ultimately into large shrubs.

Graham Stuart Thomas describes them as being mostly of a "harsh, strident tone" and says that they "cannot be recommended for inclusion with a planting of other old roses whose soft colours blend so well together".

Certainly, their bright yellow flowers do not blend with those of other old roses, but I would call them sunny and cheerful rather than harsh and strident. Coming as they do in this country before the daffodils and bluebells are over, they are a splendid addition to the spring palette.

R. primula and *R. hugonis* I had grown and loved at Bleak House. So they went in first. Then came *R. cantabrigiensis*. This beautiful little rose – brownish stems, ferny foliage, masses of tiny thorns and delicious pale gold single blooms – was a chance seedling found in the University Botanic Garden at Cambridge and thought to have been the result of a cross between *R. hugonis* and *R. sericea*. The estimate of height usually quoted is two metres, but Gordon Edwards (*Wild and Old Garden Roses*) says that his bush, after ten years, has reached a height and width of five metres. If mine does anything like as well, I shall be delighted.

At Bleak House, because I was operating a display garden, I had planted *R. harisonii* with the other Pimpinellifolias for the sake of keeping this botanical family together. In this our private garden there were no such constraints, so *R. harisonii* was planted where it belongs aesthetically – in a collection of yellow roses. It had its origins in 1830 in the garden of a New York lawyer, George F. Harison, and is thought to have been a cross between *R. pimpinellifolia* (which sets a prodigious quantity of seed) and *R. foetida*. Certainly its attractive green foliage and wealth of little double golden flowers are very welcome in a spring garden.

R. foetida 'Persiana' was included by mistake. I had ordered, for the fourth or fifth time, *R. hemispherica* (The Sulphur Rose). This is thought to have come to England from Turkey as early as 1636. Perhaps it was brought in stages from one part of the Ottoman empire to another, in the way that many plants travelled along the Old Silk Road from China to Persia. Or it may have been brought directly from Turkey by a merchant or a diplomat.

The double flowers of *R. hemispherica* are bigger than those of most of the early yellows, and the foliage is reputedly a pleasant greyish–green. I say reputedly for I have never yet seen it. Each time I have ordered it, I have received *R. foetida* 'Persiana' instead. I would dearly love to grow it. It is apparently susceptible to cold and to damp conditions, so does not do well in England. It might be happier here — if we could only get hold of it.

I have nothing against *R. foetida* 'Persiana' (Persian Double Yellow). In fact, it is delightful, with its fully double golden blooms. So I have planted another one each year for several years, following each case of mistaken identity. It was brought to England from Persia by the then British Minister in Persia and with its close relative, *R. foetida*, is historically very important, being largely responsible for introducing yellow into modern rose breeding.

On the Monet Bank, too, I planted 'Golden Chersonese', a modern hybrid, bred in the United Kingdom in 1963 by E. F. Allen, a scientist and amateur breeder of roses. It is thought to be a cross between *R. ecae* (from Afghanistan in 1880) and the mysterious and delightful 'Canary Bird' — mysterious because there have been so many and such conflicting views as to its parentage.

However this may be, both 'Canary Bird' and 'Golden Chersonese' have certainly earned their places on our Monet Bank, adding their cheerful single yellow blooms to the spring pageant.

One of the few things in the garden when we came (other than the great trees) had been a mass of cannas on one of the banks in front of the house. They are not my favourite flowers, so most of them ended their lives in the Gisborne tip. But a clump of butter-yellow ones escaped this fate, and these I planted now at the top of the bank in front of the banksia roses and interspersed with sky-blue *Salvia uliginosa* (commonly known as bog sage, but perfectly at home on this comparatively dry bank).

Clumps of blue agapanthus and yellow and tawny coloured daylilies went in then, and masses of white Shasta daisies (*Leucanthemum* × *superbum*) and, lower down along the edge of the retaining wall above the path, a quantity of soft yellow *Anthemis tinctoria* 'E. C. Buxton'. Vigorous and evergreen, it has formed a tough weed-suppressing mat.

Much later, when most of the planting had been done, I came across a plant of 'Soleil d'Or' — a miserable spindly little plant which has made no perceptible progress in the ensuing two years. Because of its historical importance I shall persevere with it and hope that, with VIP treatment in the matter of diet, water and mulch, it may eventually come good.

For 'Soleil d'Or' was the fulfilment of a dream. Over a period of sixteen or seventeen years the rose breeder, Joseph Pernet-Ducher, laboured to produce a large flowered clear yellow rose. He used *R. foetida* 'Persiana' and tried many hundreds of crosses with it and different Hybrid Perpetuals until finally, in 1900, he achieved his goal with 'Soleil d'Or'. My puny little plant has yet to put forth its first bud, so I am dependent on the descriptions of others. Peter Beales describes it as being "deep orange–yellow to tawny-gold, shaded red".

Pernet-Ducher's name will be forever associated with the history of the rose, for from 'Soleil d'Or' came many of the rich yellow, orange and coppery shades we find in modern roses.

At the northern end of this east–west bank stands an ancient hoary walnut tree — a giant of a tree, over a hundred years old, and bearing each year a prodigious crop of nuts. If it weren't for the white cockatoos, I would feel positively obliged to develop a taste for pickled walnuts. But these raucous-tongued devils descend on the trees (there is another one, just as old and just as big, on the northern side of the garden) in their hordes and strip them bare. If they ate the nuts, I think I would not begrudge them. But they don't. They simply tear them off and litter them all over the paths — a hazard for unwary feet.

However, if it bore no nuts at all, I would treasure this tree which must go right back to the early days of settlement in Gisborne.

At the south end of the bank I planted, as befits a spring colour scheme, for it flowers at the same time as the roses, a laburnum (*Laburnum* × *watereri* 'Vossii') and two plants of *Kerria japonica*. It, too, produces its buttercup-yellow blooms in spring. It is tough and hardy and receives — and asks for — no attention. (And what's more it, too, belongs to the Rose family!)

So far, so good. But I realised then that I had found no place in the garden for the spectacular, absolutely indispensable *R. moyesii* 'Geranium'. Its striking single scarlet blooms would add a touch of drama to this spring bank in the way that scarlet tulips do to a planting of spring bulbs. And in the autumn all eyes would be drawn to its prominent flagon-shaped hips. So I planted three.

The Monet Bank also offered an opportunity to add to my collection of geums and potentillas — both, again, members of the Rose family. So, at the base of 'Geranium', I planted the scarlet geum 'Mrs Bradshaw' and the golden one 'Lady Stratheden'. At the back of the bank, since it grows very tall, I put in three clumps of bronze fennel (*Foeniculum vulgare* 'Purpureum'), a perfect foil for this splash of scarlet.

And along the top of the retaining wall are clumps of *Potentilla aurea*, *Potentilla* 'Red Ace' and *Potentilla* × *tonguei*. So far I have not come to terms with the brilliant orange *Geum* × *borisii*, but that may yet come. I did sprinkle a packet of seed of the scarlet nasturtiums to tumble down over the wall. I see that they are reappearing this year — without any intervention on my part.

14   The South Side

The south side of the garden is less structured than the north and there are fewer formal touches. In fact, almost the only concessions to formality are the pencil pines set at the top of each of the short sets of steps leading from one terrace to the next. The planting on the south side preceded that on the north by more than twelve months. It predated the purchase of the additional block and there was no thought, when the south side was planned, of having separate gardens for the different types of roses. In fact, the "planning" was what might be termed haphazard.

On the morning that we took possession of Erinvale I had climbed to the highest point on the south side between the two giant cork elms. It had been no easy climb. The ground was uneven and strewn with rocks. Thistles grew over my head and there was a positive jungle of elm suckers.

I had been glad to reach the top, glad to stop for a rest, and had planned on that very first morning to erect a rose arbour here with a seat. This was essential. I had decided, moreover, that the rose arbour was to be the focal point on the south side and that all paths were to lead up to it.

I had ordered it that very day – so much for long-term planning – a conglomerate of simple Gothic arches made of metal painted dark green. And on it I decided to plant 'New Dawn' for its constant flowering and its hardiness.

Then on the boundary fence behind, 'The Edna Walling Rose' – if any roses could cope with the elm roots and the suckers, these two would.

A month or so later I did indeed plant 'New Dawn' but, being impatient, I bought cutting-grown plants from a nursery instead of striking my own. The fourth plant did look rather more vigorous and sturdy than the others right from the outset. When in spring they put on leaves and started to grow, it was obvious that this one was not 'New Dawn'. It turned out to be the rampageous almost uncontrollable *R. multiflora*, which came from East Asia in the late eighteenth century. When it flowers – which it does fairly briefly – the leaves are almost obscured by the masses of tiny white single blooms borne in huge clusters. On account of its vigour it was used for a long time as understock by many commercial rose growers. In some places it still is.

Fortunately I had planted it at the back. And behind it, on the fence, was the almost equally enthusiastic 'Edna Walling'. They will probably eventually intermingle and form an impenetrable barrier. But I decided to leave them to it, for the "garden" of our neighbour on the other side of the fence consisted entirely of head-high thistles and outsized docks. Blocking out this view had to be seen as a top priority. While 'New Dawn' is still concentrating on finding a footing among the elm roots, *R. multiflora* has covered the whole of the top and sides of the arbour. And it does look a picture in the spring!

On the whole, the south side had planned itself. The ground sloped to the south and to the west so the terraces had simply followed the natural contours of the land.

The lowest of the banks, a shallow one, I planted thickly with daylilies (*Hemerocallis*). I chose all those in the catalogue which claimed to be pink. Of course, they are not. They range from lemon–yellow, to pale orange, to deep red. There might be one or two among the forty-odd I planted that could legitimately claim to be pink. They are, nevertheless, very effective. They are hardy and need (and receive) very little attention, and where I planted forty I must now have a couple of hundred.

Along the top of this bank is a bed a couple of metres wide and thirty metres long. For instant height I placed six green metal tripods at equal intervals along the bed. On these I planted climbing roses: 'Sombreuil', 'Leander', 'New Dawn', 'Phyllis Bide', 'Souvenir de Madame Léonie Viennot' and 'Abraham Darby'.

'Sombreuil' remains, I think, my favourite white rose (and, no, I have not forgotten that paragon among white roses 'Madame Hardy'). It is ideal for a tripod or a pergola. It is not too vigorous. It flowers recurrently. I love the flat quartered shape of the blooms, and the scent is indescribable.

Then 'Leander': I am a great admirer of 'Hero' and expected that 'Leander' would match up to it. I think it does not. It is one of the very few David Austin roses I could happily do without. To be sure, it is healthy and vigorous, but I find the colour – a pale apricot – washed out and insipid. Nevertheless I shall leave it there – perhaps it is an acquired taste, and I might eventually acquire it.

Next, for no better reason than that I had a superabundance of it, 'New Dawn'. Following the mistake regarding the arbour, I had put in dozens of cuttings and most of them had taken. Of course, it is far too big for a tripod, but somehow I have managed to keep it trimmed and it is now a big sprawling shrub — and it really hardly ever does stop flowering.

Then 'Phyllis Bide' — by contrast a delicate dainty little creature with masses of tiny apricot–yellow flowers and equally tiny leaves. It is one for which the English rosarian, Peter Beales, has expressed great admiration.

'Souvenir de Madame Léonie Viennot' is definitely a mistake. I had grown her on a tripod at Bleak House, and she had been well-behaved and perfectly amenable to discipline. Here conditions must have been more to her liking. She rushed straight to the top of the tripod and then proceeded to send out long waving arms in every direction. My best endeavours have not succeeded in training her, but she does produce a spectacular display of apricot–pink scented blooms. In a moment of boredom last year, when engaged in the interminable task of deadheading her, I counted them as I cut them off. There were over six hundred.

And finally David Austin's 'Abraham Darby' — large full blooms the colour of a ripe apricot and a rich fruity scent to match. He has not yet reached the top of his tripod but is making a sturdy branching shrub. And if his flowers are large almost to the point of vulgarity, who could complain when he produces them so generously?

I find penstemons great value and have used a number of them here — mainly blues. At the back, because she grows tall, I put 'Alice Hindley' — not a true blue, more a mauve, but constantly in flower — a good companion for *Penstemon* 'White Swan', which I divided up from plants in other parts of the garden. Then two lower-growing blue penstemons: *P. serrulatus* (syn. *P. diffusus*), which produces its tubular purplish flowers for most of the summer, and *P. campanulatus*, which grows not much over thirty centimetres so is ideal for a rose bed. It bears its mauve–blue flowers throughout summer and autumn. *P. heterophyllus* 'True Blue' is possibly my favourite because it really is blue, shot through like precious silk with purple. A trim back after flowering is all that most penstemons ask. They can be divided as they send down roots, and they strike easily from cuttings. Truly, a most accommodating plant!

Last year I was given a generous present of no fewer than ten paeonies. So I planted them here. It is open, and sunny, and well-drained, and I am hoping for flowers this year. It was Margery Fish who said that a garden without paeonies was unthinkable. I still remember my ecstatic disbelief when I saw them for the first time. They came up without warning in my garden in Hobart where the climate is very much to their liking. And they are among my most cherished memories of gardens visited in the European spring — Margery Fish's own garden at East Lambrook where they grow in great wooden water butts; Cawdor Castle where massed paeonies grow in front of a wall of climbing roses; Mount Congreve in Ireland where a long wide border consists entirely of paeonies and delphiniums.

On the south side of the garden, too, is the Rugosa Bank. It is a steep stony inhospitable bank facing west, where most roses would not flourish. The Rugosas, however, are quite at home. I planted all the ones I had grown at Bleak House

— *R. rugosa* 'Alba', *R. rugosa* 'Scabrosa', 'Schneezwerg', 'Delicata', 'Belle Poite-vine', the lovely pale yellow 'Agnes', the voluptuous deep purple 'Roseraie de l'Haÿ', the ingenuous 'Lady Curzon' and, of course, 'Sarah van Fleet', my favourite among them all, despite the fact that she sets no hips.

I planted two plants of the seedling we call simply 'Maria's Rugosa' because it had its origins in Maria Fawcett's garden. It has long slender scarlet hips, unlike the rounded hips of most of the family. I added two of 'Typica' which I had not grown before. The flowers are very like those of 'Scabrosa', but deeper in colour. And deeper still is 'Rugspin', the cream stamens startling against the colour of the petals. 'Vanguard', I am told, has salmon–pink flowers, a colour not formerly found among Rugosas. My plant looks healthy, but it has not yet deigned to flower for me. She has the reputation of being very miserly with her blooms.

As underplanting on this bank I have used, among other things, a number of species gladioli. These are rapidly gaining in popularity. Small wonder, since they require absolutely no attention, preferring to be left undisturbed; they thrive in sunny dry spots and multiply with incredible rapidity. Species gladioli are very different from the cultivated varieties. The flowers are much smaller and simpler and are produced in greater numbers.

The first one I grew was *Gladiolus × colvillei*. This grows up to 30 to 40 centimetres and produces a spike of pale pink flowers early in spring. I planted it in the Gallery Garden in front of the climbing rose, 'Madame Grégoire Staeche-lin'. By the third year I had a large impressive-looking clump so I moved some to the Rugosa Bank and started to look for more varieties.

I was given a few corms of *Gladiolus tristis*, an unusual pale green in colour and with a faint but very sweet perfume. Then came *Gladiolus × colvillei* 'The Bride' — pure white flowers with green markings in the throat. In a specialist nursery I found a Nanus Hybrid, *Gladiolus × colvillei* 'Nymph', pale pink with deeper pink markings — slightly tizzy, this one — and then came *Gladiolus × colvillei* 'Ruber', deep red with a white throat. This latter I planted in front of the bright red climbing rose, 'Paul's Scarlet', and by a fortunate chance masses of self-seeded white candytuft (*Iberis sempervirens*) came up among them. The overall effect was quite stunning.

Gradually, as all the clumps in the Gallery Garden have increased, I have moved more plants to the Rugosa Bank. There, too, I planted *Tulbaghia violacea* (society garlic), which produces little umbels of violet–purple flowers over a long period in summer and autumn, and is effective against the mauve–pinks of the Rugosas. A deep purple slightly variegated form of *Iris unguicularis* looks splendid in winter in front of the heathers which flourish on this sunny well-drained bank and seems to flower for the greater part of the year. Here, too, I put the larger growing nepeta 'Blue Hills Giant' and a carpet (a rapidly spread-ing carpet!) of white gazanias.

At the end of the Rugosa Bank, where several paths meet, is a group of bold foliage plants: the yucca (*Yucca filamentosa*), which also goes by the name of Adam's needle, with its sword-shaped leaves and occasional panicles of creamy-white ecclesiastical-looking flowers; *Iris wattii*, reputedly brought to England by Major Lawrence Johnston from the wilds of Yunnan, can reach as high as two metres and has fans of broad leaves and lilac–blue flowers not unlike those of *Iris japonica*. Unfortunately, the snails like them as well as I do.

In this group, too, is *Dietes bicolor* with tough narrow evergreen leaves and pale yellow open flowers with a brown blotch on each petal. Then there is *Orthrosanthus laxus*, a member of the Iris family and native to Australia and to some parts of America. It bears clear blue flowers in summer. We have it next to *Kniphofia* 'Maid of Orleans', whose soft yellow buds open to cream. And most exotic of the group is *Puya alpestris*. The spiny blue leaves alone would warrant its inclusion in this group of foliage plants, but I am waiting expectantly for the first promised panicle of "arresting metallic blue flowers".

A hedge of French lavender (*Lavandula dentata*) edges a path above the Rugosa Bank and, above this again, very close under the larger of the two elms, is a bank we call the Species Bank. Only species roses, I thought, unused to coddling and cultivation, would survive under these conditions.

Rosa woodsii var. *fendleri* from North America makes a tall shrub covered in spring with single lilac–pink flowers and in autumn with cheerful red hips. It is suckering and spreading in exemplary fashion.

R. virginiana, again from America, will reach almost two metres. Its flowers are clear pink and single; its foliage in autumn turns every shade from gold to a deep russet red.

'Eos' is a hybrid of *R. moyesii*. Its flowers are similar to those of the superb 'Geranium', but a rather more pinkish-red. They are borne on arching canes on a shrub which can attain a height of two metres.

'Master Hugh' is a seedling from *R. macrophylla* which came originally from the Himalayas. It has some of the largest hips in the garden, flagon-shaped and a bright orange–red.

But of the roses I have planted recently, the one which has excited me most is *R. sweginzowii* (a friend with something of a complex about botanical names calls it 'Sweet and Sour'). It had its origins in north–west China. I had read about it and had been looking for it for some years. Finally I managed to get a tiny plant – so tiny I doubted whether it would survive to celebrate its first birthday. It arrived late in the winter when all my planting was done. So I put it in hastily and with insufficient thought – anything to get the poor thing's roots into the soil – at the top of the Rugosa Bank just thirty centimetres or so from the path. It grew and it flourished. With remarkable rapidity it sent up one long cane of a pleasing brownish colour and on this it bore several bright pink single blooms. The foliage is ferny and in colour a delightful deep blue–green, every bit as good as the foliage of *R. glauca* (formerly *R. rubrifolia*) which is so beloved by florists.

It continued to grow. It sent out long waving branches in every direction. They are armed with long hooked vicious thorns. The flowers were followed by amazing flagon-shaped scarlet hips which hang in huge clusters. I photographed it again and again. And it continued to grow. That path is now impassable. There is only one solution that I can see. I would not dare to move the rose in case I might lose it. So I will simply have to move the path – or put a No Through Road sign at the other end of it.

Towards the front of the Species Bank I planted a small group of tough recurrent flowering roses.

'Swany', very like a procumbent 'Sea Foam', and the Kordes rose 'Elmshorn' I had grown side by side at Bleak House to great effect. They really don't know when to stop flowering. With them I put a group of the less commonly known Hybrid Musks: 'Pax', 'Vanity', 'Autumn Delight' and 'Erfurt'.

'Pax' and 'Vanity' were bred by the Rev. Joseph Pemberton. Both grow to nearly two metres, and the rather untidy straggling shrubs are better suited to this bank than to a more formal bed. But both are invaluable. 'Pax' bears large open semi-double creamy white flowers. It has about it an aura of purity − just the sort of rose one would expect an elderly cleric to have bred. But 'Vanity' is something else. It is a brilliant lipstick-pink. One of its parents was the spectacular deep red 'Château de Clos Vougeot'. It is best planted in a dramatic group of at least three where the long arching canes can intertwine.

'Autumn Delight' was bred by Pemberton's long-time assistant and beneficiary, John Bentall. Its single white blooms with pronounced reddish stamens are a delight indeed.

'Erfurt' is a much more recent addition to the loosely connected family of Hybrid Musks. It was bred by Kordes in 1939. I was put off initially by a description in a catalogue which read "glowing pink and cream". Generally speaking I shy away from two-toned roses. But 'Erfurt' is an exception and it is, moreover, the perfect companion for 'Vanity'.

The underplanting on this bank is an irrepressible white anthemis, probably *Anthemis punctata* ssp. *cupaniana*, which seems a pretentious name for such a simple unassuming little white daisy. Its delightful grey–green ferny foliage quickly forms a dense spreading weed-suppressing mat. With it I planted a grey-leaved arctotis with flowers very much the colour of 'Vanity' but one shade deeper. And for almost all-year-round colour I struck some cuttings of the dear old mauve and brown perennial wallflower found in every cottage garden (*Erysimum* × *kewensis* syn. *Cheiranthus* × *kewensis*).

To these I added, along the stone retaining wall, the grey *Tanacetum haradjanii* syn. *Chrysanthemum haradjanii* (cuttings brought from Bleak House struck easily); *Anacyclus depressus*, a ground-hugging plant with grey–green filagree foliage and tiny white daisies, the back of whose petals are dark red; two hardy euphorbias: *E. myrsinites*, because it is evergreen and prostrate, although I did have some doubts about the bright yellow–green flowers it bears in spring; and *E. polychroma*, which grows quite bushy and literally covers itself with heads of similar yellow–green flowers − so bright, in fact, that it really was too much. It clashed violently with the Hybrid Musks and had to be moved to the Monet Bank where it is quite at home.

Alongside the path leading up to the rose arbour I planted a large number of Rugosa seedlings. The seeds from their great scarlet hips − dropped by the birds − come up in the most unlikely places. Most of those I planted seem to be seedlings of *R. rugosa* 'Alba', although a couple of them are certainly offspring of 'Fru Dagmar Hastrup'.

Below the rose arbour is a large irregularly shaped area, bounded on each side by paths leading up to the arbour, and at the base by a bed of David Austin roses. Here I wanted to grow daffodils. Like many Australian gardeners I cherished a secret ambition to naturalise daffodils in grass. Influenced by English gardens and by the poetry we were brought up on, I had mental pictures of a sheet of gold under the elm trees, fluttering and dancing, of course! This can actually be achieved, but with difficulty. Our grass grows too long and rank too quickly, and the whole patch becomes untidy and unattractive for too long before the daffodils can be mown down. Neil Robertson at New Gisborne has achieved a fine effect with mown paths through the grass, and Eve Murray at Langley has even succeeded in naturalising daffodils along the roadside under the gum trees.

But my daffodil patch is in a very prominent position and cried out for neater tidier treatment. After many experiments I overplanted the daffodils with pink evening primrose (*Oenothera acaulis*). It was described in the catalogue as "fully hardy". Fully hardy! It is totally indestructible! "Suits a rock garden," said the catalogue. That may be so in England. In Australia it needs a cow paddock.

I should not complain. It puts up with the elms. The daffodils push up through it, and I pull it out in great handfuls when it becomes altogether too much.

Last year I added to it a few clumps of *Stellaria*, otherwise known as star-wort. 'Wort' is the operative word, for it quickly spread over quite large tracts of ground, lying close to the earth and covering itself in spring with a multitude of starry white flowers. And here, too, I put several plants of *Helichrysum bellidiodes*. Almost prostrate and very hardy, it also bears masses of tiny daisy-like white flowers. And of *Prunella* (self-heal), which forms a dense spreading mat of leaves, I planted both 'Pink Loveliness' and 'White Loveliness'.

There was a time when I did not care for topiary. I saw it as stiff and unnatural. I am not sure what prompted my conversion, whether it was a protracted tour of English gardens in the summer of 1988, or whether it was a trip to Hobart from Launceston on the Midland Highway. For here, just south of Ross, one comes quite suddenly and totally unexpectedly on a hilarious group of topiarised figures at the side of the roadway. To whose genius and impish sense of humour these are ascribed, I have never discovered. Certain it is that they are one of the highlights of a memorable drive.

And then I came upon Ericvale Nursery in Tasmania, on the outskirts of the historic village of Evandale. The garden is fascinating. It is made up largely of topiarised and standardised plants — box, camellia, cotoneaster, escallonia, grapes — espaliered fruit trees, and ivy used as groundcover in beds edged with clipped box, with a view down over the Esk River and a backdrop of the towering Western Tiers.

So here I bought my first piece of topiary. It was destined to sit in the middle of the daffodil patch, and we built a little semicircular platform for it to give it some slight elevation and a fitting prominence. I think it was a peacock. In my inexpert hands it now rather more closely resembles a squirrel. But, whatever it is, it reigns supreme over the daffodils and certainly leads the eye up to the rose arbour and the exuberant *Rosa multiflora*.

A New Look for the Old Rose Garden 15

I was pleased with the Old Rose Garden. We had had a wonderful flowering in November and December. I had harboured some doubts about combining 'Rosa Mundi' and *R. gallica* 'Officinalis' in a hedge, as I had cherished what amounted almost to a conviction that to make a satisfactory hedge the roses must be all of one kind. It had only been the hedge of 'F. J. Grootendorst' and 'Pink Grootendorst', planted by that prince of landscape gardeners, Russell Page, that had given me the courage to try. When my hedge flowered last summer, I decided that it was a success.

The perennials used as underplanting, too, had put on a pleasing display. They had done as they were intended to and had provided colour when the roses were over. I had found punnets of a dusty pink Californian poppy (*Eschscholzia californica* 'Ballerina Series') – so much prettier than the usual orange, which would have been out of the question here. It had bloomed steadily for months on end.

Then, just as I was in danger of becoming smug, along came the drought. We depend on town water and, after several months without rain, the Council imposed restrictions. It came down ultimately to two hours a day with a hand-held hose. It wasn't the first time this had happened and I'm sure it won't be the last.

With hindsight I realised the folly of having centred the Old Rose Garden around a lawn. I had planted it with care. The weeds had been poisoned, the area levelled and top-dressed. Seed had been sown, then it had been watered and rolled − in fact, it had been cherished, and last year it had looked splendid.

But then came the drought. Blue skies and sunshine. Clear, cloudless day followed clear, cloudless day. And the garden grew drier and drier.

Heavily mulched, as they had been, the roses and perennials survived and looked fine. But the now dry dusty brown area that had once been my carefully nurtured lawn quite ruined the effect.

I shut myself up in the study with my ever-increasing library of gardening books and spent days searching for information and inspiration, picking up an idea here and an idea there as we gardeners do.

At the end of the week, my research supplemented by lengthy consultations with my friend Lyn Cooke, I was ready to re-plan my Old Rose Garden. The roses were to stay as they were − they were, after all, the raison d'être of this part of the garden. The perennials, too, were on the whole not a bad selection. Over the years I would cull, and add to and improve them.

But the lawn had to go. Better no grass at all than this drab unsightly apology for a lawn.

It was to be replaced by gravel. White gravel, which in this part of Victoria goes by the name of Lilydale toppings. So the grass I had nurtured so carefully was poisoned. Another drain was laid to carry away excess winter rain, and the gravel was ordered.

It was too large an expanse for unrelieved gravel, so it was decided that the narrow bed containing the rose hedge should be widened to make room for hundreds of tall bearded iris in front of the roses and a low box hedge in front of them. This was to be kept at a height of twenty centimetres.

I never cease to be amazed at the rapidity with which iris multiply. I did not need to buy any. I simply divided up the ones I had planted on the south side three years earlier. The tired old central rhizomes were discarded and the new offsets planted and by the next spring they were bravely flowering. And iris and box need no watering.

Then, in the centre of the area that was to be gravelled, a long rectangular bed was made. A low dry-stone wall was constructed around it to raise its level by about thirty centimetres. We filled this space, having no spare topsoil, with the contents of five very big compost bins, our entire compost for twelve months. A rich diet indeed!

In the spring an Old Rose Garden, for the rest of the year this entire area was to take on a Mediterranean flavour. I found four standardised grapes and planted them in the corners of the raised rectangular bed.

Prostrate rosemary was planted in each corner under the grapes to trail down and soften the dry-stone wall. The rest of the bed was filled with various kinds of iris, planted symmetrically. *Iris pallida* was a must for its variegated foliage,

silvery green and white. It produces its delicate pale mauve blooms only spas-
modically, but they are worth waiting for. I included a good deal of *Iris graminea*,
the low-growing little 'plum tart iris', named for its scent on a hot sunny day;
Iris pumila in colours of palest blue (the colour of the rosemary) and white.
I included, too, a variegated salvia with foliage of a pale and a deeper green
and a rich plum colour. For the centre of the bed I found a large terracotta
jar − not the harsh orange colour that terra cotta often is, but a pale apricot.
And by the greatest good fortune it has, at its broadest point, a circlet of grape
leaves.

Apart from the grapes, which are accorded an occasional drink, none of the
plants in this bed is ever watered and they are all doing well.

Extra trees were needed to give shade from the north and west. This, too,
would cut down on the amount of water needed by the roses and perennials.
In keeping with the Mediterranean theme, and because they are evergreen and
so serve also as a windbreak − and because they conjure up nostalgic memories
of Greek islands and sun-drenched Italian vineyards − it was decided to plant,
behind the rose hedge, a row of olive trees.

A low bank drops down behind the hedge to the lowest terrace and it was
on this level, just at the base of the bank, that the olive trees went. The bank
itself has been planted thickly with the cheerful little evergreen autumn-flowering
bulb, *Zephyranthes candida*; with *Oxalis hirta* which opens its tiny mauve
enamelled flowers in the autumn sunshine; with the prostrate white thyme
(*Thymus serpyllum* 'Albus'); and with the Australian native, *Scaevola*, whose
bright green foliage and constant succession of mauve−blue flowers are a delight.

It was this year of drought, too, which led me to look further for more grey
foliage plants for other parts of the garden.

A year or so earlier I had found in a local nursery a delightful blue−grey,
lacy-leaved cypress from Kashmir (*Cupressus himalaica* var. *darjeelingensis*). I
had given it a bed of its own shared only with several plants of the dark red
Gallica rose, 'Charles de Mills'. Grown on its own roots, it had suckered to form
quite a thicket. I planted, as a border round the whole bed, lamb's ears (*Stachys
byzantina* syn. *S. lanata*). I love its woolly grey leaves, but don't care so much
for the spike of purple flowers. This is fortunate, because the leaves tend to
deteriorate if the plant is allowed to flower. So it is best to cut the flowers off
in the bud. The plant needs virtually no other attention.

Artemisia canescens I put along the top of a dry-stone wall where its fine lacy
foliage perfectly matches the grey lichen on the stones. It is low-growing and
spreading, and is the ideal accompaniment for red or pink roses. I have since
used it extensively as it is so hardy. As is often the case with grey foliage plants,
it bears unattractive bright yellow flowers which have to be removed in order
not to ruin the total effect.

From Lambley Nursery I recently received another very promising artemisia,
Artemisia ludoviciana 'Valerie Finnis' with deeply divided silver foliage. I have
planted it under the dark red David Austin roses, 'Othello' and 'The Squire',
along with the deep blood-red potentilla 'Hamlet'.

Tanacetum haradjanii syn. *Chrysanthemum haradjanii* I had grown and loved at Bleak House. It is one of the most interesting, as well as one of the hardiest, of all the grey plants. It trails happily down over stone walls and sends out roots as it travels along a bed, so that it is a simple matter to find young plants to move to other parts of the garden.

The taller growing *Chrysanthemum ptarmiciflorum* (now re-named *Tanacetum ptarmiciflorum*) is indispensible. It has the great advantage that its flowers, instead of being the usual harsh yellow, are a pristine white and very decorative. It needs little attention apart from cutting it back fairly hard after flowering.

Much more aristocratic, though just as undemanding, is the shrubby *Sideritis candicans*, which has strange textured felted leaves of such a pale grey as to be almost white.

On top of dry walls, exposed to unrelenting sun, the little grey-leaved shrub, *Convolvulus cneorum*, is flourishing. Its pink-tinged buds open white and the flowers are borne from spring to late summer.

At the end of the Monet Bank we made a hedge of *Teucrium fruticans* (shrubby germander) with aromatic grey–green leaves, white underneath, and pretty soft-blue flowers in summer. It strikes readily from cuttings and grows quickly.

I have always intended – an intention which is strengthened by each hot, dry summer – to plant a hedge of that old friend wormwood (*Artemisia absinthium*). I do prefer the much more romantic name of lad's love. There is a particularly good 'improved' form that goes by the name of 'Lambrook Silver' – no doubt from the garden of Margery Fish to whom we owe so many fine plants. It, too, grows easily from cuttings, needs no attention except for an occasional trimming, and is even said to repel slugs, aphids and fleas!

The Rose Tunnel 16

The sun was shining on a day in late November the following year when we set out for Beechworth, high in the mountains of north–eastern Victoria. But by the time we reached Romsey, barely half an hour's drive away, the clouds were gathering, and as we drove into Kilmore the storm broke. Thunder and lightning and torrential rain, so heavy that the windscreen-wipers couldn't cope with it, and visibility was almost nil. Had I been driving I would have felt compelled to pull off.

But we were due in Beechworth by noon. Impulsively, I had agreed to give a talk at the Beechworth Garden Festival. So Bill kept driving. At first we thought it was a passing storm but, as mile followed mile and the rain showed no sign of easing, we reconciled ourselves to an unpleasant trip. Long before we reached Beechworth I had decided that no-one in his right mind would go out on a day like this unless he absolutely had to. Certainly no one would venture forth to attend such a frivolous thing as a talk on roses.

It was no better at Beechworth. I had looked forward to seeing Tour de Malakoff Nursery, set up some eight or nine years ago by my friends Jenny and Frank Gadler, enthusiasts both, who had bought their very first roses and a veritable library of rose books from Bleak House. We did walk resolutely round the beautifully tended garden, but the paths were awash and the roses hanging their heads and looking thoroughly miserable.

The hall had been set up with great care, generous bowls of roses everywhere in anticipation of a good crowd. But the rain continued relentlessly and by two-thirty (half an hour after the scheduled starting time) the organisers resigned themselves to the sad fact that forty people were all that were coming.

It was decided that we should start. Only then was it discovered that the slide projector was out of order. The globe had blown and no-one had thought to bring a spare one.

There followed another frustrating half-hour while one of the committee went home to get a replacement. The audience was (understandably) restless and I was having difficulty in keeping up an inconsequential patter.

It was after three by the time we finally got started. But the enthusiasm had gone — mine and the audience's. And I had to shout to be heard above the noise of the rain on the iron roof. There was no microphone.

Only a handful stayed for lukewarm tea and biscuits and at five we set out on the four-hour drive home. More than once, feeling cold, decidedly damp and thoroughly dispirited, did we both reiterate that this was positively the last time I would ever agree to speak — moreover with no fee — to an uncertain audience at a long distance from home. As we reached Lancefield we heard on the car radio that Gisborne had received the brunt of the storm. Trees and powerlines were down, roofs blown off and shops flooded.

We reached home just before ten o'clock. The old house, veteran of hundreds of such storms, had stood up to it well, as had the giant oak on the bank above. We resolved to leave it till the morning to look further. We would have a night-cap and go to bed. It was too dark, in any case, to see anything.

We were up early and set out, filled with silent apprehension, on a tour of inspection. On the south side all was well. A few branches had broken off the old elms, but there was no serious damage. It was quite another story on the north side. One of our only two eucalypts had snapped off just three or four metres above the ground. The whole crown of the tree lay athwart my olive trees and the hedge of 'Rosa Mundi' and R. gallica 'Officinalis'.

In almost total silence — I think he secretly feared an outbreak of hysteria — Bill got the chainsaw and I a small handsaw and we started work cutting the tree into moveable pieces. All morning we cut, dragged the cut branches down to the drive, loaded them on to the old truck and made trip after trip to the tip.

I still find it hard to believe that, when all that great weight had been lifted off, the nine little olive trees still held their slender branches erect. The roses had been battered and broken, but they would recover, as would the iris. The olive trees had been my main concern.

The remaining eucalypt had a decided list to the south. It had lost one huge branch and I was firmly of the opinion that the whole tree should be removed before the same thing happened again. The next time we might not be so lucky.

So the tree surgeon was contacted to remove the trunk of the first tree, and his opinion was sought as to the fate of the other. I was glad when he said it should go. He arrived the following day with ropes and tackle — and a stump muncher — and by nightfall both trees were, as Bill would say, history.

Not the least of my regrets was that we would no longer enjoy the visits of an itinerant koala — a solemn venerable old fellow — who had been in the habit of making a brief stay from time to time. He would arrive under cover of darkness and, apprised of his presence by the frantic barking of Willy at the foot of his tree, we would find him high up in the branches, munching contentedly and totally indifferent to Willy's incessant clamour.

How he negotiated the streets of Gisborne I never knew, nor where he lived between visits. But we had enjoyed his company — I had photographed him many times as he looked solemnly down from his secure height. With the eucalypts gone, there would no longer be any inducement for him to visit us.

All this drama occurred only a week before the weekend when we were to open the garden under the Victorian Garden Scheme. The tree surgeon, his helpers and equipment had reduced that part of the garden to a quagmire and, to make matters worse, the rain continued unabated for the whole of that week.

On the appointed Saturday morning I consoled myself with the thought that very few people would be foolish enough to visit a spring garden in the rain. It would be Beechworth all over again. It was hardly worth putting out the "Garden Open" signs.

I rang Neil Robertson, whose garden was open on the same weekend, and was somewhat comforted to hear that his garden, which is very flat, was in a similar condition. He suggested roping off the section where the eucalypts had been. Of course we had insufficient rope, so we resolved simply to warn any visitors intrepid enough to come, to keep away from that part.

Over eight hundred people came through the garden that weekend. By Sunday evening many of our grass paths were in much the same condition as the slope where the eucalypts had been. At least two smartly dressed women were seen leaving the garden with their high-heeled shoes held in their hands and their costly white slacks marred, possibly irrevocably, by muddy brown stains.

The following week was, of course, warm and sunny. I went around the garden assessing the damage. Some of the grass paths would have to be gravelled. This was a relatively small matter. The eucalypt slope was something else.

As I stood for the hundredth time contemplating the devastation it suddenly occurred to me that what I had seen as disaster had in reality been a stroke of incredible good fortune. I had a row of lilacs parallel to the fence line and opposite them, at a distance of about four metres, the row of olives. Now that the eucalypts had gone, there was nothing in between. I could never in cold blood have taken the decision to remove them. But fate had stepped in and done it for me.

I had always wanted a rose tunnel. I had looked with admiration tinged with envy at the great arches spanning the main path in front of the house in Monet's inspired and exuberant garden at Giverny; and at the laburnum walk (too much photographed and copied) in Rosemary Verey's garden, Barnsley House. On a humbler scale, I had envied the wisteria tunnel at Buda, the home of a gifted Hungarian silversmith in Castlemaine in central Victoria. There had seemed to be no place at Erinvale, our garden of slopes and terraces, where such a thing would be possible.

And here it was. Made to order! The main recollection I had of our wet and miserable morning at Tour de Malakoff Nursery was of the many fine arches and arbours and the handsome entrance gates made by Frank Gadler. I rang him forthwith and ordered five metal arches. They were to be graded in width from two metres for the one at the bottom of the slope to one and a half metres for the one at the top. This would give a sense of perspective and make the tunnel look longer than it actually is.

It took Nick Flens some four or five weeks to complete the project. Of course it was more complicated than it had at first appeared. It always is! The ground slopes in two directions, both to the west and to the south, so there was a lot of levelling to be done if the arches were to sit squarely. I designed a wide flight of steps curving up from just above the sunken garden to the top of the rose tunnel. Stone retaining walls had to be built on the west side. This necessitated many more trips with the old truck to the Bleak House quarries. Thank goodness we had them! Then the whole path and the steps had to be gravelled to avoid any more accidents on wet days.

Roses had to be ordered. I cannot recollect how many times I designed and redesigned the planting. This was the boldest feature of the whole garden. It had to be right. The roses had to be vigorous enough not only to reach the top of the arches but ultimately to extend horizontally from one arch to the next. But they must not be so big as to be uncontrollable. Colour is always, with me, a matter of prime importance. The roses would be in flower at the same time as the 'Rosa Mundi' and *R. gallica* 'Officinalis' hedge which ran parallel at the top of a low bank in the Old Rose Garden. So the roses must be pink or white.

After weeks of indecision I decided on three Alister Clark roses – not out of any misplaced patriotism, but because they best met my requirements. 'Daydream' is one of the loveliest climbers I know – pale pink and single and crowned with golden stamens. 'Gwen Nash' is similar but a slightly deeper shade of pink. Alister described it as "the most beautiful thing in decorative pinks I can hope to produce". And it was described in the 1931 American *Rose Annual* as "the most beautiful rose I ever saw; the sheer beauty of a plant in full bloom is enough to take one's breath away". It is thought that 'Gwen Nash' may be one of the parents of 'Daydream', but this is still in the realm of the uncertain. The third rose for my tunnel would be the voluptuous deeper pink 'Kitty Kininmonth'. All three are recurrent.

To be effective a rose arch really needs the same rose to be planted on each side. I planned that the first and fifth arches would be clothed by 'Daydream', the second and fourth by 'Gwen Nash' and the middle one by 'Kitty Kininmonth'.

Just beyond the last arch, so that you look straight into it as you come up through the tunnel, 'Jessie Clark' was already clothing the fence and climbing with gay abandon into the nearby aspen trees. Named after Alister's dearly loved niece, she is one of the first roses to bloom in the spring. She does not repeat the performance, so just a little further along the fence I planted 'Cicely Lascelles', who goes steadily on through the summer. I planted Alister's 'Golden Vision' at the foot of an old plum tree alongside the steps and another at the foot of a silver birch. They are covered in spring with great semi-double pale yellow roses which fade to nearly white. And at the foot of an aspen halfway up the steps, I put a rose which I found in the garden of Glenara, Alister's home, weaving its way up through an old lilac. Soft gold, the colour of the stamens of 'Daydream' and 'Gwen Nash', it may well be, according to the only available descriptions, 'Traverser'. But there is insufficient evidence to name it with any degree of certainty. It is without doubt a hybrid of *R. gigantea*, and so well at home in this company.

Later I planted hundreds of daffodils between the rose tunnel and the base of the bank (which is crowned by the 'Rosa Mundi' and 'Officinalis' hedge), and overplanted them with more creeping thyme (*Thymus serpyllum* 'Albus'), native violets and more of the violet–blue Australian native, *Scaevola*. I always have a slightly guilty feeling about my lack of enthusiasm for natives, and am glad when I can find a suitable role for one in this garden of exotics.

There were already on the bank, planted the year before, quantities of the starry white autumn-flowering *Zephyranthes candida* and the enamelled mauve *Oxalis hirta*. To these I added, under the lilacs, masses of golden *Sternbergia lutea*. Each autumn when they flower they bring back pictures of the carpet they made under the old orchard trees in Louie Wilson's garden at Camnethan.

I found some more interesting cranesbills – 'Criss Canning', a hybrid from *Geranium himalayense; Geranium pratense*, a soft, misty, lilac–blue; and *Geranium macrorrhizum* 'Ingwersen's Variety', for all its cumbersome name a charming little pale pink and white bloom. This overplanting is gradually thickening and shortly I hope that this area, mulched in winter by oak leaves put through the muncher, will be relatively maintenance free.

From Tim Barbour's topiary nursery in Tasmania came two circles of ivy which I planted in square pots at the shady foot of the steps and the project was completed. What had been a rather dull corner of the garden had become, thanks to a mighty storm, one of the most interesting.

17 Of Steps and Stairs

Other than the front steps, there are two flights which lead down from the level of the house to the front garden at street level.

The first leads down from the Gallery Garden and is entered through an archway covered by the little pink Noisette rose, 'Champney's Pink Cluster'. I decided to edge these steps with pink roses. I wanted to try training climbing roses over hoops to form railings.

So on each side of the steps we used thick polythene pipe bent over to form overlapping hoops. At ground level they were fed into galvanised water pipe sunk into the earth to keep them firm. Over these hoops I planned to train the climbing roses.

The choice of roses for this purpose was difficult. On each side, at the top of the steps, I planted the very constant-flowering gloriously-scented rose–pink 'Blossom Time'. It is a bit stiff and needs encouragement to extend horizontally, but it is still there, and flourishing.

On the next hoops I planted Climbing 'Dainty Bess', for no better reason than that I love its pale pink single flowers with their distinctive red stamens. It was not a success. It grows slowly and was quickly left behind by 'Blossom Time'. It is stiff-stemmed and unyielding, and its foliage is sparse and undistinguished. Overall it is an awkward looking plant, not worthy of such a prominent position. It has been moved to another part of the garden where its deficiencies will not be so noticeable.

On the next hoops I planted 'Swan Lake' (white, of course). It was a disaster. It grew thick and dense. It was quite intransigent and refused to be trained in any direction. And when it did consent to put forth a flower, it was, by anyone's standard, ordinary. After a year or so I dug out both plants and gave them away. In their new home I hear that they are doing well and are greatly appreciated.

On the bottom hoops I planted two of that dear little, unpretentious looking rose with the ridiculous name of 'Pinkie'. They had to be planted in the shade of a giant rhus tree on one side and, on the other, a huge bush of japonica (*Chaenomeles japonica*) of the kind generally referred to as 'Apple Blossom'. It had resisted all Bill's strenuous attempts to dig it out.

'Pinkie' thrived. It grew, and flowered with enthusiasm. It is pliant and amenable. Moreover, it is virtually thornless. It found its way along the hoops with scarcely any help from me. I bought four more (it strikes easily from cuttings, but I was so delighted with its achievements that I was too impatient to wait). These took the place of both 'Dainty Bess' and 'Swan Lake'. So now, thanks almost entirely to 'Pinkie', our railings are well on the way to being clothed and might, I think, by next spring be deemed a success.

Outside these climbers I planted, on each side, a thick border of *Santolina chamaecyparissus* (cotton lavender), which is growing in neat little mounds and needs little attention beyond the occasional clipping and the removal of its harsh yellow flowers before they clash with the roses.

The southernmost set of steps leads down from one of the terraces to the pond made when the initial terracing was done. It is not a big pond − I would have preferred a large dam, but there was insufficient room − though it is quite attractive and is home to twenty or so goldfish and several large pots of water-lilies. On the bank at the back, and on both sides, it is thickly planted with white agapanthus − a cool sight on hot summer days.

At the top of these steps, I planted on each side one of the pencil pines known as 'Skyrocket', with attractive blue foliage. Their tall straight lines are a valuable contrast to the foliage of the other shrubs and the roses. Outside each of these, and on the same level, is a huge, free-standing bush of Alister Clark's great rambler 'Cherub'. These two bushes cover themselves with a dense mass of tiny semi-double pink and white roses for several weeks in early summer.

It was below these that I planted on each side of the steps two *Pyrus salicifolia* 'Pendula' (four in all). I love everything about them − their silver foliage, their tiny white flowers, their strange contorted shapes. So I planted them despite the discouraging remarks of Robin Lane Fox.

It was not long after I had put them in that a friend, be it said a gardener of great repute, remarked casually that really the weeping silver pear was a specimen tree and should only be planted singly.

Shortly after this I read in one of the better gardening magazines that the weeping silver pear was better not planted at all since it had become a gardening cliché!

I have never been able to sympathise with the mentality that turns away from something beautiful simply because others have also found it so. In a mood of defiance, then, I continued to rejoice in my four, and have not for a moment regretted them.

I saw recently in Helen Dillon's inspired and inspiring garden in Dublin, across the other side of the garden, what I took at a distance to be *Pyrus salicifolia*. On closer examination it proved to be the equally lovely but more symmetrical silver–grey *Eleagnus angustifolia*. I only wish I had room for four of those, too.

This slope down to the pond tends to be damp. Water seeps through slowly from somewhere far up the hill. So I planted the whole slope, among the pear trees, with the Japanese water iris (*Iris kaempferi*) in colours of white, pale pink, pale blue and mauve. Their great flat, saucer-shaped flowers are pure delight. They come after the tall bearded iris are over and before the white agapanthus round the pond have opened their first buds.

On the drier southern edge of the slope I put in clumps of the giant garlic (*Allium scorodoprasum*). The round mauve flower heads remind me always of the onion towers of Bavarian churches. If picked before they start to die off they are very effective in dried arrangements, or simply hung upside down from the beams in the kitchen.

The tree mallow (*Lavatera thuringiaca* 'Rosea') grows on this slope, too, its pink blooms a perfect foil for the silver foliage of the pears. Also the later, rarer, paler pink and more beautiful form *Lavatera thuringiaca* 'Barnsley' but this one must not be cut back too hard after flowering.

Pink cranesbills have sown themselves here and last year, adding to my Sorbus collection, I planted two of the lovely *Sorbus cashmeriana* (what truly wonderful things come out of Kashmir!), which I had first seen growing in the rose garden at Sissinghurst – palest pink flowers, followed by clusters of white berries in autumn.

On top of the bank which divides this slope from the rose-clad steps, I planted, since I did not want to see both sets of steps simultaneously, three *Exochorda* and two *Rhaphiolepis* (Indian hawthorn). Both are hardy. Both are lovely. Both belong, as do so very many lovely things, to the very extensive Rosaceae family.

The *Exochorda* comes out in a veritable cloud of snow-white blossom in spring, *Rhaphiolepis* over a long period in spring and early summer in enchanting little pink-tinged single blooms on a tough little evergreen shrub with glossy dark green leaves.

Ixias have seeded themselves beside the steps – mostly the pink and white candy-striped ones, which are the first of the family to bloom in spring, and the pure white one which comes last.

And, trailing down the steps and weaving its way among the trees and shrubs, is that ubiquitous little pink and white erigeron which goes in Britain by the enchanting name of 'Daisy gone crazy'!

Willy decided early on that this pond had been installed solely for his delectation. So he can be seen on hot days, especially just following his impassioned pursuit of the postman, hurtling down the steps and taking a flying dive into the water to the undoubted detriment of the waterlilies and, I feel sure, to the infinite terror of the goldfish.

Gladiolus × *colvillei* 'Ruber' grows at the feet of the climbing rose 'Paul's Scarlet' with *Iberis sempervirens* for contrast.

'Elmshorn' is hardly ever out of flower. In the foreground is *Artemisia canescens*.

The blue poppy, *Meconopsis betonicifolia*, in the kitchen garden at Inverewe. 'New Dawn' is in the background.

Margery Fish's "pudding trees" at East Lambrook Manor with *Skimmia japonica* in the foreground.

The Australian Garden in summer. *Nepeta* × *faassenii* forms a soft border contrasting with the brightness of the Alister Clark roses.

The sculptures are a striking feature of the Italian Garden at Mount Stewart outside Belfast.

Lawson cypress have been clipped to form arches leading into the Spanish Garden at Mount Stewart.

Clipped trees and box edges lend formality to mixed plantings of roses and perennials at Hatfield House outside London.

The Alister Clark Stakes are run each year at Moonee Valley and the winning horse is garlanded in roses. Naturalism won in 1992.

The Australian Rose 18
Garden

It was not long after the redesigning of the Old Rose Garden that I decided
to make, on the second terrace on the north side of the garden, an Australian
Rose Garden.

There are, of course, no roses native to Australia, for that matter to the southern
hemisphere, but I had at Bleak House established a special garden for the roses
of the great Australian hybridiser, Alister Clark. Over a period of some eight
years I had devoted a good deal of time to the searching out and planting of
his roses.

For Alister Clark was no ordinary rose breeder. Where most of our breeders
have aimed at producing "a really good red" or "an unfading yellow", Alister
Clark had a much wider and more ambitious aim. Influenced by his experiences
in Ireland and in the countries of the Mediterranean, he thought that it should
be possible in our temperate climate to breed roses that would flower throughout the year.

He imported the best garden roses (he had no interest in show roses) from
Europe, and established them in his beautiful twenty-five acre garden at Glenara

203

on the outskirts of Bulla, adjoining what is now Melbourne's airport at Tullamarine.

The most significant rose in his breeding programme was not one of the European roses, but the great creamy-coloured single rose, *Rosa gigantea*. Its home is in the Himalayas and in Burma where it climbs to heights of twelve metres through trees. It had been little used by European breeders because it is susceptible to cold.

Unfortunately, after Alister's death in 1949 many of his roses were lost. He had released well over one hundred and twenty. There is really nothing strange or unusual in this. So many new roses are released each year that very many of them have only a short life on nursery shelves before being pushed out to make room for others. A glance at nursery catalogues of fifty years ago gives an idea of just how many, once highly acclaimed, are now no longer available.

Another significant factor is that Alister Clark bred roses for the garden, not for the show bench. Nurserymen tend to stock only those roses in great demand, and those in demand are those promoted by the rose societies, those which have won prizes in shows.

Many of the roses which are lost in this way are of no lasting significance. But this is not the case with those of Alister Clark. For he did succeed – with 'Lorraine Lee' and 'Nancy Hayward', and almost to the same extent with 'Squatter's Dream' – in breeding roses that would bloom all year round.

There is a plant of 'Nancy Hayward' growing on a fence on the steep hill leading down into Bulla (when approached from the north) which is never without a flower. Bill started to bet me, every time we approached the hill on our way down to Melbourne, that this time there would be no rose. He lost every time, until finally he gave up and awarded the victory to 'Nancy Hayward'.

Towards the end of Alister Clark's long life he wrote in one of the annuals of the Rose Society that he hoped some younger man might carry on his work where he had left off. For it is with the second generation bred from *R. gigantea* that his success was achieved. The first generation crosses – 'Courier', 'Golden Vision', 'Jessie Clark', 'Mrs Richard Turnbull', 'Tonner's Fancy' – glorious as they are, and worthy of a place in any large garden – bloom only in the spring. 'Lorraine Lee' and 'Nancy Hayward' were both bred from 'Jessie Clark'. If his work was ever to be continued it was essential to find and preserve as many of Alister Clark's roses as possible.

So when I left Bleak House, the special garden devoted to Alister Clark's roses was one of my greatest regrets. John Nieuwesteeg, the rose grower, and I, working sometimes separately, sometimes together, had found about thirty of the roses – chiefly from the families of the women the roses were named after. The friends who initially leased Bleak House from me were good gardeners and rose enthusiasts, but they did not have this special interest, nor did they have the time, with a nursery to run and a large garden to maintain, to search for more of the roses.

The collection of Alister Clark roses had been one of the first collections established and registered with the then newly formed Ornamental Plant Collections Association (OPCA). Based on an English model and established by some of the staff of the Royal Botanic Gardens, Melbourne, this organisation has as its aim the preservation of significant garden plants from extinction. It is not only roses that disappear from cultivation. The story is much the same whichever plant variety you turn to.

Rather than lose the collection, I decided to re-establish it at Erinvale. The acquisition of the additional block of land had given me the space to house it. So much for Bill's fervent hope and my firm avowal that we would make no gardens on this block but plant trees only!

The second terrace was ideal. It is open and sunny, facing north and far removed from the big trees in the old part of the garden.

With the experience gained in the making of the Old Rose Garden, I decided that there would be no "lawn". We made a wide bed the whole length of the terrace on the eastern side at the base of the slope leading down from the top terrace. On the west side I had already planted the groundcover roses which were well on the way to covering the slope leading down to the Old Rose Garden. I decided to widen this bed and to plant here seven pillar roses, widely spaced. This would lend height and create a visual barrier between the old roses, with their soft, muted colours, and the Australian roses, clear, bright and sometimes almost strident. I read a marvellous description by Anthony Sampson where he described the colours of the old roses as "subtle as a water-colour". The Australian roses are in many cases, to continue his analogy, "as obvious as poster paint"!

I used the green metal tripods I had designed for Bleak House. Because the site is (unfortunately) exposed to north winds, we cemented the bases into the ground. The roses chosen for the tripods were not all Australian roses. After all, they would be visible also from the Old Rose Garden below. I selected that old favourite, Alister Clark's 'Black Boy' (reasonably successful); Climbing 'Iceberg' (hardly ever out of flower and every garden must have one); Climbing 'Shot Silk' (a coppery pink and very floriferous); Climbing 'Madame Abel Chatenay' (a deliciously fragrant soft pink bloom, but the plant, alas, turned out to be the bush form not the climber so it will have to be moved); Climbing 'Souvenir de la Malmaison' (her usual unreliable self, hopeless in spring and delightful in autumn); 'Ophelia' (moderately successful, but I would like more flowers); and 'Madame Butterfly' (like 'Madame Abel Chatenay' she turned out to be the bush form, not the climber, so I have recently replaced her with the exuberant constantly flowering lipstick-pink 'Zéphirine Drouhin').

At the south end of this long bed, not on a tripod, for no tripod would be big and strong enough to contain her, I planted the climbing form of the widely beloved buttonhole rose 'Cécile Brunner'.

Here, too, I planted three *Amelanchiers* (that rose family again!), two of *Amelanchier canadensis* and one of *Amelanchier lamarckii*. Small, graceful trees, they are covered with tiny white blossoms in spring, and the young leaves are a delightful and distinctive shade of rosy–fawn (how difficult it is to give an accurate idea of colour). In autumn they turn wonderful shades of scarlet and russet–red.

Now came the vexatious question of what degree of formality I wanted in this part of the garden. The gravel immediately precluded any suggestion of "cottage garden" or total informality. But I did not want, in this Australian country garden with a backdrop of mares and foals grazing on the hill opposite, to try to emulate a formal English rose garden. As is so often the case, a compromise had to be found.

I turned again to Margery Fish and her garden at East Lambrook. It is a garden I feel I can relate to because it is not too large; it is difficult to relate to the vast expanse of a Stourhead or a Mount Congreve! I find myself returning to East Lambrook Manor (in imagination) again and again, and going over and over the slides I took on that magical summer morning when I was fortunate enough to be almost the only visitor in the garden.

One of the slides I love best is of Margery's "pudding trees" which she described as "shapely little cypresses (*Chamaecyparis lawsoniana* 'Fletcheri') . . . just tall and distinct enough to emphasise the curving path as it winds up to the orchard above" and kept by judicious pruning to "their neat shape of little pointed puddings".

The Lawson cypress is a much maligned tree. I had seen it very successfully cut into tall arches in the Spanish Garden at Mount Stewart. And so, undoubtedly influenced by both Margery Fish and Mount Stewart, I decided to plant, alternately with my pillar roses, seven of what the nursery described as *Cupressus torulosa minima* — a smaller form of *Cupressus torulosa* which attains a height of not much more than two metres. This would emphasise the break between the Old Rose Garden and the Australian Garden and introduce just the desired degree of formality. Clipped trees are used for this effect in many English gardens and I felt that the *torulosas*, with their natural pyramidal growth, would achieve it without the need of clipping. I have to report that, so far, they are doing well.

Right down the length of the terrace, to break the expanse of gravel we built up a narrow bed, not more than a metre wide, but some forty metres long. In this I set, at equal intervals, four large goblet-shaped sandstone pots. And in these I planted four of what the same nursery called *C. torulosa nana*, the dwarf form of the *torulosa*, four perfectly shaped pyramidal pointed little trees which echo the shape of the taller *torulosas* and tie the whole design together.

Between the pots, symmetrically spaced, I planted three 1.4 metre standards of the Kordes rose 'Heidesommer'. It bears large clusters of small creamy-coloured single blooms with golden stamens right through spring and summer. And it has a scent of gardenias.

One of the problems of holding a collection of any sort of plant is that you cannot make long-term planting plans. You must plant as you find. If you find a deep yellow rose and the only spare spot you have at the time is beside a vivid pink, that is just too bad. In it must go. But I did want some sort of harmony in this very colourful garden.

So I filled the whole long bed between the big pots and the standards with Alister Clark's delightful little, low-growing border rose, 'Suitor'. It grows to not much more than thirty centimetres and it is in flower from spring until it is hit by the first frosts in June. The little double roses are borne in huge clusters, opening bright pink (he was certainly a man for bright colours) and fading to almost white.

Here, too, between the roses, I planted white lilies, and hundreds of bulbs of *Iris xiphium*, violet–blue and gold. The iris flowers before the first buds open on the roses, so this gives us a complete change of colour-scheme for a few weeks.

Edging the big main bed was the subject of a good deal of thought and indecision. Box was too formal for this bright, exuberant company. But again I wanted a note of harmony. Finally I decided on catmint (*Nepeta* × *faassenii*). The bed is raised up with a low stone wall, so all along it I planted dozens of roots of *Nepeta* (obtained by splitting up a couple of very big clumps). The blue–green foliage and mauve flowers, which it bears in abundance, contrast with and soften the colours of the roses. And, if cut back after its first flowering, it will repeat the whole performance a couple of times over.

Then in the middle of the long main bed, starting at the base of the bank, we built a wide, generous flight of steps leading up to the top terrace.

Here then were the bones of the Australian Rose Garden.

19   *Sheila Bellair*

We had been so busy at Erinvale, both in the house and in the garden, that there had been no time to continue with the hunt for Alister Clark's lost roses. This is a time-consuming business, involving letters, endless phone calls and miles of driving, only to find in many cases that the clue one had been following led nowhere.

Now, with a new home established for these special roses, I was filled with the desire to find more of them. So in the long winter evenings of 1990 I started putting notes together again, and making a card index for all the Alister Clark roses I had ever heard of and any description or references to them I had been able to find from old *Rose Annual*s, nursery catalogues and early Australian rose books. A poor resource it proved to be, but better than nothing.

For most of the roses there were only the scantiest descriptions — "red, semi-single, scented" or "pink, long-stemmed, vigorous" . . . nothing by which one could possibly hope to identify a rose. Ultimately one depended on the families where a member had had a rose named after her. "Her" — for Alister seldom named his roses after men — mostly they were after women — or racehorses.

I was checking through my cards for the hundredth time one evening. "Bellair", I said, "Sheila Bellair. What an unusual name."

Bill, born and bred in Victoria, has an encyclopaedic knowledge of all things Victorian. It transpired that he knew a John Bellair.

"An old fellow, he'd be. Eighty at least." That was just the age-group I was interested in. Alister Clark died in 1949 and most of those who had known him well were in their eighties.

So I rang John Bellair, now living at Upper Beaconsfield. He was, indeed, in his eighties, but with all his faculties unimpaired. Yes, Alister Clark had named a rose after his sister, Sheila. She had been delighted. A pretty pink, it was, he said, with not many petals. This tallied with the description I had from an old *Rose Annual* which said: "Hybrid tea, released 1937. Large, semi-double, open, pink, bushy."

The rose had been released just before Sheila was married, her brother said, and she had planted it in the garden of a house she and her husband had built at Balliang. Callendale it was called.

So the following week I drove to Balliang — a funny, sleepy little town in the neighbourhood of Bacchus Marsh in central Victoria. I had been there only once before to pick up a young dog, a blue heeler bitch who had a poor reputation and was desperately in need of a home. When I saw her, cowering in the back of a kennel and alternately whimpering and growling when approached, I had no great hopes for her. But I agreed to give her a month's trial. By the end of the month we had made no progress and she had twice, entirely without provocation, bitten Don, who helped me in the garden. We were forced to admit defeat. Even Willy, whose canine charm is proverbial, could make no headway with her.

So Balliang held no happy memories for me, and I drove down its dusty main street with no great feelings of optimism. The first call was the Post Office, for I had no idea who now owned Callendale or whether, in fact, it was still there at all.

The Post Mistress was helpful. She gave me directions and the name of the present owner who, she said, was a keen gardener and active in the local garden club. My spirits rose.

The house was approached by a long drive bordered by tired dusty old cypress pines, but this opened out to an expanse of red gravel in front of the house. There was no-one at home, but one glance at the garden dispelled any hopes I might have cherished. The only roses were planted in strictly geometrical beds and pruned ruthlessly to a uniform height of thirty centimetres. Bare earth between the bushes and concrete edgings completed the picture. Surely 'Sheila Bellair' would never have submitted to such a fate. No rose bred as early as 1937, and certainly none of Alister Clark's, would have a place here.

I did ring the owner of Callendale that evening and all my fears were confirmed. They had cleared out "all those old things" in their first year there and replaced them by modern roses which she would be very happy to show me if I cared to come back in the spring.

So that was the end of that lead. I rang John Bellair again. He was sorry and disappointed, but not vanquished. Sheila had moved later to a property outside Echuca and he was sure she would have taken cuttings of the rose with her. She had had a great friend in the town, the widow of a local solicitor, and she was still there. John was sure that she would be able to help.

I made my initial contact that same evening. Ellen was more than happy to talk about old times, the days she had spent with Sheila, and the pride Sheila had taken in the rose named after her. Ellen knew exactly where it grew — behind the house, near the swimming pool. She could see it now, and the lovely arrangements of pink roses in a silver rose bowl that Sheila had always had on the dining-room table.

The property was owned now, she said, somewhat disparagingly, by "horse people". They would know nothing of roses, but she, Ellen, would go out and see them and find out whether the rose was still there. I expressed my warm appreciation and forebore to mention that Alister Clark, too, had been something of a "horse person".

Next week she rang back, full of excitement. The rose was there. It was not in flower, but the "horse people" had no objection to our taking a few cuttings. It took me six months and untold phone calls to arrange a suitable day. Either it was too cold, or it was too hot, or the roses weren't out, or it was bushfire weather, or Ellen had a cough, or the "horse people" were too busy.

Finally we made it. I picked Ellen up in Echuca and we drove out together. It didn't look promising. The drive was lined with horse floats. It was dusty and unkempt, the garden overgrown and the house needing paint. Still, I argued, this did not mean that the rose was not there. Alister's roses were notoriously tough. And Ellen was undaunted. Round the back of the house we went, and down to the swimming pool.

"There," cried Ellen, flinging out her arm in a gesture of triumph, "There it is! 'Sheila Bellair'!"

My heart sank. Rising tall and majestic out of a sea of nettles and docks, crowned with at least a dozen clear pink blooms, was a perfectly splendid bush of 'Sunny South'. There is no mistaking 'Sunny South' once you have seen it. Of all the roses he bred or grew at Glenara it was Alister's favourite. At the time of its release it had achieved tremendous popularity. Growing to over two metres, it made a fine hedge, with its large, semi-double pink flowers "flushed carmine" as the catalogues said.

I could not bring myself to tell Ellen she was wrong, that all our planning had been for nothing. She was so sure, and so happy to have been able to help.

So I took cuttings — cuttings I did not need, for I had plenty of 'Sunny South' — and I took some for Ellen, too, and showed her how to take them. I wrapped the cuttings carefully in wet newspaper and put them in plastic bags brought for the purpose.

It was just as we were leaving that I had a sudden flash of inspiration. "Did Sheila have any other roses in the garden, Ellen?" I asked.

"Only two," came the reply. "She really wasn't a gardener. There was one more just here and one outside the kitchen door."

From the undersized bush beside 'Sunny South' I could get only three cuttings, so starved and neglected it was. And though I told myself it was hoping against hope, I could not dispel a lingering thought that perhaps Ellen had

The scarlet hips of the Rugosa rose 'Scabrosa' make a fine table decoration.

'Château de Clos Vougeot', possibly the loveliest of all red roses.

Roscoea cautleoides growing under roses in Helen Dillon's garden in Dublin.

'Scarlet Meidiland' with *Artemisia canescens* spilling over the wall at the base of the Red Bank.

The soft blue Australian native, *Brachyscome*, weaves its way through a yellow potentilla.

This low-growing *Moraea* flowers beneath the David Austin rose, 'Heritage'.

The Red Bank with *Stachys byzantina* in the foreground, *Artemisia canescens* along the wall and the giant leaves of the cardoon forming a background for the red David Austin roses 'Othello' and 'Prospero'.

Alister Clark roses in the Australian Garden in November.

mixed them up. After all, she was over eighty. Sheila had been dead for many years. It is easy enough to mix up plants in one's own garden, let alone in some-one else's. Especially when they are growing side by side.

When we got back to Echuca I helped Ellen plant her cuttings at the end of the vegetable garden, against a rickety paling fence. We put in ten and I am confident that by now she must have a perfectly splendid hedge of 'Sunny South', for as a rule every piece strikes.

My own cuttings I put carefully in the glasshouse and, in due course, I had fifteen beautiful little plants of 'Sunny South'. We raffled them in aid of the Peter MacCallum Cancer Institute each time a group of visitors came to the garden.

The cuttings from the rose outside the kitchen door struck too, but when they flowered they turned out to be a rather ordinary red which I have never identified. Of the three taken from the poor little bush so dwarfed by 'Sunny South', two pined away and died. The last I watched over with tender, loving care. It was my last hope. After long waiting roots did form and I potted it up in potting mix. And one morning months later I came out and found the dearest pink semi-single rose, the colour of a sun-ripened peach, revealing when open a trace of pale yellow round the golden stamens, and perfectly fitting the description of 'Sheila Bellair'.

20 *The Search is Resumed*

And so, given new impetus by the finding of 'Sheila Bellair', the search for the lost roses of Alister Clark was resumed in earnest. The urge to collect is a strong and inexplicable one. Most of us have it, to a greater or a lesser degree.

As more of these roses were found and added to the garden, it became increasingly difficult to confine them to the second terrace.

I was mindful of my undertaking when we bought the second block that I would not make a garden there. I had made what I had thought was an unshakeable resolution that at least the top terrace would be given over entirely to trees.

And so trees had been planted in wide sweeping semicircles — *Crataegus, Malus, Prunus, Sorbus*, medlars (*Mespilus*) and quinces (*Cydonia*) and, after reading Hugh Johnson where he speaks of "the frivolity of the flowering cherry" — one weeping cherry.

At the top of the wide steps leading up from the second terrace, a short path leads to a simple summerhouse. For here is the best view in the whole garden — better even than that from the rose arbour on the south side. From here one looks down over a sea of trees, a tapestry of different textures and colours, to the church spires of Gisborne, and across to the idyllic scene of mares and foals on the opposite hill.

Round the summerhouse, with the object of covering all but the entrance, I had planted five 'Lamarque', which ranks very high on my list of favourite roses, and one (I could afford only one) *Clematis armandii* 'Apple Blossom' which is just as entrancing as I had been assured it would be.

And behind the summerhouse, partly to add strength to my collection of deciduous trees, partly to screen the summerhouse from the street behind, and mostly to link the top terrace with the second one, I planted fifteen *Cupressus torulosa* in a broad semicircle − not *torulosa minima* or *torulosa nana* which I had used on the second terrace, but the genuine article which, I am told, will ultimately reach a height of more than fifteen metres.

But the Alister Clark roses were insistently demanding more room. So I started with the fences. A high fence had been built right round the second block for Willy's convenience, a replica of the one on the south side. Since this had to be clad, the Alister Clark climbers and ramblers seemed a logical choice.

First 'Cherub' and 'Gladsome' because of their vigour. Little 'Cherub' looks like Dresden china and is almost indestructible. I had found it first − a huge mound of it − at the National Trust property, Clarendon, near Evandale in Tasmania. Nestled in a corner of the back garden where two walls meet, it was at least three metres high and equally wide.

I had to employ all my powers of persuasion to coax three ten-centimetre pieces from the curator, a dour but indecisive soul who was reluctant to allow even the smallest particle of the Trust's property out of her hands. The day I reached home, John called in. He suggested I plant two of the cuttings and he would make three buds from the third. My cuttings did grow, but John's budded plants reached maturity much faster and by the following winter were sturdy plants. Later we were sent budwood purporting to be 'Cherub' from Trevor Nottle in South Australia. It was identical to our own. And later still we found it again in Dame Nellie Melba's old garden.

'Gladsome' is more plebeian − typical small rambler's blooms of a robust undistinguished rosy colour. But planted side by side, the two have shot up the fence in great style. Later I added a ring-in, 'Kew Rambler', released by Kew Gardens in 1912. One of its parents was the vigorous, bright pink 'Hiawatha', so it holds its own with the Clark roses, both for colour and vigour. With the assistance of Clark's lovely cream 'Milkmaid' they have almost succeeded in entirely blocking out Erinvale Close.

On the north fence is a mixture of 'Cicely Lascelles', 'Doris Downes' and 'Jessie Clark', with the old purple rambler, 'Veilchenblau', for contrast and a couple of plants of 'Francis E. Lester' because I had propagated more than I needed and had a few left over.

All we need now to complete the planting on this fence is 'Harbinger'. We had it at Bleak House but have not yet planted it at Erinvale. Unlike most climbers and ramblers, the *R. gigantea* hybrids do not strike easily from cuttings, so it is a matter for budding. Mary Chomley sent me a photograph of a splendid specimen growing in her garden at Casterton in western Victoria.

She promised to send some budwood the winter before last. Then came a letter of apology. 'Harbinger' had grown so out of control that it was "pushing the roof up and the old room sideways" so, to effect repairs, it had been necessary to cut it right to the ground. By next year it will probably have reached the roof again and she will, I feel sure, send budwood.

One of the highlights of this part of the garden is 'Gwen Nash'. It was named after the daughter of one of Alister's closest friends, Albert Nash, with whom he used to play golf on Nash's private golf course at Bullarto. And very competitive golf it was, too. Alister frequently recorded his wins and losses in his diary.

I had used 'Gwen Nash' on the rose tunnel, but because she is so lovely and because Alister himself had such a high regard for her, I felt that an Alister Clark garden without 'Gwen Nash' would be incomplete.

It was Eve Murray, a daffodil breeder, a lifetime lover of plants and gardens and a colleague of Alister's, who first put me in touch with the Nash family. From this introduction came the inevitable mistakes but, ultimately, this grand discovery.

'Countess of Stradbroke' had never been quite out of circulation. She turned up in various places. A great double deep red fragrant climber, she was hailed in the American *Rose Annual* of 1939 as "probably the finest climbing rose in the world". The Countess may not be able to defend that title today, but she is undoubtedly worth a place in the garden.

'Courier' and 'Tonner's Fancy' are both still flourishing at Glenara. 'Courier', for want of more adequate support, has entwined herself round two or three other climbers which were in a similar predicament. The whole towering structure is held together by a positive jungle of smilax — but in spring when they burst simultaneously into flower it is one of the sights of Melbourne.

'Tonner's Fancy' is pure delight. Released in 1928, it is compared in the *Rose Annual* of that year with 'Devoniensis' — "globular, fragrant, white tinged pink in the opening bud". It was named after George Tonner, a keen gardener from Ballarat, who persuaded Alister to release it. Alister had hesitated to do so because the flowering period is so short, and so early that the buds are sometimes frosted. We should be eternally grateful to George Tonner.

Alister himself wrote of this rose: "'Tonner's Fancy' is much the best formed flower of all my *gigantea* seedlings and I fancy that was why George Tonner begged me to issue it. It is also a glorious grower with great foliage; unfortunately the flowers come so early that they at times get caught by the frost; but if it never flowered, its foliage alone would make it worth having." (*Rose Annual*, 1932)

'Tonner's Fancy' is not easy to establish. It is one of the many *gigantea* hybrids that will not strike from cuttings. John budded it and gave me three sturdy plants. One died almost instantly. The second struggled, but after two years it has at last sent up one strong shoot. The third I planted on a shady, sheltered bank. This is apparently to its liking for it has shot up and is well on the way to the top of an old apple tree.

Many of the leads followed up in this interminable search end in disappointment. Many end in uncertainty. In many cases there is simply insufficient proof.

I have a whole bed full of "possible Alister Clarks", the majority of which will in all probability never be confirmed. Among these is 'Peggy Bell'.

Alister had a friend at Kyneton, another daffodil breeder, Hugh Dettman. Both he and Dr Groves of Kyneton "tried out" roses for Alister to determine whether they should be released.

In a letter of Alister's I found reference to the fact that 'Edith Clark', 'Busybody' and 'Peggy Bell' were doing well in Dettman's garden. Hugh Dettman is long dead. So I rang his daughter and obtained permission to visit his one-time garden. The house had been let ever since his death. It is a rare tenant who cares for the garden. These had not. Of this once loved and well-tended garden nothing remained save for a tangle of rank grasses and weeds, a few tired and dejected rose bushes and – in the midst of this desolation – a royal purple clematis which had climbed to the very top of an old tank-stand.

I took cuttings from nine or ten of the better-looking rose bushes – those which did not look terminally ill – but I did not hold any great hopes of them. I knew that 'Edith Clark' had been here, but the only description of her was "double fiery red". Many, many roses would fit this inadequate description. It would be impossible to identify her without some more circumstantial evidence. 'Busybody' would be easier – "rich, orange–yellow buttonhole rose" – but when my cuttings took, I found nothing that fitted that description.

'Peggy Bell' was described as resembling, in colour and form, 'Betty Uprichard' (pronounced U-prichard). After long searching I found a colour photograph of 'Betty Uprichard' in an American book, *Roses of the World in Colour*, by Horace McFarland. It could have been a photograph of my rose from Dettman's garden. Given that we knew it was growing there and doing well, I think we might almost be safe in concluding that we have 'Peggy Bell'.

I visited Dr Groves's home while I was in Kyneton – one of those solid, foursquare old bluestone houses for which the district is renowned. Dr Groves had been first and foremost a lover and grower of sweet peas, but he, too, had "tried out" roses for Alister. This garden is cared for. Many roses have been planted since Dr Groves's days, but the present owner had bought direct from him and could point out those that were there when she bought the house. Among these were a couple of deep reds. 'Mrs W. R. Groves', released in 1941, is described simply as "deep red; foliage good" – not much help. The rose had been presented to the Kyneton Rose Society and presumably her husband would have planted one. But was it, in fact, one of the two old reds we found here? And if so, which one? Nothing but uncertainty here. So these two are condemned to sit indefinitely in the bed of "possible Alister Clarks"!

A visit to Banongill near Skipton produced more uncertainty. In fact, nothing more than a rather whimsical story and a vague possibility. Alister Clark had been a regular visitor to Banongill. Indeed, he exchanged daffodil bulbs with the Fairbairns, who owned Banongill at that time, and it is more than probable that some of those daffodils which put on such a brave show at Banongill today are Alister Clark's. He almost certainly had a hand in the replanning of the rose garden in the 1920s.

I visited Banongill at the end of the season when little was in flower. But 'Borderer' was still putting on a good display, and with it a tiny white cluster rose which just possibly could be 'Powder Puff' (Alister referred to it as "a dear little white", and added casually, "I think it came from 'Comtesse Dusy'"). Among the others, a dark, dark red semi-single stood out. Alister had loved reds and, on impulse, and with nothing particular in mind, I took cuttings of this one. When it flowered for the first time for me, I looked up all my records to see if there was any description that fitted. I came upon 'Mrs Philip Russell' bred in 1927 from 'Hadley' and 'Red Letter Day' and described as "semi-double dark red, shaded black, pillar or large bush". And in the 1931 *Rose Annual* another description: "a dark red rose, as dark as any rose grown".

Now Mrs Philip Russell, known as Cissie Russell, was a great gardener and a friend of Alister. She had lived at Mawallok so was a close neighbour and friend of the Fairbairns. Alister had wanted to name a rose for her and she had expressed a strong preference for a dark red. She died in 1927, the year the rose was released, and Alister visited her, so the story goes, a couple of days before her death and told her about the rose he was naming for her.

It is a charming story — perhaps no more than that. Certainly not admissable as evidence in a court of law. But if it is true, what more probable than that Cissie Russell's friends, the Fairbairns, should plant it in their new rose garden! It is tempting to hope that we may one day find some proof and that this dark red beauty may indeed turn out to be 'Mrs Philip Russell'.

A Red Bank 21

Finally I have planted a red bank — after years of passing over all things red in nursery catalogues because red sat so uneasily in my old rose borders with their muted colours of pink and mauve, blue, white and palest primrose. The deep purplish-red of the old Gallica roses I had come to terms with — 'Charles de Mills' and 'Cardinal de Richelieu' were old favourites and occupied places of honour. They were quite at home with the smoky lavenders of 'Anaïs Ségales' and 'Jenny Duval', and the deep purple shot with dusty pink of 'Reine des Violettes'. But the more recently bred clear definite reds were out of place in this company. I had almost convinced myself that it was a colour I had no liking for in any case — despite the fact that my garden education had begun with Gertrude Jekyll.

But there remained a hankering, which amounted at times almost to a compulsion, to plant some scarlet roses — not among the old roses for they could not contribute to that atmosphere of gentle nostalgia — but in a place of their own.

Then in the English summer of 1989 I visited Hidcote for the first time. I don't know how much this influenced me — I suspect a great deal. Of course,

I had read about the famous red borders. And they were just as exciting, as dramatic and compelling as I had expected them to be.

I was there when the cannas were at their best, and the dark red bronze-leaved dahlias. The scarlet *Geum* 'Mrs Bradshaw' was putting on her usual splendid display, as was the scarlet lobelia 'Queen Victoria'. The huge fiery red poppies were just opening their first buds and I couldn't help wishing I had been there in the spring to see the scarlet and purple tulips. Or in the autumn to see the leaves of *Acer platanoides* 'Crimson King' beginning to turn. As it was, the deep red foliage of a cherry plum (*Prunus cerasifera*) formed a marvellous background to the red border. I think it may have been the variety known as 'Pissardii', whose leaves turn nearly purple. This cultivar comes from a sport found in the garden of the Shah of Persia by a French gardener by the name of Monsieur Pissard — a fittingly romantic origin.

But I had only one day at Hidcote, and only half an hour to spend in the red borders. So I carried home with me no detailed picture but a vivid overall impression of something rich and royal, exciting and challenging.

Some months after I returned to Australia I found, in a copy of the Royal Horticultural Society's *The Garden*, an advertisement for a garden tapestry kit entitled "The Red Border" by Sarah Beecham, based upon the red borders at Hidcote. With winter approaching, when it is too cold to garden much after four-thirty and the warmth of the log fire beckons, I find tapestry a relaxing evening occupation — almost as good as thumbing through nursery catalogues and making impossibly lengthy lists for next spring. So, hoping perhaps to relive those all too few hours spent at Hidcote, I sent for Sarah Beecham's "The Red Border" and worked at it steadily through the winter of 1990. As the weeks went by, those dark velvety greens, fiery reds and royal purples really got to me. I started to put ticks against some red plants in the nursery catalogues and by the onset of spring I was truly committed to the idea of a red garden.

There was one corner which we had not yet touched. Below one of the giant cork elms on the south side, which had contributed greatly to our decision to buy the property in the first place, the ground slopes steeply towards the Rugosa Bank. This slope faces west and is fully exposed to the sun from eleven o'clock onwards. Up to this time it had been covered only by rank grasses, elm suckers and thistles, and really presented an enormous problem. Had it been a flatter area, I am sure I would simply have poisoned the weeds, sown some grass seed and kept it mown to discourage the suckers. But it was far too steep for that. So it had continued to be the Cinderella of the garden, passed by with averted eyes.

The preceding spring, below the bank I had made the bed for *Cupressus himalaica* var. *darjellingenis* syn. *C. cashmeriana*, edged with *Stachys lanata* and including 'Charles de Mills' and 'Great Western' (Chapter 15). It was probably the presence there of the greys and reds that made me view our problem bank increasingly in the light of a potential red garden.

The bank is not only exposed and hot. I expect that the elm takes every bit of moisture and nourishment from the soil. If I wanted to plant red roses there — and this was, of course, in reality the whole purpose of the red garden —

we would need some good, deep soil. So Nick built, with his usual consummate skill, a beautiful stone wall about ninety centimetres high and sweeping in a long curve round the base of the bank to the boundary fence.

This fence had been planted, a couple of years before, with rambling roses: 'Albéric Barbier', 'Goldfinch' and Alister Clark's soft creamy 'Milkmaid', bred from the Noisette rose, 'Crépuscule', and showing distinct signs of her parentage. And it was here that we had built our three large compost bins to save pushing barrows up and down the hills. Now we had our reward — three huge bins full of two-year-old compost, exceedingly rich and rare. All of this we put behind the stone wall, making a level base to the bank about one metre wide.

Into this satisfying loam I proceeded to plant my red roses. Right at the top of the bank, because it grows to two metres, I put David Austin's 'Red Coat'. Its single red flowers remind me of 'Scharlachglut' ('Scarlet Fire'), a Kordes rose. But whereas 'Scharlachglut' blooms only in the spring, 'Red Coat' flowers continuously right through summer and autumn. Below it I put in more of David Austin's roses. The bank is in a very prominent position and I wanted colour there for as long as possible. So in went two each of 'The Knight', 'The Squire' and the midnight red 'Othello'. I hesitated over 'Prospero' because I had grown it before and it had seemed not very robust. Finally I decided in its favour, and it has not looked back.

A visit to The Perfumed Garden resulted in my placing an order for two more: 'Wenlock', a plum red, and 'William Shakespeare', darkest red, double and quartered and bearing a strong resemblance to 'Charles de Mills' himself.

To the David Austins I added what is, to me, probably the loveliest of all red roses, the deep dark mysterious 'Château de Clos Vougeot' bred in France by the redoubtable Pernet-Ducher in 1908; a couple of plants of Swim's more conventional, but very rewarding, 'John S. Armstrong', and Meilland's dark red 'Tassin'; two of 'Rosemary Rose' bred in the Netherlands in 1954, its flattish flowers not unlike those of the old Centifolias; and two of the perennial favourite 'Etoile de Hollande', largely for its remarkable fragrance. Then I added one of the old Moss roses, 'Nuits de Young', also known as 'Old Black' as it is one of the darkest reds of all.

Next, so mixed are the motives that lie behind the making of a garden, I could not resist putting in 'Lilli Marlene' for no better reason than that she takes me back to sentimental evenings spent in old inns on the banks of the Neckar River during my student days in Heidelberg. I had not even seen her in flower. Fortunately she has turned out to be an outstanding deep velvety red, the flattish flowers being borne in clusters over a very long period.

Then there is 'Mrs Reynolds Hole'. And what rosarian could resist a rose bearing the name of that grand old English clergyman who occupies such a prominent position in the history of the rose? In the days when the clergy were mainly younger sons of fine old families and had time for hunting, shooting, fishing and other such pastimes, Dean Hole grew roses and toured England encouraging gardeners to show their roses in the Rose Shows inaugurated by him. Such was his contribution to the cultivation of the rose that the Dean Hole Medal, awarded annually in England for service to the rose, is regarded as the highest honour a rosarian can achieve. It has been awarded twice to an Australian, once to Alister Clark and once to the late Dr A. S. Thomas.

Finally, encouraged by the success of the groundcover roses in other parts of the garden, I planted, at the steepest point in the bank, the Rugosa hybrid, 'Red Max Graf'. This flowers only in spring, but it produces bright cherry red hips and its lush green foliage promises to give a dense cover. At the bottom of the bank, to spill over the wall, I put one of Meilland's landscaping roses, 'Scarlet Meidiland'. It has fulfilled all my expectations, bearing little scarlet roses in big clusters for months on end.

We built a winding flight of steps over against the boundary fence leading up to the foot of the elm. At the bottom of the steps I planted Kordes's 'Dortmund'. I had not seen it growing. It was listed as a shrub rose. But it grew so fast and exhibited such unbounded enthusiasm that before long I had to look for an arch to train it over. I found a Gothic-shaped metal one and Nick erected it at the bottom of the steps. 'Dortmund' seems content with the arrangement. Single red, with a white eye, and with dense dark shiny foliage, he flowers long and generously.

So much for the roses. But my Red Bank was not to be restricted to roses. During those long winter evenings while I had worked away at my Hidcote tapestry, I had continually turned over plans for this garden, selecting and rejecting, mixing and matching. This was to be no pale replica of the Hidcote borders. In our hot climate I did not want a "flowery inferno". Nor did I have a backdrop of copper beech. Instead I had my splendid statuesque old elm and, beyond it, silver poplars along Jacksons Creek.

There was to be no orange in my garden — no daylilies — and no cannas either, or dahlias. These were not for me, I decided. The colour scheme was to be basically red, purple and grey. And everything I planted on this hot steep exposed bank would have to be hardy. It was no site for weaklings or delicate subjects which needed pampering.

Right at the top of the bank, nearest to the elm, I decided to plant buddlejas. One of my most vivid memories of summer visits to London is of the buddlejas growing, totally neglected, in the old bomb sites which have still not been cleared. They flower bravely amidst the desolation. So if anything could contend with the elm roots, they would. I selected *Buddleja davidii* 'Black Knight' (as dark a red as its name suggests) and *Buddleja colvilei*, more of a cherry red. Then, for contrast, or perhaps because it is my favourite of this family, I put in the lilac *Buddleja alternifolia* (the fountain buddleja) with the deep red clematis 'Elsa Spath' to wind its way through it. There was no two-year-old compost for these hardy fellows, just a handful of Osmocote in the bottom of the hole and a thick mulch of old horse manure and straw from our ever-friendly racing stable.

For dark foliage, I planted at the top of the steps the deepest red of the smoke bushes, *Cotinus coggygria* 'Royal Purple'. And then came the greys.

Wanting to create a bold feeling of spaciousness, of drama and largesse, I put in three of the giant silver-leaved cardoons (*Cynara cardunculus*). I do not let it seed when the striking blue thistle-like flowers come out, but cut it down to the ground at this stage. The clumps are increasing nicely.

Salvia argentea's grey leaves are decorative even in winter. And from the Centifolia garden I moved a few seedlings of the majestic *Salvia forskaohlei* with its huge grey–green leaves and spires of purple flowers. *Eryngium alpinum* 'Blue Star' went in here too. Opening a metallic grey, the flowers change as they age to a deep, vibrant blue.

I divided clumps of *Campanula glomerata* and *Campanula latifolia*. Both of these are almost indestructible; they flowered steadily through last summer and autumn, and are forming a good thick cover.

On the steepest and most inhospitable part of the bank I planted the cherry-red *Achillea* 'Paprika' and the little Australian native, *Brachyscome iberidifolia*. This tolerates both heat and drought and comes in several shades of pink through to deep purple. It was the last-named that I wanted. It is making a dense mat and is covered, almost perpetually, in tiny daisy-like flowers.

Artemisia canescens, planted along the edge, is spilling over the wall, its grey foliage blending with the moss and lichen on the old quarry stones. *Artemisia ludoviciana* 'Valerie Finnis' I used again for its superb indented leaves. Its popular name is the very fitting 'Silver Ghost'. I discovered recently, quite by chance, that Valerie Finnis (Lady Scott) is an alpine expert and has a fascinating garden in Northamptonshire.

Senecio greyi came from much nearer home. I saw it in Neil Robertson's garden at New Gisborne. Its deep green leaves with their white wooly undersides were the perfect complement for an unnamed pale pink rose. Neil gave me cuttings, all of which took, so I now have five little rounded bushes along the steps. I hope to keep them that shape, and never to let them flower − the flowers are, as usual, a rather objectionable yellow.

I put in a few bulbs of vallota lilies (from South Africa). Their clear scarlet is ideal and, fortunately, they don't like being disturbed, so can be left in the same spot for some considerable time. And then I did, after all, plant a dahlia. David Glenn, at Lambley Nursery, persuaded me of the necessity of including it in this planting. It is the same one that I saw at Hidcote, 'Bishop of Llandaff'. Its dark red foliage is almost as striking as the small (for a dahlia) emphatic red flowers.

David was so enthusiastic about it that I finally said, "Oh, well, if it's as good as that, I'll have five."

"You will not," came the prompt reply. "You'll have one. I'm rationing them, one to a customer." So one I have, and I am cherishing it and hope to be allowed a companion for it next year.

And then I discovered *Allium christophii*. I had seen it often in those glorious photographs of English herbaceous borders but had never been able to buy it. Now here it was. So, in a fit of wild extravagance, I bought four. I have read that the flowering head can reach a diameter of twenty centimetres and carry up to eighty of its star-shaped little flowers. They are striking in a mixed border and ideal with roses as they do not grow too high. This was the beginning of a collection of alliums which now includes, among others, the spectacular *Allium giganteum* and the tiny blue *Allium cyaneum*.

There was little room left on the bank when I made an exciting find. One of the Alister Clark roses which I had so far found no trace of was 'Mrs Harold Brookes', released in Victoria in 1931.

John Brookes, her son, had told me that his mother had lived outside Woodend in a house called Doyswood. So, following his instructions, I set out to find it. The house was gone, burnt down, and a new one built in its place. The old fellow who now owns the place spoke little English, but I managed to discover that there had been some roses there, and he had dug a few of them out and planted them in front of his new home. Without much hope, I took cuttings of the three roses there. 'Doyswood No. 2' flowered first — quite a pretty, if undistinguished, salmon–pink. Not what I was looking for. 'Doyswood No. 1' flowered next and was identical. Two months went past before 'Doyswood No. 3' opened its first reluctant bud and it was bright red.

I had three cuttings struck, so I planted two and gave the third to John and Marion Brookes to watch. John was sure he would recognise it, by the foliage and scent as well as by the flower. After all, he had grown up with it. It was an exciting day when he rang to say that this was it. And he was relying not only on his own memory. His sister from Sydney had been visiting him. He had not mentioned the rose. But when they went round the garden, she stopped in front of it and said: "You didn't tell me you had 'Mrs Harold Brookes'." So she occupies the last space on my Red Bank. The second plant went into the Alister Clark garden.

I think the bank might be termed a success. New treasures have a way of turning up: a blood-red potentilla, fortuitously named 'Hamlet', has been planted under the deep red rose, 'Othello', and a burgundy aster, 'Sir Winston Churchill' (reputedly named by Sir Winston himself), has its home under the *Cotinus*, together with the purple *Salvia* × *sylvestris* 'Ostfriesland'; and the silver curry plant (*Helichrysum angustifolium*) with its pungent scent is close by.

But when a strange little rose called 'Léonie Lamesch' turned up I had to call a halt. She was one of the first polyanthas, bred, before her time, in 1899. Her strange bronze–red flowers with their yellow centres would have been at home on the Red Bank but there was, quite simply, no more room. She would have looked fine, too, with the strange old *Rosa chinensis* 'Mutabilis' but there was no room there, either. So 'Léonie Lamesch' must sit in a plastic pot in the work area until I can find a suitable home for her.

And those Indispensable 22
English Roses

They are planted throughout the garden, those English roses of David Austin — on the front terraces, on the south terraces, at the base of the daffodil patch (where I had vowed to plant no roses) — everywhere except among the old roses and the Australian roses. Each time I think I have done with them, I find another which I simply cannot live without.

I started by planting a few of my favourites — 'Hero', 'Canterbury', 'Cymbeline', 'Lucetta' — on the front terraces where the Hybrid Musks hold sway — 'Penelope', 'Cornelia', 'Felicia', 'Menja'. But space is limited there.

It was when I was putting in the big mixed beds on the south side that I came upon 'Heritage'. It was immediately apparent that this rose warranted a place of honour. So I planted it halfway up a flight of steps. It hangs its aristocratic pale pink cupped blooms over the steps where they cannot be missed and where the glorious scent can be appreciated to the full without the need of stepping into the bed. At its feet is a clump of moraea, pure white with a brilliant peacock blue eye.

At the same time I found 'Belle Story'. When she flowered, her pale pink semi-double blooms opening flat to reveal a wealth of golden stamens, she was immediately promoted to near the top of the favourites' list. Unfortunately I had planted her towards the back of the bed, beside Kordes's newly imported 'Rosendorf Sparrieshoop'. I had grown 'Sparrieshoop' for years and was acquainted with its rapacious ways. But this new edition outdid even the original. I think I planted it partly for its name 'Sparrieshoop, Village of Roses' — Sparrieshoop being, of course, the small north German town where the Kordes family first established their rose nursery. 'Rosendorf Sparrieshoop' has grown apace and flowers prolifically but is threatening to strangle 'Belle Story' entirely. I have pruned it quite hard this year and, as an additional safeguard, I have planted another 'Belle Story' towards the front of the bed. It is all very well to have the David Austin roses interspersed among other roses where their constant flowering is so valuable, but perhaps they should also have at least one place of their own.

A winding path leads down from the Centifolia Garden to the bottom of the rose tunnel — the path originally marked out by Willy on his forays through the garden. It is not a brilliant position for roses, as it is shaded for a good part of the day. But beggars can't be choosers, and I was once again running out of space. The David Austin roses have not minded. In fact when I walked round the garden at the very end of May this year, with winter setting in and the days becoming shorter, the roses that were still bravely flowering were the David Austins and the Alister Clarks.

At the top of the path, peeping over the hedge into the Centifolia Garden, is 'Dapple Dawn'. *Centifolia variegata* bears the nickname 'Village Maid'. This could just as easily be applied to 'Dapple Dawn'. A sport of 'Red Coat', and growing just as tall, its wealth of simple single rather ingenuous pink blooms, borne throughout the season, entice one to continue along the path. Beside it is the more restrained and sophisticated apricot pink 'Jacquenetta'.

Below them a big old pear tree hangs over the path. A curved stone wall makes an alcove under it, and here I put two little iron chairs and a low round table — a perfect, secluded place for lunch when the flowers of 'Dapple Dawn' mingle with the pure white pear blossom in early summer. *Clematis* 'Nellie Moser' is making her way up through the pear tree and through a red-leaved prunus, and on the opposite side of the path an aged plum tree is festooned with *Clematis montana*.

Beyond the prunus, surrounded by deep blue *Scilla peruviana* and a soft pink tritonia (*Tritonia rubrolucens*), is the pristine white 'Swan'. It seems to appreciate the sheltered position as this ensures that its flowers are protected from damaging winds.

And beyond 'Swan', and in sharp contrast to her purity and refinement, is the sensuous voluptuous 'Immortal Juno'. And immortal I think she might well prove to be. Her huge flowers — reminiscent of the hats seen on Melbourne Cup day — are deep pink shot through with violet tonings as some of the old roses are. And she bears them untiringly, sending out long canes which, if pegged down, will flower along their entire length.

Opposite 'Swan', on the other side of the path, is a wealth of riches: 'Hero', growing tall and reaching for the sun; 'Canterbury', with her huge open flamboyant pink blooms; 'The Reeve' — anyone could be excused for taking this more restrained fellow with his gentle cupped blooms for an old rose. Then 'Chianti', rapidly growing into a big shrub. It might flower only in spring, but what a flowering! The wealth of darkest red full quartered heavenly scented blooms beggars description. I have to visit it every day during the flowering season, so as not to miss one day of its beauty. On the bank below it I have put *Viburnum plicatum tomentosum*, one of my favourites in that large and decorative family. And further down the slope is *Pseudocydonia sinensis*, an exquisite and aristocratic relative of the common quince. It grows eventually into a small spreading tree and bears pale pink flowers in spring (before 'Chianti') and, as one would expect, large golden fruits in autumn.

Back on the path, beyond 'Chianti', is another old pear tree that I nearly chopped out, clothed now by the delicate palest pink full flowers of the modern climbing rose, 'Pierre de Ronsard', the flowers flushed faintly green in the shade. And beyond it, where the path curves round to meet the lower end of the rose tunnel, I found a place to plant a second 'Constance Spry'. I put a decorative arch there to give her some support and she is weaving her way steadily across it towards a golden ash.

'Constance Spry' is one of the earliest of the David Austin roses, named for her in appreciation of the role she played in bringing the old roses back into our gardens. For it was she, together with Vita Sackville-West and Graham Stuart Thomas, who first sought out the old roses, which were fast disappearing from cultivation, and championed their cause. She did not mind that they flowered only in the spring. "I would rather have perfection once than a well-maintained level of something else," she said.

Most of us think of Constance Spry as a flower arranger. She was this — par excellence — but she was many other things besides. She lectured in Health in Ireland. She was a successful headmistress of a school in London's East End. She owned a flower shop and established a school of cookery. Her rose is worthy of her and deserves a place of honour.

Foxgloves grow along this path and drop their seeds into the bank below, where they mingle indiscriminately with white valerian and *Campanula latifolia*. Cherry-coloured ixias are multiplying rapidly at the foot of a *Prunus serrula*, grown for its bark, which has the glow of polished mahogany. White watsonias are forming big clumps, as are deep purple babianas. Three big brown Aladdin jars, over a metre high, are placed at intervals along the path at the foot of trees. They are filled with tulips, which provide colour when the trees are still bare and the roses have not yet come into bud. I do not lift the tulips every year. Time is too short. But every third year I take them up, sort them, replace the best ones in the pots (with new potting mix) and plant the immature bulbs in big plastic pots in the work area to grow on.

In the shade provided by the golden ash (*Fraxinus excelsior* 'Aurea') a patch of *Dicentra* 'Stuart Boothman' is spreading steadily. Its fern-like blue–green foliage and dusty pink flowers make it a perfect companion for the roses.

And then, when there was no more space along my David Austin path, I came upon a picture of the newly released 'Wild Flower' — a tiny clear yellow single rose, like a buttercup. It reminds me of the little yellow species roses — *R. hugonis*, *R. primula* and 'Canary Bird' — that come so early in the spring. But where they flower only once, 'Wild Flower' blooms steadily all through spring and summer.

I knew that I had to have it. But bright clear uncompromising yellow is not easy to place. It is certainly not at home with pinks, and would have been quite out of place along my David Austin path — even if there had been room.

And then I found other yellows I wanted to plant, especially 'Symphony'. Released by David Austin in 1991, it bears masses of soft yellow fragrant rosette-shaped blooms all summer. And there was 'Bredon'. I had childhood memories of my uncle, who had a mellow baritone voice, standing at the piano on Sunday evenings and singing "In summer time on Bredon"! What I really needed was a whole bed of yellow roses — a bed of summer sunshine.

I had only one place for a new garden — a corner on the south side where two banks met. These unclothed banks had troubled me for some time. So we made a bed the shape of half a semicircle, a quadrant in fact. The curved side was built up with a dry stone wall almost to the height of the banks (which formed the two straight sides). We filled it with a base of oak leaves (the compost bins being already filled, it was a way of using them). Then compost and topsoil.

I ordered three of 'Wild Flower' and, because they are low-growing, reaching little more than .5 metre, I planted them along the top of the wall. Here, too, I put three of 'Francine Austin', named after David Austin's daughter-in-law. It grows slightly taller — to .8 metre. Its small flowers are pure white and borne in long sprays. 'Queen Nefertiti', only released in 1992, is slightly taller again and her flowers are softest yellow. (I do wonder how Her Majesty came to be included among David Austin's very English roses!)

A few taller roses were needed for the back of the bed. Here was a place for 'Moonbeam'. It grows to 1.3 metres and flaunts its great white semi-single blooms with their boss of golden stamens over a long period. There was room for two.

There was need for something stronger at the back of the bed. I decided on 'Ellen' — a rich golden apricot. Was she named, I wonder, for Ellen Willmott? She is a perfect example of Austin's achievement in combining the form of the old roses with a colour never found among them. So two of 'Ellen' — I wish there had been room for three.

But there was space for only one more towards the back of the bed and I simply had to include the incomparable 'Troilus', although I already had one in the garden. Its colour has been described as "honey-buff". In shape it reminds me of 'Souvenir de la Malmaison' — large, and cupped, and quartered.

I had bought my first 'Troilus' at The Perfumed Garden the year before. I had gone there to pick up one rose only, 'William Shakespeare', which had not been ready at the time my others had been despatched.

The display garden was a picture, the roses at their peak, planted in beds of one colour and edged with low rosemary hedges. Somehow, in next to no time, nine large pots were assembled beside the car. Now, we were in Bill's

ALISTER CLARK ROSES

my Johnson'.　　　　'Australia Felix'.　　　　'Baxter Beauty'.　　　　'Black Boy'.

orderer'.　　　　'Cherub'.　　　　'Cicely Lascelles'.

ountess of Stradbroke'.　　　　'Courier'.　　　　'Daydream'.

'Diana Allen'.

'Dividend'.

'Doris Downes'.

'Editor Stewart'.

'Fairlie Rede'.

'Flying Colours'.

'Gladsome'.

'Glenara'.

'Golden Vision'.

'wen Nash'.

'Jessie Clark'.

'Kitty Kininmonth'.

'Lady Huntingfield'.

'Lorraine Lee'.

'Mab Grimwade'.

'Margaret Turnbull'.

'Marjory Palmer'.

'Mary Guthrie'.

'Milkmaid'.

'Mrs Albert Nash'.

'Mrs Fred Danks'.

'Mrs Harold Alston'.

'Mrs Harold Brookes'.

'Mrs Maud Alston'.

'Mrs Richard Turnbull'.

'Nancy Hayward'.

'Peggy Bell'.

'rinceps'.   'Restless'.   'Ringlet.'

corcher'.   'Sheila Bellair'.   'Squatter's Dream'.   'Suitor'.

unlit'.   'Sunny South'.   'Tonner's Fancy'.   'Zara Hore-Ruthven'.

POSSIBLE ALISTER CLARK ROSES

'Cracker'.

'Edith Clark'.

'Emily Rhodes.'

'Herbert Brunning'.

'Janet Morrison'.

'Lady Somers'.

'Nancy Wilson'.

'Nora Cunningham'.

'Queen of Hearts'.

'Traverser'.

car on this occasion. He is a man not given to impulse buying – I think few men are. Nor does he carry plants in his car. I was relieved when the nine pots had been (with considerable difficulty) stowed in the boot.

And then I saw 'Troilus' – a superb plant, in full flower, in a 35-centimetre pot. Of course we bought it. And it had to sit on the back seat with Willy. I travelled the whole way home with my heart in my mouth in case he overturned it. He didn't. I think he is beginning to understand about plants.

But it had not been accorded the picked spot in the garden, which I felt it deserved. So here, in this new planting, was the perfect opportunity.

Space had been reserved in the middle of the bed – centre stage – for 'Symphony'. And beside it was room for two of 'Bredon'. David Austin speaks with great enthusiasm of this little rose, which he says could be described as a floribunda, as it produces so many flowers in each big spray. It is a buff yellow.

Then in my local nursery I found 'Minilights'. Like 'Wild Flower', it reminds me of the early yellow species roses – small single flowers, so bright as to look enamelled. And, like 'Wild Flower', it is recurrent. I still had space at the front of the bed, so I bought three of 'Minilights'. I am not such a purist as to mind that it is the odd man out in this bed of English roses. In fact, I was delighted when I found that it was bred by the firm of Dickson in northern Ireland, the same firm as gave us the superb 'Irish Elegance' and 'Dame Edith Helen'.

Having assembled such a fine collection of roses for this garden, I decided to search for some new and interesting perennials to put with them.

At the back of the bed, as it grows quite tall, I planted a new achillea, 'Coronation Gold'. I value the achilleas for their tough constitutions and the very small demands they make on the gardener – just the occasional removal of spent flowers. This one has attractive grey–green foliage and white buds which open yellow.

The artemisias are valuable for much the same reason. I now have quite a collection. This time I ordered *Artemisia stelleriana*, a new one to me, which was described as having "intensely silver oak-shaped leaves". The flowers, as with so many grey-foliage plants, are of no consequence.

Then *Erodium chrysanthum* – fern-like silvery leaves and creamy-yellow flowers. And a dwarf sisyrinchium growing to no more than ten centimetres – ideal for under roses – and bearing pure white flowers over a long period. Its popular name is 'May Snow', botanically it is *Sisyrinchium idahoense* 'Album'.

My enthusiasm for the cranesbills continues to grow, and I always keep an eye out for any I have not got in the garden. This time I found *Geranium renardii* – just right for the colour scheme in this bed. It likes some shade, so I put it where the two banks meet and a little copse of aspens (*Populus tremuloides*) cast a shade for part of the day. It has rounded matt-green scalloped leaves with something of the texture of felt. Its white flowers have a tracery of faint violet veins.

I found another member of the Iris family, *Synnotia villosa*. It comes from South Africa, grows about twenty centimetres high and produces delightful creamy–yellow and mauve flowers in abundance.

Potentilla megalantha also grows not more than twenty centimetres high. It produces clear yellow blooms in summer and has unusual matt-green slightly hairy leaves. At the back of the bed I planted a few lupins: 'Noble Maiden' — white, of course, and 'Chandelier', a soft yellow.

On a visit to Helen Dillon's garden in Dublin I saw, for the first time, *Roscoea cautleoides*, and fell instantly in love. It grows not much over fifteen centimetres tall and produces masses of creamy–yellow flowers, not unlike those of *Iris pumila*. In fact, I thought it must belong to the Iris family. But it does not. It is classed as a tuberous perennial related to ginger. It came originally from western China and flowers through summer and early autumn. I think I rang every Victorian nursery I have ever had dealings with in my search for it — only to be disappointed. Finally I found it in the catalogue of Woodbank Nursery in Tasmania. They had only three little tubers left so I have planted them near the back door, where I cannot possibly lose them. When my stock increases they will go in with the yellow roses — I cannot imagine a more suitable underplanting.

In the meantime, for instant and constant colour throughout summer, I bought eight punnets of that viola sold as 'Antique Shades' (a tawny blend), a change from the blue I so often plant with yellow.

Some more Australian Roses 23

Some years ago I heard the story of how, on one sunny morning in Brisbane in 1906, Mr Leslie Corrie, president of the Queensland Acclimatisation Society, set out with his five-year-old daughter, Penelope, to visit his colleague, John Williams. Mr Williams was about to release a new rose.

They found him at work in his garden in the aptly named suburb of Sunny-bank. He had various classical names in mind for his new rose, but when the little girl saw it — and when John Williams noted her delight in it — he decided there and then to name it 'Penelope'.

That little girl is now in her ninety-third year and lives in the central Victorian town of Castlemaine. When she had first mentioned to me some years earlier a Tea rose named 'Penelope', I had thought at once of the well-known Hybrid Musk rose of that name bred in England by the Rev. Joseph Pemberton in 1924. But she assured me that there was another, earlier, Queensland-bred rose of that name.

I thought little more about it, being persuaded that by now it would be out of circulation — as are so many of our early roses — and quite unobtainable.

Then an article in the Australian *Rose Annual* of 1931 brought it to mind once more. There was 'Penelope' listed under the roses released in 1906 and described as follows: "A variety of exceptional beauty; flower of medium size, full, with high pointed centre; colour unique and remarkable; lower petals rich dark red and centre creamy white; quite distinct from any other rose. Received Award of Merit from National Rose Society, England."

I rang Penelope Corrie in Castlemaine and determined to see if I could find her rose. After many letters and phone calls I finally obtained a plant from Roy Rumsey in Sydney.

It was the finding of 'Penelope' and her subsequent splendid performance in the garden that prompted me to search for more of our early roses.

Then I made the acquaintance of 'Carabella' − 'Cara Bella' her breeder called her. She came as a gift in a parcel of roses from South Australia with a note saying simply: "Try this. It's good."

So I did try it. And it is good. In fact, for length and continuity of flowering, it is one of the best in the garden. It has a strange little flower, pale pink and white, in shape more like an azalea bloom than a rose − but its little flowers are borne in great clusters and for months on end. The foliage is plentiful, light green and attractive − and there are almost no thorns. If I had room for more hedges, I would plant a hedge of 'Carabella'. It grows tall but doesn't mind being cut back. In fact, it doesn't seem to mind anything much. I grew it at Bleak House, where it had inadequate drainage and stood for months with its feet in a bog. Where other roses would have pined away, it soldiered bravely on. Where I grow it at Erinvale, at the top of the Rugosa Bank, it has insufficient water and is exposed to north wind. It is impervious to this and, backed by a hedge of French lavender (*Lavandula dentata*), which also blooms for months on end, is one of the stand-bys of the garden.

'Carabella's' manifold virtues led me to enquire about her breeder. I could find little. His name was Riethmuller and he lived in Sydney, at Turramurra. As is the case with all of our rose breeders except Alister Clark, he seems to have regarded rose breeding as a hobby, for he released few roses − perhaps twenty. Most of them are now lost.

'Gay Vista' achieved some measure of fame. Released in 1960 it, too, bears large trusses of single pink flowers with a white centre, as many as fifty blooms to a cluster. It, too, was described as being suitable for hedges. Thanks to Deane Ross, it is now obtainable again. Mine has not yet attained hedge proportions, but it is doing well.

The great German rose breeder, Wilhelm Kordes, in his book entitled simply *Roses* and published in 1964, does not accord so much as a mention to Alister Clark, but he speaks favourably of 'Gay Vista' and also of another of Riethmuller's roses, 'Titian'.

Unlike the other Riethmuller roses we have, 'Titian' bears large flamboyant flowers of a vibrant carmine−pink. It is readily available and can be treated either as a pillar rose or as a large shrub. I have recently planted two of 'Titian' between two 'Nancy Hayward' − I may need to plant two 'Iceberg' as well to tone them down. On the bank behind is the bright pink groundcover rose, 'Rosy Carpet'. There may be a need for sunglasses in this corner of the garden!

'Honeyflow' is not unlike 'Carabella', but a paler pink, almost white, and it seems less vigorous. Likewise, 'Claret Cup', which is dark red with a white eye. Then there is 'Spring Song' — as joyous as its name suggests, a vigorous bush, tirelessly producing great clusters of small rich carmine–pink blooms, and 'Kwinana', a striking single bright red.

Of Riethmuller's other roses little trace remains. This is tantalising for Riethmuller, like Alister Clark, appeared to have had a broad aim in view. Except for 'Titian', his roses have a similarity of form, stemming no doubt from the fact that he used one rose, the little-known 'Gartendirektor Otto Linne', extensively in his breeding programme. His roses are characterised by their attractive foliage and a great profusion and long duration of flowering. As hedge roses or as shrubs at the back of a border they are hard to beat.

Australia has produced other rose breeders. But at no time have we had a full-time rose breeder to compare with the famous breeders of England, France and Germany. Even Alister Clark, who comes nearest to this, would have been surprised had he been described as a professional rosarian. On his marriage certificate he listed his profession simply as "gentleman". His rose breeding was fitted in as time allowed between racing, hunting, golf, fishing, shooting, polo playing, photography, daffodil breeding and supervising the care of his very beautiful ten-hectare garden.

Most of our rose breeders have turned to it as a hobby to be pursued in their retirement or at weekends, and have worked in their own back gardens — nothing to compare with the huge nurseries, extensive trial grounds and professional equipment and staff of the European breeders.

But one or two other Australian roses have made their mark overseas, most notably Patrick Grant's 'Golden Dawn'. Produced in 1929 from 'Elegante' × 'Ethel Somerset', 'Golden Dawn' according to Hazelwood's, one of the leading nurseries of the day, "forged its way into the first twelve roses in England, America, Australia and New Zealand". It was described as being "a rich sunflower yellow . . . which tones to lemon yellow as the flower fades". It is Deane Ross, again, who has put this rose back on the market.

Grant produced only two other roses that we know of, 'Salmon Spray' and 'Midnight Sun', both of which appear to have been lost.

Then there was William Adamson, a Scot, who was head gardener at Talindert, the property of James Manifold at Camperdown. A gentle retiring man, a lover of gardens and of poetry, he produced one notable rose, a rich red climber, 'Miss Marion Manifold'. T. A. Stewart (the editor of the *Rose Annual*, after whom Alister Clark named a superb red rose) described 'Miss Marion Manifold' as "undoubtedly one of the finest climbing roses in the world" which "has done much to make Australian roses known". Thanks largely to George Jones of Geelong it is now available again.

This is no history of Australian rose breeding. There are many other names which will be remembered: the roses of Ron Bell, George Dawson and Eric Welsh are popular today and will assuredly grace our gardens for many years to come, although their names are largely unknown outside this country.

But if Australia has produced few internationally acclaimed roses and few internationally recognised rose breeders, she has certainly produced some unusual ones. At meetings of horticultural societies and garden clubs, lectures on horticultural topics, workshops and seminars, the audience is invariably predominantly feminine. And yet, despite the fact that women are now represented in all professions and callings, from the High Court bench to the racetrack, there has yet to emerge one world famous woman rose breeder.

Australia can currently boast four women who, although not prolific rose breeders, and certainly not known outside this country, have produced a handful of fine roses.

Mrs Fitzhardinge, working in Sydney in the 1920s and 1930s, bred some ten or so roses which were at the time highly regarded. Two only are now available, and even they have to be sought out in specialist rose nurseries: 'Lubra', a dark red, and 'Warrawee', a very beautiful silvery pink. An interest in Australian history manifested itself in the naming of some of her roses: 'Captain Bligh', 'Governor Phillip', 'Sirius'.

Mrs Fitzhardinge's aim might have been similar to that of Alister Clark. Perhaps she was influenced by him, as he was at that time enjoying great success. She wrote in the *Rose Annual* of 1932: "Few of these (her own roses) will ever grace the gardens of the general public, but the crosses may be of interest to those bent on the happy quest of hoping to raise roses stronger and more suited to our land of sunshine."

More recently two women in central New South Wales have become involved in what is to them a fascinating hobby. We have two of Marguerite Parkes's roses in the Australian garden. 'Jenny Brown' was bred from 'Dainty Bess' × 'Pink Favourite'. All rose growers know and love 'Dainty Bess', but all too often the bush is spindly and a "poor doer". 'Pink Favourite', with the indefatigable 'New Dawn' in its breeding, must have lent it strength and stamina, for 'Jenny Brown' bears its single bright pink blooms steadily throughout the summer.

'Sharon Louise' flowers as prolifically as any rose in this part of the garden — big pale pink classical flowers on a sturdy bush. With 'Queen Elizabeth' and 'Virgo' as her parents, this was surely to be expected.

The one Marguerite Parkes believes to be her best is 'Pink Angel', which has so far proved very elusive. I live in hopes of finding a plant one day.

From Myrtle Robertson in Bellingen we have 'Miss Rita', a delightful pink Hybrid Tea, perfectly shaped and generous with her blooms, another true daughter of 'Queen Elizabeth'.

And from Myrtle Robertson, too, comes 'Cousin Essie', a seedling from Riethmuller's 'Honeyflow'. This makes her second generation Australian. Her pale pink buds open to white and the blooms, like those of 'Honeyflow' and 'Carabella', are borne in huge clusters. If given room, she will grow into a large attractive shrub which is almost perpetually in flower.

More recently Myrtle has bred a delicate pink cluster rose which she has called 'Fairy Floss' — tiny, perfectly shaped roses in long sprays on a vigorous shrub.

Quite by chance I came across an entirely charming daughter of 'Iceberg' called 'Iced Parfait'. It has the same fresh green foliage as 'Iceberg', the same perfectly shaped double blooms and the same light fragrance. But 'Iced Parfait' is pink — a delicate pale Dresden-china pink.

'Iceberg' is a German rose. Its name in Germany is 'Schneewittchen' ('Snow White', the same who lived with the seven dwarfs) and it was bred by that great firm of Kordes and released in 1958.

I was interested to find out who had bred 'Iced Parfait' and intrigued when I discovered its breeder is an eighty-year-old nun from Launceston, Sister Xavier.

Sister Xavier has loved roses all her life. When she was at St Finn Barr's convent, the Dean of Launceston encouraged her to plant roses in the convent garden. Soon she had more than three hundred growing there. She became a member of the Tasmanian Rose Society, and following in the footsteps of earlier English churchmen, Dean Hole of Rochester and Bishop Darlington, she also became a keen exhibitor at rose shows. In fact, she won the local championship five times with 'Ena Harkness'.

Then she became interested in breeding. She got hold of the books of the late Dr A. S. Thomas of Melbourne and studied his methods carefully. As many amateur breeders do, she started by planting self-pollinated seeds, but soon she went further.

'Iceberg' grew in the convent garden, and next to it was a thriving bush of the soft pink floribunda rose 'Pink Parfait', which bears great clusters of lightly scented flowers for months on end. And Sister Xavier noticed that 'Pink Parfait' sets great quantities of seed. So she used the pollen from 'Iceberg' to set seed on 'Pink Parfait'.

Twelve of her seeds germinated and they were all different. She kept the six strongest bushes and discarded the rest. Later a careless gardener threw away five of these and she was left with only one bush. This was released ultimately as 'Iced Parfait'.

This was eighteen years ago. Sister Xavier was seeking neither fame nor fortune — she just loves roses.

When I came across the name 'Kookaburra' in a rose catalogue a few years ago, I thought that here was certainly another Australian-bred rose. I went looking for it without delay but all my hopes were dashed when I finally got through to the importer.

"Oh, no," he said. "It's not Australian. It's a Kordes rose. You see it came to us with the impossible name of 'Vogelpark Walstrade'. Now who's going to buy a rose with an outrageous name like that? So I gave it a new one!"

I have to add that it is a particularly beautiful semi-single pink rose and I bought it as a standard this year and am glad of it. What's more, the only place I had room for it was in the Australian garden!

We who live in the south of this great continent and enjoy an almost Mediterranean climate, think of Queensland gardeners as growers of hibiscus and frangipani rather than roses. Yet I met a gardener recently who lives in Brisbane and whose passion is roses. He grows over two hundred of them in his two-hectare garden. So I asked John which were his favourites (a question I always dread myself, as the answer changes almost daily).

He named 'Maria Callas'. I had grown her once in the garden of a tiny cottage I had owned in Castlemaine. She had, with prodigious speed, rushed up to the top of the fence, and her large scented many petalled bright pink flowers had nodded across into my neighbour's garden. It was the beginning of a beautiful gardening friendship. So I had fond memories of 'Maria Callas'. She achieved such popularity in the USA that she was given the name of 'Miss All-American Beauty'. No wonder John found her irresistible.

Predictably 'Iceberg' was the next rose he named. It is known and grown by rose-lovers the world over. It is not surprising that it has been nicknamed "the rose of the century".

"Then," John went on, "there's 'Lady Flo'." I pricked up my ears. I had never even heard of a rose called 'Lady Flo', let alone seen it. It must, I assumed, have been bred in Queensland. Here, perhaps, was a hitherto unknown Queensland rose breeder. There had been some in the early years of this century — John Williams, for example, who had bred 'Penelope'.

'Lady Flo'! The rose would be, without doubt, one of those currently popular tawny-apricots — pumpkin-coloured, in fact. John went on to describe its scent and its fine form. "And the colour?" I asked expectantly, and was conscious of a sense of deep disappointment when he said it was pink. Of the breeder he knew nothing, but referred me to the nurseryman from whom he had bought it.

A lengthy search and many interstate phone calls finally elicited the information that it had been bred in the USA by Jackson and Perkins, brought to Australia, renamed for commercial reasons and released in Queensland only. Disillusioned I cancelled the order I had, in my initial excitement, placed for it.

Of course, I didn't leave the spaces reserved for it empty. Instead I planted the Brundrett Centenary Rose, bred by the Brundrett family nursery to commemorate one hundred years of growing and selling roses for Australian gardeners. A landscaping rose, having 'Sea Foam' in its ancestry, it bears clusters of pink blooms on a low-growing procumbent bush. In the second space reserved for 'Lady Flo' I planted 'Joyce Edmonds'. A lifetime gardener and a tireless worker for Heritage Roses in Australia, Joyce is a very fitting person to have this lovely rose named after her. A sport of 'Scarlet Queen Elizabeth', it bears large many-petalled coppery–pink blooms in great numbers on a sturdy bush. It was put on the market in 1992 by John Nieuwesteeg who grows such robust rose bushes in his outstanding nursery at Coldstream.

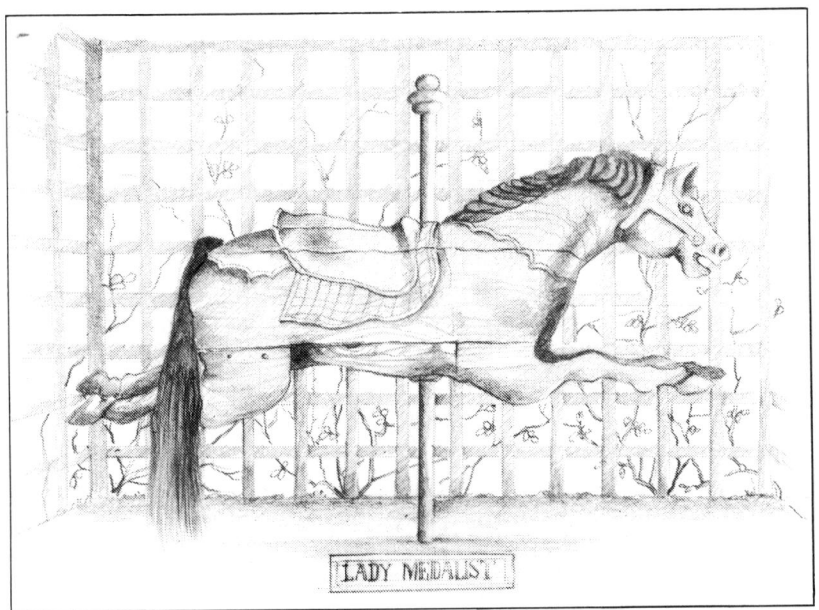

LADY MEDALIST

The Fate of the Top Terrace 24

And so, as their numbers grew, the Australian roses forged their way inexorably on to the top terrace.

First a bed was made along the top of the bank to house the little plants John Nieuwesteeg and I had collected as budwood two years earlier from Hugh Dettman's and Dr Groves's gardens. After all, they had to be planted somewhere. Some of them might turn out in the end to be Alister Clark's.

Others were added to the number. Alister's apricot–pink 'Mab Grimwade' turned up, and George Dawson's vibrant orange 'Olive McKenzie'. So a narrow curved "temporary" bed was made for them. Walter Duncan sent me, from buds given him by David Ruston, two little plants of a mystery rose whose tag read 'Gwen Cunningham'. Now Alister Clark bred 'Gwen Nash' and 'Nora Cunningham', but not 'Gwen Cunningham'. The semi-single pink flower is exquisite. So, of course they, too, must be grown on and looked after in case the mystery can ultimately be solved.

And then even the summerhouse was taken over. 'Lamarque' was doing beautifully there, providing both shade and scent for the seat beneath, that seat from which one can enjoy such a panoramic view down over Gisborne.

We were on a fishing holiday in Tasmania. At least, Bill was fishing. I was poking about enjoying the scenery, the old towns, the Georgian buildings, the antique shops and the gardens.

In the historic and picturesque town of Ross is a colourful character called "The Village Toymaker". I visited him with a friend who wanted to order a rocking horse for a new grandchild. I, having no interest in rocking horses, was wandering rather aimlessly about the workshop when I came upon a bigger, more sturdy, rustic-looking horse, a horse from a merry-go-round, perhaps. I asked about him.

"Oh, he's the Moonee Valley horse," came the answer. "He's not for sale. They wanted three horses for the Committee room and I sent this fellow over as a sample. They decided to go ahead, and this one, being unfinished, was sent back to me."

I had recently been to Moonee Valley — the running of the Alister Clark Stakes is, for me, one of the highlights of the year — and I had noticed the horses in the Committee room: a galloper, a hurdler and a trotter. Indeed, it would be hard not to notice them, their jockeys are painted in such glowing colours.

So now, of course, I felt absolutely compelled to acquire this horse for the Alister Clark garden. I explained to the toymaker our involvement with Alister Clark and hence with Moonee Valley. I described his roses in graphic terms. I felt he must understand how desirable it was to site this horse in their midst.

Finally he acquiesced. The horse was equipped with a new, flowing tail and several coats of marine varnish to protect him against the weather, and shipped over to Melbourne. The summerhouse was the perfect place for him, situated as it is in a central position and right at the top of the steps. So there he stands now, in all his glory, with a placard below saying "Lady Medallist" — the name of Alister's first successful rose, bred in 1912, and one of his most successful racehorses. As yet we have found no trace of the rose.

Of course, the seat had to be moved. It found a new home farther along the bank where it will be shaded ultimately by *Sorbus vilmorinii* with its decorative pink berries and *Sorbus hupehensis*, and where the view over Gisborne is unimpaired.

And then it transpired that we needed a Kitchen Garden. And what more suitable place for it than the highest point of the top terrace? It faces north, basks in sunshine all day, is perfectly drained and sheltered from the cold south winds by a rapidly growing young cypress hedge — planted not by us but by our predecessors, so already well established.

I think, when I started out, I had no clear idea of whether I wanted a vegetable garden or a herb garden. What I ended up with might more properly be described as a potager.

As had been the case with all this garden, the site needed terracing. A lad with a bobcat made five shallow terraces and we constructed rough retaining walls, using the irregularly shaped stones thrown up by the bulldozer when the original terracing was done.

At the eastern end, the highest end, we had a small arbour built and on the long northern side a pergola to serve as entrance from the garden proper. Here, at the very outset, I was presented with an opportunity to plant red climbing roses. This was irresistible and I chose two of those heavenly velvety 'Château de Clos Vougeot'.

Over the arbour, to create an illusion of coolness on hot summer days, I planted two sultana grapes — but intermingled with them is the dramatic scarlet single rose, 'Altissimo', which flowers all summer through. Under the arbour, on a carpet of prostrate thyme (*Thymus serpyllum* 'Albus'), I placed an old red cedar garden seat. I cherished visions of us sitting here, glass in hand, on warm summer evenings, watching the sun go down over Gisborne.

On either side of the arbour I planted, mainly for its scent, which is like no other, but also for its very attractive silver-backed dark green leaves, a Russian olive (*Elaeagnus* × *ebbingei*). For their colour — I find it hard to resist colour — I put, one on each side of the seat, two old terracotta chimneypots planted with the miniature rose, 'Orange Cascade' — not orange at all, but a soft warm gold. And beside each chimneypot I planted a miniature pomegranate (*Punica granatum* var. *nana*), chosen for their scarlet flowers and golden fruit. Nature, with her unerring sense for what is appropriate, but with a complete disregard for symmetry, planted — but on one side only — an Italian lavender (*Lavandula stoechas*).

The whole needed to be defined and contained. So on three sides — the cypress hedge made up the fourth — I planted my hedge of white *Escallonia*, white instead of the more frequently seen bright lipstick-pink. *Escallonia* 'Iveyi' covers itself with pure white flowers in summer, a striking contrast to the small glossy dark green leaves. We cut it at least twice a year to keep it at a height of about .8 metre so that no sun is excluded from the garden.

I planted English gooseberries (for jam) with garlic (for the dramatic effect of the great round flower heads, as well as for its culinary virtues) and nearby a mass of dark red primulas.

After some searching, I managed to find a well-grown espaliered apple and a plum. These I placed in the beds on either side of the long east–west path. Espaliered trees take up so little room and lend a satisfying air of structure to the garden. In front of them, each year, I grow tomatoes (the low-growing kinds that don't need staking) and capsicums. I start them in individual pots in the glasshouse and plant them out on Melbourne Cup Day (between races) when all danger of frost is past. The little beds are bordered with parsley and, in the corners, for use with the tomatoes I plant a couple of clumps of basil.

Climbing beans are planted on tripods made of wooden garden stakes — scarlet runners for the flowers and Purple King, whose dark purple beans turn green when you cook them. And snow peas, which bear so prolifically and grow so quickly.

Under the pergola I put an old wrought-iron gate, painted dark green — not that we needed to shut anything either in or out. But gates are an important part of garden furnishing and one of the quickest ways of creating an atmosphere.

In the very centre of the garden (if a slightly irregular rectangle can be said to have a centre) I set a small statue of Ceres, the Roman goddess of agriculture and of all the fruits of the earth. On her arm she carries a sheaf of wheat and seems to embody all my hopes for this part of the garden.

Then there is a bed of silver beet, the kind with the marvellous red stems, bordered with apricot violas. And a large bed of strawberries. The very many birds who make their home in our garden love these and, while I don't object to their helping themselves within reason, I really felt they transcended the limits last year. So when I saw in a local gallery a wooden black and white bird (I think he is a magpie) with wings that rotate in the wind, I felt it was worth a try. We fixed him to the top of the arbour and as the wings go round they keep up a steady whirring noise; I almost believe it has had the desired effect.

There is a little hedge of Russian tarragon (*Artemisia dracunculus* var. *inodora*) and large clumps of chives. When these reach the stage where they need to be divided, the excess is used in the rose gardens where the soft, mauve flowers complement the pink and red roses and where, perhaps, they also help to keep pests at bay.

As for rosemary, I might almost say, with Sir Thomas More, that

> I let it run all over my garden walls
> Not only because my bees love it
> But because 'tis the herb
> Sacred to remembrance.

It is the old pale blue *Rosmarinus officinalis*, which has been a feature of herb gardens for centuries, that I plant, not the deeper coloured 'Blue Lagoon' which I can never regard as the genuine article. And prostrate rosemary (*R. officinalis* 'Prostratus') trails over the retaining walls. It has even been claimed that there is an affinity between roses and rosemary. I have read that in the gardens which border the Nile and owe their fertility to the rising of that ancient river, the rose gardens are edged with rosemary. And the gardeners declare that rosemary keeps the roses healthy. They even go so far as to say that an ailing rose will be restored to perfect health if a bush of rosemary is planted nearby. Perhaps it is a fairytale. If so, it is a charming one and I mean to put it to the test this year.

I planted another olive tree and round it zucchini vines, and each year I scatter between them seeds of scarlet poppies. Here, too, is a bay tree (*Laurus nobilis*), a little hedge of rue (*Ruta graveolens* 'Jackman's Blue') for its delightful blue–green foliage, and a mass of golden ixia. I have always regretted that in a moment of frugality I refrained from buying a standardised bay and settled for an ordinary one. Perhaps it is not yet too late to remedy this error, for my bay tree is still small, quite small enough to be moved, and Christmas is not far off.

And speaking of Christmas, I found a few years ago, in an "antique shop" in Hobart, an old wooden wheelbarrow. This was no ordinary wheelbarrow, but one with the most pleasing proportions, and it had never known a touch of paint. On an impulse I bought it, having at that time no real plans for it.

The dealer was, as is the nature of dealers, very accommodating, and assured me that there would be no difficulty at all in having it sent back to Melbourne. So when Christmas came and I was asked, as I nearly always am, what I would like, there by the greatest good fortune was a wooden wheelbarrow, just the very thing for the Kitchen Garden. So it stands now, where the path widens at the bottom of the garden at the opposite end to the arbour, and I fill it each spring with big terracotta pots full of scarlet and white geraniums, which bloom all summer through.

25 *A Place of Never-Changing Peace*

I lay in bed this morning and listened to a blackbird sing. Up and up went her notes, telling of her sheer joy at being alive on such a morning in spring.

Perhaps it was the same little bird who is with me each day in the garden, hopping along, her head on one side, watching with her keen black eye for any worm I might turn up. Never more than a foot or two away, she knows no fear.

I think it must be the same little bird who nests each year on a ledge high up in the back of the grotto, that strange little, distinctly sentimental Victorian grotto which had so attracted me on that day five years ago when we had first seen Erinvale. It was built, perhaps, by the woman solicitor who had lived alone at Erinvale some forty years ago, and loved it and left her mark upon it. She it was, I feel sure, who had planted many of the fine trees.

It is just a little grotto, built of stone and overhung with ivy. And right at the back, on a ledge sheltered from wind and storm, is the nest where the blackbird each spring hatches out her young. They were there now. Yesterday I had seen three hungry mouths over the edge of the nest. Perhaps it was their presence which made her sing so joyfully.

Her song was infectious. And presently I found myself out of bed and stealing out quietly so as not to disturb Willy, whose exuberance would have shattered the stillness of the morning.

Through the dew to the little arched bridge over the sunken garden I went — that sunken garden which at one time in the garden's history had been a big lily pond. Its banks were cracked now by the invasive roots of overhanging trees and by the bamboo Bill had hacked out with such perseverance. I could not bear to remove the trees, so we had turned it into a sunken garden with three little ponds in it — mossy stones, a mass of ferns and hellebores, drifts of white honesty (*Lunaria annua*) and primroses, with cyclamen along the edges — and the little boy with his platter looking down on it all. And, overhanging it, the old plum tree whose first buds had been opening yesterday. In a day or two it would be a cloud of white against the blue sky. Another day or two and it would be gone until next spring.

And there, at the foot of the plum tree, where yesterday had been nothing, was a clump of crocus. Overnight their fragile mauve chalices had pushed their way through the damp earth and there they stood now, washed with the dew of the morning.

I was reminded of Elizabeth von Arnim, who relates in *A Solitary Summer* how she had gone out into her garden quite alone at three o'clock one morning and had discovered there a "wonderful, unknown world". She found herself "almost frightened by the awful purity of nature when all the sin and ugliness is shut up and asleep, and there is nothing but the beauty left".

From across the road came the whinny of a mare calling her foal. And there they stood under the oak trees — three mares and three foals — waiting patiently for the bread we sometimes bring them.

My mind went to Barnsley House and a visit I had paid there in the early English summer. I had gone not knowing quite what I hoped to find. Certainly I had not realised that Barnsley House is an integral part of the village of Barnsley, a tiny village with little stone cottages, mostly dating from the seventeenth century. They are built only a few feet back from the winding road, each with its carefully tended front garden, many of them with *Clematis montana* 'Rubens' in full flower reaching right up to the second storey windows. A squat towered church dominates the village, and everywhere one comes upon those wonderful walls made of Cotswold stone.

We have all seen pictures of the famous laburnum walk, and of the gracious seventeenth century house. I knew of Mrs Verey's interest in garden history and was prepared for the knot garden and the intricate little herb garden with its diamond shaped beds, and for the vegetable garden designed like a French potager with box edges, espaliered apple trees and standardised English gooseberries.

But I had seen no mention of what was, to me, one of the most significant features of the garden. At the end of the laburnum walk is a sundial. It is present in all the photographs of course, but its significance cannot be appreciated unless one reads the inscription.

Placed there in 1973 by Rosemary Verey and designed by Simon Verity, it was a present from Mrs Verey to her husband, David Verey, on his sixtieth birthday. The lines inscribed on it speak volumes about this garden, such a personal creation. Written by John Evelyn in 1660 it reads:

> As no man be very
> miserable that is
> master of a Garden
> here; so will
> no man ever be
> happy who is not
> sure of a garden
> hereafter . . . where
> the first Adam fell
> the second rose.

It was a Sunday afternoon when I visited Barnsley House, a still sunny day which had brought forth a large number of garden visitors. The nursery was doing a brisk trade in plants from the garden, topiary and Mrs Verey's books. I wondered how she felt about the chatter and the clatter, the loud laughter, the high heels, the superficial comments. And yet, this is all part of having a garden, for gardening is, of all occupations, the most solitary and the most companionable. There are times when a garden must be private and times when it must be shared.

Gardening has no age limits — I thought of my little three-year-old grand-daughter planting her first nasturtium seeds in the back garden, and of my friend, Eve Murray, ninety-three this year and still gardening from a wheel-chair. There are no barriers in a garden — no social, no racial, no intellectual barriers. Instead, amongst real gardeners (as distinct from those who dabble in it), there is an infectious camaraderie, a warmth, a generosity, an instant rapport.

I had gone back to Barnsley House (with permission) at six o'clock the following morning. I walked up the narrow country lane which runs between the formal garden and the potager, a lane with a high stone wall on one side and a hedge on the other, and ending in the picturesque old farm buildings which form the background to the potager and proclaim the relationship of the garden to the surrounding countryside.

The sun was just coming up, little black-faced lambs were calling for their mothers in the field beyond, and doves were cooing unceasingly from the huge chestnut trees which line the drive. The garden was full of pink and white tulips — planted in mixed borders and in stone tubs and urns. The magnolia in front of the Doric temple was still in flower. The first of the paeonies were out. The laburnum walk was in bud as were the roses espaliered on the high stone walls — the whole garden was full of promise and a sense of expectation.

All around me was that atmosphere of harmony and serenity which charac-terises a great garden. A wealth of historical knowledge lies behind the making of this garden — the garden of an architect and a plantswoman working together to create something of rare beauty.

With my mind still running on Barnsley House and the black-faced lambs, I gave the mares their bread, the foals shying away on their long gangling legs as Willy released now by Bill came bounding across to say good morning. But not even Willy could shatter the peace of this spring morning.

I thought of another of that great community of gardeners, who have worked to create a thing of beauty and have written to share their joy in it. I thought of Lady Vyvyan working over long years in her garden in the south of England and leaving for us her *Letters from a Cornish Garden* in which she wrote:

"Whenever you see a tuft of moss in a crevice, or a tree habitually looking up to the sky, or a daffodil, nodding and erect while it stands as herald to the spring, you will know that, so long as the moss, the flower and the tree are with us, there is hope for mankind in this troubled world."

Appendixes

A. Roses for Various Purposes

The following lists are not intended to be exhaustive. They include simply the roses I have found most successful and most pleasing under our conditions.

Roses for Hedges

'Irish Rich Marbled' — Small pale pink blooms, ferny foliage, tiny black hips. Spring only. One of the Scotch Burnet roses.

'Pink Grootendorst' ('The Carnation Rose') — Mid-pink with frilled petals, no hips. Recurrent. A Rugosa hybrid.

Rosa rugosa alba — Single white blooms, disease-free foliage, splendid hips. Recurrent.

R. rugosa 'Scabrosa' — Single magenta with creamy stamens, fragrant, splendid hips. Recurrent.

'Sarah van Fleet' — Double pink blooms, disease-free foliage. Constantly in flower. Another Rugosa hybrid.

'Stanwell Perpetual' — Softest pink, scented blooms, grey-green, ferny foliage. Very recurrent.

Roses as Edges to a Bed

'Ellen Poulsen' — Small cherry-coloured double blooms. Recurrent.

'The Fairy' — Small pale pink, double blooms in clusters. Recurrent.

'Green Ice' — Tiny double white blooms, tinged green. Recurrent.

'Nozomi' — Tiny pale pink, single blooms, tiny red hips. Somewhat recurrent.

Roses as Shrubs in a Border

R. × alba 'Semi-plena' — Milk-white blooms, grey-green foliage, hips. Spring.

'Belle Story' — Soft pink, open blooms with pronounced golden stamens, fragrant. Very recurrent. A David Austin rose.

'Buff Beauty' — Clusters of soft apricot-gold roses on a spreading bush. Recurrent.

R. centifolia variegata ('Village Maid') — Palest pink blooms, striped deeper, fragrant. Spring.

'Charles de Mills' — Grand dark red, flat, quartered, strongly scented blooms. Spring.

'Complicata' — Large bright pink, single blooms on a vigorous shrub. Spring.

'Cymbeline' — Palest pink with a touch of grey. Double, fragrant blooms borne constantly through summer. A David Austin rose.

'Fantin-Latour' — Soft pink, double, deliciously fragrant blooms. Spring.

'Frühlingsgold' (Spring Gold) — Softest, creamy-yellow nearly single blooms paling to cream. Spring.

'Frühlingsmorgen' (Spring Morning) — Clear pink single blooms, paling to cream in the centre, maroon stamens. Some repeat bloom.

R. glauca — Small, single bright lilac-pink blooms, purplish stems, grey-blue foliage, hips. Spring.

'Heidesommer' (Summer on the Heath) — Small creamy-white blooms in clusters, scent of gardenias. Recurrent.

'Heritage' — Softest pink, cup-shaped blooms, richly fragrant. Produced throughout the summer. A David Austin rose.

'Hero' — Rich apricot-pink blooms, wonderfully fragrant. Produced all summer on a tall shrub. A David Austin rose.

'Ispahan' — Semi-double, light pink, fragrant. Blooms over a long period in spring.

'Königin von Dänemarck' ('Queen of Denmark') — Soft pink, double, sweetly fragrant blooms. Spring.

'Madame Hardy' — Medium sized, pure white, quartered blooms with a green 'eye'. Spring.

'Maigold' — Apricot-gold, semi-single, fragrant flowers on a large shrub-climber. Spectacular in spring. Some repeat flowering.

'Penelope' (Hybrid Musk, 1924) — Creamy-pink, semi-double, scented blooms. Good repeat flowering.

'Rosa Mundi' — Pink and white striped blooms. Spring.

'Shropshire Lass' — Palest pink, large, single, fragrant blooms with marked stamens. Spring. A David Austin rose.

R. sweginzowii — Small, single bright pink flowers, blue-green foliage, brilliant flagon-shaped hips. Spring.

'Vanity' — Bright lipstick-pink single blooms on a sprawling shrub. Throughout summer.

R. willmottiae — Grey-green, ferny foliage, small lilac-pink flowers on a tall, arching shrub. Spring.

Climbing Roses for Pergolas, Arches, etc.

'Albéric Barbier' — Creamy white, double, beautifully scented blooms. Spring. Very vigorous.

'Altissimo' — Single striking scarlet blooms. Throughout summer.

'Château de Clos Vougeot' — Deepest red, strongly scented. Recurrent.

'Desprez à fleur jaune' — Creamy yellow, strongly scented, few thorns. Continuously in flower.

'Devoniensis' ('The Magnolia Rose') — Parchment colour, strongly scented. Continuously in flower. One of the very best.

'Gloire de Dijon' — Buff yellow, strongly scented. Recurrent.

'Lady Hillingdon' — Apricot-gold, strongly scented. Recurrent.

R. laevigata ('The Cherokee Rose') — White single blooms, glossy dark green foliage, very thorny. Spring only.

'Lamarque' — Creamy-white, lemon-scented blooms, beautiful foliage, vigorous. Very recurrent. (See also Roses to Ramble through Trees.)

'Madame Alfred Carrière' — White, flushed pink, wonderfully scented. Very recurrent.

'Madame Grégoire Staechelin' — Clear pink, spectacular in spring (only), good hips.

'Meg' — Salmon-pink, single. Spring only.

'Mermaid' — Pale yellow, single, vigorous, very thorny. Recurrent.

'New Dawn' — Pale pink, fragrant, very floriferous. Continuously in flower.

'Sea Foam' — Small white double blooms in clusters, versatile. Constantly in flower.

'Sombreuil' — Creamy white, quartered, gloriously scented. Very recurrent. One of the very best.

'Souvenir de Madame Léonie Viennot' — Coppery-pink, well scented. Recurrent.

'Zéphirine Drouhin' — Very bright pink, scented, virtually thornless. Continuous flowering.

Vigorous Rambling Roses for Windbreaks, over Tanks, Sheds, etc.

'Albertine' — Salmon-pink, deliciously scented. Early summer.

R. banksiae banksiae — Tiny white, sweetly scented blooms. Early spring.

R. banksiae lutea — Masses of tiny butter-yellow blooms. Early spring.

'The Edna Walling Rose' — Clusters of small blooms (single), palest pink fading to greenish-white. Early summer.

'Félicité et Perpétue' — Tiny pale pink buds opening white in masses. Early summer.

'Francis E. Lester' — White single blooms splashed with pink, strongly scented, bright red hips. Early summer.

'Sanders' White' — Small double white blooms in clusters, attractive dark green foliage. Early summer.

'Veilchenblau' — Deep purple semi-double blooms streaked white and borne in large clusters. Early summer.

Roses to Ramble through Trees

'Bloomfield Courage' — Masses of dark red small single blooms. Early summer.

R. brunonii (The Himalayan Musk Rose) — Small single white blooms in clusters, grey-green foliage. Spring.

'Lamarque' — Creamy-white double blooms, lemon-scented. Recurrent. (See also Climbing Roses.)

'Rambling Rector' — Small, semi-double, creamy-white flowers with golden stamens, fragrant. Spring.

'Tea Rambler' — Small soft pink, fragrant, double flowers. Spring.

'Wedding Day' — Small single white blooms with yellow stamens in large trusses. Early summer.

Roses as Ground Cover

R. bracteata — Large single white, scented blooms with an abundance of golden stamens, glossy dark green foliage, very vigorous, roots as it goes. Flowers throughout summer.

'Heidekönigin' (Queen of the Heath) — Apricot-pink, fragrant, double blooms, good foliage. Throughout summer.

'Max Graf' — Bright pink single blooms. Spring. A Rugosa hybrid.

'Repandia' — Small single pale pink blooms, small hips, vigorous. Slightly recurrent.

'Snow Carpet' — Tiny, double white blooms. Recurrent.

Alister Clark's Australian-bred Roses

'Borderer' — Good for edging a bed. Small, double, scented salmon-pink blooms throughout the season.

'Cherub' — A vigorous rambling rose. Small pale pink blooms in huge clusters. Spring.

'Cicely Lascelles' — Climber. Clear pink, semi-double blooms, scented. Very recurrent.

'Daydream' — Shrub-climber. Softest pink, single blooms. Recurrent.

'Doris Downes' — Climber. Large, semi-double clear pink blooms. Spring.

'Editor Stewart' — Shrub rose. Clearest bright red blooms with wavy petals. Constantly in flower.

'Gwen Nash' — Climber. Semi-single soft apricot-pink blooms with golden stamens. Recurrent.

'Jessie Clark' — Climber. Large soft pink, single blooms. Magnificent in spring.

'Kitty Kininmonth' — Climber. Huge, bright pink double blooms in spring. Some repeat flowering.

'Lorraine Lee' — Available as bush or climber. Apricot-pink, deliciously scented blooms. Almost always in flower.

'Milkmaid' — A vigorous rambling rose. Masses of double creamy-white scented flowers. Early summer.

'Mrs Fred Danks' — A large bush. Mauve-pink, large, semi-double blooms. Very recurrent.

'Squatter's Dream' — Small single gold blooms in clusters. Very recurrent.

'Suitor' — Good for edging a bed. Tiny, rich pink, double blooms in big trusses. Hardly ever out of flower.

'Sunlit' — Hybrid Tea rose. Soft, apricot-pink, scented blooms. Very recurrent.

B. Perennials and Self Seeding Annuals for the Rose Garden

As with the lists of Roses for Special Purposes, these lists are in no way intended to be exhaustive. They are quite simply the plants which have given me the most satisfaction when planted in rose gardens.

Plants are listed by their botanical names, as some have no common names. When several species or hybrids are equally suitable, the genus name only is given. Common names have been added to the botanical names when they are very well known or when the common name is different from the name of the genus.

Tall
Althaea rosea (hollyhock)
Physostegia virginiana 'Summer Snow'
Salvia argentea
Salvia uliginosa (bog sage)
Tanacetum ptarmiciflorum syn. *Chrysanthemum ptarmiciflorum*

Medium Height
Alyssum saxatile
Anemone hupehensis (Japanese anemone)
Anthemis tinctoria 'E. C. Buxton'
Aquilegia spp. and hybrids
Borago officinalis (borage)
Campanula latiloba
Campanula persicifolia
Chrysanthemum parthenium now called *Tanacetum parthenium* (feverfew)
Eschscholzia hybrids (Californian poppy)
Euphorbia polychroma syn. *E. epithymoides*
Geranium pratense
Geum 'Mrs Bradshaw'
Geum rivale 'Leonard'
Helleborus spp.
Hemerocallis spp. and hybrids (day-lily)
Lavandula spp. (lavender)
Lychnis coronaria 'Alba' (white lychnis)
Nigella damascena (love-in-the-mist)
Paeonia spp.
Penstemon 'Evelyn'
Penstemon 'White Swan'
Polemonium caeruleum
Rosmarinus officinalis (rosemary)
Ruta graveolens (rue)
Salvia sclarea (clary sage)
Salvia transcaucasica (white sage)

Low Growing
Ajuga reptans 'Variegata'
Alchemilla mollis
Aquilegia bertolinii
Campanula portenschlagiana
Campanula poscharskyana
Dianthus 'Beatrix'
Dianthus 'Mrs Sinkins'
Geranium himalayense
Geranium sanguineum var. *striatum*
Iberis sempervirens (candytuft)
Lobularia maritima (alyssum; sweet Alice)
Nepeta × *faassenii* (catmint)
Penstemon heterophyllus 'Blue Gem'
Primula auricula (auricula)
Primula vulgaris (English primrose)
Prunella grandiflora 'Pink Loveliness'
Prunella grandiflora 'White Loveliness'
Pulmonaria angustifolia
Pulmonaria officinalis
Pulmonaria 'Sissinghurst White'
Rosmarinus officinalis 'Prostratus' (prostrate rosemary)
Satureia montana (winter savory)
Stachys byzantina syn. *S. lanata* (lamb's ears)
Tanacetum haradjanii syn. *Chrysanthemum haradjanii*
Thymus 'Albus' (white thyme)
Thymus 'Coccineus'
Thymus 'Lars Hall'
Thymus pseudolanuginosus (woolly thyme)
Veronica gentianoides
Veronica teucrium
Viola spp. and hybrids, in single colours

Iris are particularly suited to growing with roses. I have listed the ones we also grew separately.
Iris gracilipes
Iris graminea (plum tart iris)
Iris innominata
Iris kaempferi now called *I. ensata* (Japanese water iris)
Iris pallida
Iris pumila
Iris setosa nana
iris, tall bearded
Iris tingitana
Iris unguicularis syn. *I. stylosa*
Iris xyphium

C. Alister Clark Roses

Since the publication of *A Hillside of Roses* interest in Alister Clark's roses has grown. Many gardeners have joined in the search and many have come forward with roses which are believed to be of his breeding. But evidence is minimal. Descriptions are scanty and he left so few records that any new discoveries must be treated with caution.

It is tempting to believe for instance that the red rose planted in the garden at Craiglee by Jessie Clark, Alister's niece, must be the same red rose he named for his wife Edith Clark.

But we have no real justification for this assumption. Jessie planted many roses at Craiglee. Most of them have not survived. Certainly this rather undistinguished little red rose does not conflict with the description we have of 'Edith Clark' but there are many other roses which would fit it just as well.

The following appendix contains two lists of roses. The first is a list of those Alister Clark roses which have been identified with as great a certainty as we can hope for. Thanks are due to many members of the families who had roses named for them and to Mrs Ruth Rundle, the present owner of Glenara.

The second list describes roses which are thought to be Alister Clark roses but for which adequate evidence is still lacking.

Many of the roses in the first list are now available commercially (thanks to John Nieuwesteeg) and are being widely grown.

Many of the slides are my own. One or two were taken by photographers from *Your Garden* and some by Garry Aitchison. For the use of these I am very grateful.

List I

'Amy Johnson' — Climbing H. T. 1931. 'Souvenir de Gustav Prat' × ?. Large, cupped, fragrant, pink blooms. Vigorous.

'Australia Felix' — H. T. 1931. 'Jersey Beauty' × 'La France'. Small, semi-double, cupped, fragrant flowers of silvery pink, on a low bush. Very recurrent. Plant came to us (without a name) from the Alstons and Eve Murray. Fits the description of 'Australia Felix' and distinctive shape of petals corresponds with old photographs. 'Sweet Seventeen' and 'Fancy Free' seem to be similar, and until our plant was identified I called it 'Alister Clark's Pink Floribunda'!

'Baxter Beauty' — Sport of 'Lorraine Lee' and not registered by Alister himself. Described by T. A. Stewart as follows: "originated at Baxter, Victoria. The colours of this rose are most difficult to describe. There are a number of shades, varying from a light yellow to sulphur, overlaid on the outside of the petals with splashes of light salmon pink . . . It has all the good qualities of 'Lorraine Lee' in growth and winter flowering propensities."

'Black Boy' — Climbing H. T. 1919. 'Bardou Job' × 'Etoile de France'. One of his first great successes. Large, semi-double, fragrant, dark red blooms. One of the few which never went out of commerce.

'Borderer' — Polyantha. 1918. 'Jersey Beauty' seedling. Semi-double to double salmon-pink. Very low-growing. Excellent border rose. Found at Delatite and at Wombat Park, Daylesford.

'Cherub' — Very vigorous rambler. 1923. 'Claire Jacquier' seedling. Small, semi-double, cupped, pink blooms in big clusters. Spring only.

'Cicely Lascelles' — Climbing H. T. 1937. 'Frau Oberhofgärtner Singer' × 'Scorcher' (one of Clark's). Large, semi-double, open, pink blooms of great beauty borne abundantly from spring to autumn. Our plant came from Cicely Lascelles herself. This rose has been planted now at Royal Melbourne Golf Club as she was a great golfer.

'Countess of Stradbroke' — Climbing H. T. 1928. 'Walter Clark' × unnamed variety. Dark, glowing crimson, double blooms highly scented and very recurrent. Described in American *Rose Annual* of 1939 as "probably the finest climbing rose in the world".

'Courier' — 1930. Probably *R. gigantea* × 'A. Joseph'. Blooms palest pink on white ground borne in clusters on a vigorous climbing plant, spring. Still at Glenara.

'Daydream' — Climber or pillar rose. 1925. Probably 'Souvenir de Gustav Prat' × 'Rosy Morn' or 'Gwen Nash' (both Clark roses). Pale pink, single blooms with golden stamens, borne recurrently. Clark likened it to a waterlily. Still growing at Glenara. An outstanding climbing rose.

'Diana Allen' — H. T. 1939. 'Mrs Aaron Ward' × unknown. Smallish double, mid-pink flowers with distinctive pointed petals. Has been likened to a carnation. Identified by David Ruston.

'Dividend' — H. T. 1931. 'Franz Deegen' × unknown. Double, globular, golden yellow blooms, lightly scented. Found through Alice Jeffries.

'Doris Downes' — Climbing H. T. 1932. Very large, semi-double, cupped, fragrant, extremely beautiful blooms borne profusely but not recurrently. Dame Elisabeth Murdoch has a fine specimen at Cruden Farm.

'Editor Stewart' — H. T. 1939. Allen Brundrett described it in the 1939 *Rose Annual* as: "a splendid, free-flowering, red pillar rose with large wavy petals and beautiful young red foliage. Semi-double, but when open it is immense and the wave in the petals is unique . . . honours the name of our editor to whom we owe so much."

'Fairlie Rede' — H. T. 1937. 'Mrs E. Willis' × unknown seedling. Large, full, fragrant, pale pink flowers. A classic shaped rose. Fairlie Rede lived on the Peninsula outside Melbourne and grew flowers commercially. 'Mrs Willis' is a New Zealand bred rose.

'Flying Colours' — 1922. *R. gigantea* hybrid. Large, single, not very fragrant, pinkish-red flowers similar to 'Nancy Hayward' but softer in colour. Very vigorous, non-recurrent climber.

'Gladsome' — Very vigorous rambler found at the Alstons' home at Oaklands Junction. Given to the Alstons by Clark. Large clusters of mid-pink, small blooms in spring.

'Glenara' — Large bush or pillar rose. Released in 1951 after Clark's death and named after his home. Large, semi-double, deep rosy-pink blooms. Constantly in flower. Still in Glenara and at the Alstons' home.

'Golden Vision' — 1922. *R. gigantea* × 'Maréchal Niel'. Semi-double, fragrant blooms of Maréchal Niel yellow fading to nearly white. Still at Glenara.

'Gwen Nash' — Climbing H. T. 1920. 'Rosy Morn' × ?. Exquisite, large, semi-single, cupped fragrant blooms of a soft, glowing pink with prominent golden stamens. Alister called it "the most beautiful thing in decorative pinks I can hope to produce".

'Harbinger' — Very vigorous climber. 1923. *R. gigantea* hybrid. Large, single, soft pink flowers. Growing at the Chomley's property in the Western District of Victoria.

'Jessie Clark' — 1915. Probably *R. gigantea* × 'Madame Martignier'. His first great success. Very large, single roses of clear pink borne very abundantly on a vigorous climber. Early spring.

'Kitty Kininmonth' — Very vigorous climber. 1922. *R. gigantea* × unnamed seedling. Very large, semi-double, slightly fragrant flowers of rich, glowing pink with golden stamens. Sometimes recurrent. Came to us from the Kininmonths of Mount Hesse.

'Lady Huntingfield' — H. T. 1937. 'Busybody' (Clark rose) × ?. Large, double, fragrant, rich golden-yellow flowers. Vigorous, bushy plant, very recurrent.

'Lorraine Lee' — H. T. 1924. 'Jessie Clark' × 'Captain Millet', so second generation hybrid *R. gigantea*. Double, open, very fragrant rosy-apricot flowers almost perpetually. His best-known rose. Available as bush or climber.

'Mab Grimwade' — H. T. 1937. 'Souvenir de Gustav Prat' × ?. Double, chrome yellow, shaded apricot. Fragrant.

'Margaret Turnbull' — Climbing H. T. 1931. Large, double, slightly fragrant, mid-pink, very recurrent. Our plant came from the Turnbull family.

'Marjory Palmer' — Polyantha. 1936. 'Jersey Beauty' × ?. Double, very fragrant, rich pink flowers in clusters on a short, bushy plant. Very recurrent. From Eve Murray and Wombat Park.

'Mary Guthrie' — 1929. 'Jersey Beauty' × 'Scorcher' (one of Clark's). Small, single, open, fragrant, vibrant lipstick-pink flowers in clusters on a low-growing bush. Our plant confirmed by Mary Guthrie herself.

'Milkmaid' — 1925. 'Crépuscule' × unnamed variety. Medium-sized, semi-double, open, creamy flowers in clusters on a very vigorous rambler. Still growing at Glenara.

'Mrs Albert Nash' — H. T. 1929. Very dark red, one of the darkest in the garden. Very recurrent, fragrant. Our budwood came from the Nash family.

'Mrs Fred Danks' — H. T. 1951. Parentage unknown. Very large, semi-double, fragrant flowers of an unusual pink tinged with violet. Tall, upright bush, very abundant bloom. Our plants from Tid Alston and Eve Murray.

'Mrs Harold Alston' — Climbing H. T. 1940. Semi-double clear pink pillar rose. Recurrent. Our plant came from her niece, Tid Alston.

'Mrs Harold Brookes' — H. T. 1931. 'Frau Oberhofgärtner Singer' × 'Firebrand'. Large, double, fragrant, very bright red flowers borne recurrently. Our plant found at her old home and identified by her son John Brookes and his sister.

'Mrs Maud Alston' — Also known as 'Mrs Alston's Rose', was growing in the Alston's garden (also in Marjory Palmer's garden at Terang). Perhaps it is one he gave the Alstons to "try out" as it is nowhere listed as having been officially released. It is a delightful, cherry-coloured small rose, borne in huge clusters and hardly ever out of flower — a valuable addition to the rose garden. It is available commercially.

'Mrs Richard Turnbull' — Extremely vigorous climber. *R. gigantea* hybrid. Flowers are single, white with golden stamens. Scent is superb. Flowers prolifically in early spring. Our plant came from the Turnbull home and from the Alstons.

'Nancy Hayward' — Very vigorous climber. 1937. 'Jessie Clark' × ?, so second generation from *R. gigantea*. Large, single, vivid lipstick-pink flowers. Almost perpetually in flower. Confirmed by Nancy Hayward herself.

'Peggy Bell' — H. T. 1929. Mid to salmon pink. Free flowering. Compared by *Modern Roses* to 'Betty Uprichard'. Our plant is from Dettman's garden where it was known to be growing.

'Princeps' — 1942. Very large, fragrant, red pillar or climbing rose. Our plant from Alston's garden.

'Restless' — Tall bush. H. T. No date of release. Very dark velvety red with magnificent scent. Very recurrent. Our plant from Eve Murray.

'Ringlet' — Climbing. H. T. 1922. 'Ernest Morel' × 'Betty Berkeley'. Medium-sized single pink flowers with white centres borne in clusters. Constantly in flower. We treat it as a large shrub. From Eve Murray.

'Scorcher' — Climbing. H. T. 1922. 'Madame Abel Chatenay' × unnamed seedling. "Large, semi-double, open, slightly fragrant, brilliant scarlet-crimson. Vigorous climber to 10 ft. Non-recurrent." (*Modern Roses*) Notes kept by Alister's gardener, Sharp, suggest that the unnamed parent was *R. moyesii*. The plant we have came from a winery at Coldstream and an old garden at Alexandra. It corresponds to a coloured photograph in *Roses of the World in Colour* (1937) by Horace McFarland, long-time editor of the American *Rose Annual*.

'Sheila Bellair' — H. T. 1937. 'Miss Mocatta' × ?. Large, semi-double, open, mid- to salmon-pink flowers with golden stamens. Our plant from her own garden.

'Squatter's Dream' — 1923. A seedling from a *R. gigantea* seedling. Semi-single, open blooms from saffron-yellow to apricot on a bushy, thornless plant. Constantly in flower.

'Suitor' — No date of release. Probably 1940s and possibly never officially released. Small bright pink flowers which fade to nearly white on a very low-growing bush. In flower from early spring to onset of winter. Our plant from Alston's garden.

'Sunlit' — H. T. 1937. Small, double, pale apricot-pink flowers on a compact bush. Very highly acclaimed in America at time of release.

'Sunny South' — H. T. 1918. 'Gustav Grünerwald' × 'Betty Berkeley'. Large, semi-single, fragrant blooms, pale pink, flushed carmine on a very tall bush. Very profuse bloom, recurrently. Widely used for hedges. Alister's favourite of all the roses he grew.

'Tonner's Fancy' — 1928. *R. gigantea* seedling × unnamed variety. Large double, exceptionally beautiful flowers, white tinged pink in the bud. Foliage outstanding. Flowers briefly in early spring. Our plant from Glenara where it is still growing.

'Zara Hore-Ruthven' — H. T. 1932. 'Madame Abel Chatenay' × 'Scorcher' (one of Clark's). Large, double, fragrant, rich pink flowers, borne recurrently.

List II

'Agnes Barclay' — A fragrant Hybrid Tea released in 1927 and described in *Modern Roses* as "yellow and reddish salmon". Alister's records suggest that it is a cross between 'Comtesse Dusy' and 'Crépuscule' and a coloured advertisement dated 1927 shows a semi-double soft salmon-pink rose with marked yellow stamens.

'Cracker' — This little rose was found in a garden previously owned by Marjory Palmer who had spent a good deal of her life at Dalvuii. She planted a rose garden at Terang which still has a number of Alister's roses in it, including 'Marjory Palmer', 'Mrs Maud Alston' and 'Sunny South'. This rose is planted as a hedge at the back of the rose garden. It fits the description of 'Cracker', which was advertised as a hedge rose, but proof is needed.

'Doris Osborne' — H. T. 1937. 'Madame Abel Chatenay' × ?. Semi-double, open, ruby-cerise flowers, free bloom. A rose fitting this description was found in Hugh Dettman's garden at Kyneton. He regularly "tried out" roses for Alister. There is no proof.

'Edith Clark' — 1928. 'Madame Abel Chatenay' × unknown seedling. A red rose fitting the inadequate description of 'Edith Clark' (named after Alister's wife) came to us from Craiglee, near Bulla. It was planted by Jessie Clark (Alister's niece), when she went to live there after her marriage to William Johnston. There is no real proof of identity.

'Emily Rhodes' — A climbing Hydrid Tea bred from 'Golden Ophelia' and 'Zéphirine Drouhin' and described as "large, double, cupped, fragrant pink with abundant bloom".

'Herbert Brunning' — A brilliant red Hybrid Tea released in 1940 and named in honour of a well-known rosarian. This rose came to me from Brunning's grand-children Judy Clark and Ken Dean who have had it growing in Sydney since their grandfather's day. As it came from his family it can be assumed that the name is correct but we cannot verify our plant until it flowers.

'Janet Morrison' — Climbing H. T. 1936. 'Black Boy' × unknown seedling. Large, semi-double, open, fragrant, light red flowers with intermittent bloom. We have a rose which fits this rather sketchy description but I know of no proof.

'Lady Somers' — A Hybrid Tea released in 1930, a cross between 'Comte de Rochemur' and Alister Clark's own 'Scorcher'. It is a clear pink, open and slightly fragrant.

'Mrs Hugh Dettman' — A climbing Hybrid Tea released in 1930 and described in *Modern Roses* as "bright apricot yellow". Hugh Dettman lived in Kyneton and the rose released under this name was found in his now-neglected garden. Its colour — a soft buff — does not conform to the description in *Modern Roses* so, lacking further evidence, it must be treated with reserve.

'Mrs Norman Watson' — A climbing Hybrid Tea released in 1930, a cross between 'Radiance' and Alister's 'Gwen Nash'. It is a vigorous pillar rose described in *Modern Roses* as "deep cherry pink". The rose released under this name bears all the marks of an Alister Clark rose but Mrs Watson's family have some doubts.

'Mrs W. R. Groves' — A deep red Hybrid Tea released in 1941. Dr Groves was a medical practitioner in Kyneton and the rose released under this name was found growing at the front door of the house where he lived. The property is no longer in the Groves's hands and the description in *Modern Roses*, "deep red, foliage good" is hardly sufficient to allow us to identify it with any certainty. It may be the rose named after Dr Groves's wife, but it equally well may not be.

'Nancy Wilson' — H. T. 1940. "Silvery pink blooms with a darker shade on the inside of the petals. Seedling from 'Antoine Rivoire'" is the description in Hazelwood's catalogue. The rose came to me with this name attached, but I know of no proof.

'Nora Cunningham' — A climbing Hybrid Tea released in 1920, a seedling from 'Gustav Grünerwald'. *Modern Roses* describes it as 'large, semi-double, cupped fragrant flesh pink, centre paler, foliage wrinkled, light. Vigorous climber free bloom, sometimes recurrent." A more detailed description than we usually get. This may well be the right rose.

'Queen of Hearts' — A climbing Hybrid Tea released in 1920, a cross between 'Gustav Grünerwald' and Alister's 'Rosy Morn'. *Modern Roses* gives the following description: "Bud globular, flower large, double, cupped, fragrant rich pink, foliage dark. Very vigorous climber, free recurrent bloom." The plant I have in my garden conforms to this description. It is the vivid pink Alister seems to have been so fond of.

'Traverser' — Vigorous climber. 1928. *Modern Roses* describes it as "well-shaped, yellow and cream" and the 1939 *Rose Annual* as "extra strong climber; beautiful pale yellow nearly double flowers cover the plant in spring." Such a rose grows still at Glenara up a huge lilac bush and into the trees above. Our plant came from there, but we have no positive proof of identity.

D. *Short List of Nurseries who Supply Old Roses*

Balyarta Fragrant Gardens, Highfields, Queensland 4352

Brundretts, Narre Warren, Victoria 3805

Bungendore Garden Centre, Bungendore, NSW 2621

Cloyne's Nursery, Cooma, NSW 2630

Colonial Cottage Nursery, Dural, NSW 2158

Country Farm Perennials, Nayook, Victoria 3821

Hilltop Nursery, Guildford, Victoria 3451

Liberty Gardens, Orange, NSW 2800

Mistydown, Balmoral, Victoria 3407

Nieuwesteeg's Rose Nursery, Coldstream, Victoria 3770

Ring of Roses, Maling Road, Canterbury, Victoria 3126

Ross Roses, Willunga, South Australia 5172

Silkie Gardens, Kilmore, Victoria 3764

Stoneacres Farm, Drysdale, Victoria 3222

Swane's Nursery, Dural, NSW 2158

The Perfumed Garden, Mt Eliza, Victoria 3930 (David Austin Roses)

The Rose Arbour, Malvern, Victoria 3144

The Rose Garden, Nairne, South Australia 5252

The Rose Garden, Watervale, South Australia 5452

Treloar's, Portland, Victoria 3305

E. *Some Rose Societies*

Heritage Roses Australia Inc

The National Rose Society of Australia

The Queensland Rose Society Inc.

The Rose Society of NSW Inc.

The Rose Society of South Australia Inc.

The Rose Society of Tasmania Inc.

The Rose Society of Victoria Inc.

The Rose Society of Western Australia Inc.

Heritage Roses New Zealand

Heritage Rose Foundation, USA

Royal National Rose Society, UK

Bibliography

Thomas, Graham Stuart (1955) *The Old Shrub Roses*, Phoenix House, London.
—— (1962) *Shrub Roses of Today*, Phoenix House, London.
—— (1965) *Climbing Roses Old and New*, Phoenix House, London.
—— *The Graham Stuart Thomas Rose Book* (1994) John Murray, London. (Revised and enlarged single volume edition of the above three books.)
—— (1991) *The Art of Gardening With Roses*, Henry Holt & Co, New York.

Austin, David, (1992) *Old Roses and English Roses*, Antique Collector Club, Woodbridge, Suffolk.
Beales, Peter (1987) *Classic Roses*, Collins Harvill, London.
—— (1988) *Twentieth Century Roses*, Collins Harvill, London.
Brown, Jane (1990) Sissinghurst, Portrait of a Garden, Weidenfeld & Nicolson, London.
Bunyard, Edward (1978) *Old Garden Roses*, Earle M. Coleman, New York. (Facsimile of 1st edition, 1936.)
Darlington, *Bishop* H.R. (1911) *Roses*, T.C & T.E.C. Jack, Edinburgh.
Dickerson, Brent C. (1992) *The Old Rose Advisor*, Timber Press, Portland, Oregon.
Edwards, Gordon (1975) *Wild and Old Garden Roses*, Readers' Union (David & Charles), Newton Abbott, U.K.

Foster-Melliar, *Rev.* A. (1910) *The Book of the Rose*, Macmillan, London.
Garnett, T.R.(1990) *Man of Roses*, Kangaroo Press, Kenthurst, N.S.W.
Gibson, Michael (1981) *Shrub Roses, Climbers and Ramblers*, Collins, London.
Griffiths, Trevor (1983) *My World of Old Roses*, Vol. I, Whitcoulls, Christchurch, N.Z.
—— (1986) *My World of Old Roses*, Vol. II, Thomas Nelson, Melbourne.
Harkness, Jack (1978) *Roses*, Dent, London
Hole, *Rev.* S. Reynolds *Dean* (1869) *A Book About Roses*, William Blackwood, Edinburgh.
—— (1872) *The Six of Spades*, William Blackwood, Edinburgh.
Jekyll, Gertrude (1902) *Roses For English Gardens*, Country Life, London.
Kordes, Wilhelm (1964) *Roses*, Studio Vista, London.
Le Lièvre, Audrey (1980) *Miss Willmott of Warley Place*, Faber & Faber, London.
Le Rougetel, Hazel (1988) *A Heritage of Roses*, Unwin Hyman, London.
McFarland, Horace (1936) *Roses of the World in Colour*, Cassell & Co, London.
—— (1926) *The Rose in America*, The Macmillan Co, New York.
Nottle, Trevor (1983) *Growing Old-fashioned Roses in Australia and New Zealand*, Kangaroo Press, Kenthurst, N.S.W.
Page, Russell (1983) *The Education of a Gardener*, Collins, London.

Paul, William (1903) *The Rose Garden*, 5th ed., Kent & Co., London.

Pemberton, *Rev.* J. (1908) *Roses, Their History, Development and Cultivation*, Longmans, London.

Phillips, R. & Rix, M. (1988) *Roses*, Pan Books, London.

Ross, Deane (1972) *Shrub Roses in Australia and New Zealand*, Rigby Ltd. Adelaide.

—— (1985) *Rose Growing for Pleasure*, Lothian, Melbourne.

Sackville-West, Vita (1968) *Garden Book*, Michael Joseph, London.

Scott-James, Anne (1975) *Sissinghurst, the Making of a Garden*, Michael Joseph, London.

Shepherd, Roy (1978) *The History of the Rose*, Heyden, London

Steen, Nancy (1967) *The Charm of Old Roses*, Angus & Robertson, Sydney.

Thomas, A.S. (1950) *Better Roses*, Angus & Robertson, Sydney.

—— (1983) *Growing Roses: a Complete Guide to Growing & Showing Roses in Australia*, Thomas Nelson, Melbourne.

Other Books

Chatto, Beth (1988) *Beth Chatto's Garden Notebook*, J.M. Dent & Sons, London.

Chivers, S. & Woloszynska, S. (1990) *The Cottage Garden*, John Murray, London.

Cuffley, Peter (1983) *Cottage Gardens in Australia*, Five Mile Press, Melbourne.

Fish, Margery (1956) *We Made a Garden*, Faber & Faber, London.

—— (1980) *Ground Cover Plants*, Faber & Faber, London.

Hobhouse, Penelope (1985) *Colour in Your Garden*, Collins, London.

Jekyll, Gertrude (1982) *Colour Schemes for the Flower Garden*, Country Life, London.

Johnson, Hugh (1984) *Encyclopaedia of Trees*, Mitchell Beasley, London.

Latymer, Hugo (1990) *The Mediterranean Gardener*, Frances Lincoln, in association with The Royal Botanic Gardens, Kew, London.

Lloyd, Christopher (1985) *The Well-chosen Garden*, Michael Joseph, London.

Lyte, Charles (1989) *Frank Kingdon-Ward, The Last of the Great Plant Hunters*, John Murray, London.

Massingham, Betty (1966) *Miss Jekyll, Portrait of a Great Gardener*, David & Charles, Newton Abbott, U.K.

Mathew, Brian (1981) *Bulbs*, Collins, London.

—— (1973) *Dwarf Bulbs*, Garden Book Club, London.

Nottle, Trevor (1984) *The Cottage Garden Revived*, Kangaroo Press, Kenthurst, N.S.W.

Pescott, R.T.M. (1968) *Bulbs For Australian Gardens*, Thomas Nelson, Melbourne.

Royal Horticultural Society (1989) *The Gardeners' Encyclopaedia of Plants & Flowers*, ed. Christopher Brickell, Dorling Kindersley, London.

—— *The New Royal Horticultural Society Dictionary of Gardening* (1992), editor-in-chief, Anthony Huxley, Macmillan, London.

Scott-James, Anne (1981) *The Cottage Garden*, Allen Lane, London.

Thomas, Graham Stuart (1984) *The Art of Planting*, J.M. Dent & Sons London.

Van der Spuy, Una (1978) *Gardening With Trees*, A.H. & A.W. Reed, Sydney.

Von Arnim, Elizabeth (1899) *The Solitary Summer*, Macmillan & Co, London.

Vyvyan, C.C. (1972) *Letters From a Cornish Garden*, Michael Joseph, London.

Watts, Peter (1983) *Historic Gardens of Victoria*, O.U.P., Melbourne.

Wilkinson, Jennifer (1989) *Herbs and Flowers of the Cottage Garden*, Inkata Press, Melbourne.

Index

of plants, people and places

Plant names in the index have been revised where possible (with *see* references), to show current botanical usage. The principal authorities used were *The Graham Stuart Thomas Rose Book* and *The New Royal Horticultural Society Dictionary of Gardening*.

Fine Garden Writing

from

HYLAND HOUSE

Hyland House is home to Australia's most entertaining, knowledgeable and admired garden writers. If you've enjoyed Susan Irvine's book, we can wholeheartedly recommend these other authors to you as well.

Sarah Guest

Sarah has been described by the *Sunday Age* as the 'best and most entertaining garden writer in Australia'. Her effortless way with words, and keen, infectious wit can be enjoyed in three books from Hyland House: *Flowers for the Australian Cottage Garden Border*, *Flowers from Old Adam's Garden* and the colourful *Flowering Perennials*.

Penny Woodward

Few authors can claim to have produced a definitive book in their lifetime, let alone two. *Penny's Woodward's Australian Herbal* was unanimously acclaimed as the best book ever written on herbs for Australian conditions and she has capped that success by producing the definitive work on garlic, onions and the rest of the allium family: *Garlic & Friends*.

Of this book, garden authority T.R. Garnett has written: 'I doubt whether any comparable book about a single group of vegetables has been written anywhere in the world'.

Gwen Elliot

For over 30 years, Gwen has promoted the growing of Australian native plants. Her message has always been simple: Australian plants are best suited to Australian gardens and their flowers can look just as beautiful as those of introduced species. Author of such bestselling titles as *Australian Plants for Art & Crafts* and *Australian Plants for Small Gardens and Containers*, Gwen's masterwork is the recently published *Gwen Elliot's Australian Garden*, a colourful and encyclopaedic guide to growing Australian plants.

Esther Wettenhall

'The more one considers a garden to belong to not only us, but to a whole world of other living creatures, the more absorbing and fascinating the planning and growing of such a garden becomes.' So says Esther at the start of her celebrated book *The Bush Garden*, a rewarding and often moving chronicle of a lifetime's work creating a garden of Australian plants. Like so many gardens, Esther's becomes over the years an embodiment of her hopes and dreams.

As Gwen Elliot says in her introduction, this is a book 'which begs to be read outdoors in spring or summer, near a pond or birdbath and under the cool shade of a large tree'.

All of the books mentioned above can be ordered through your local bookshop or direct from Hyland House Publishing, 'Hyland House', 387-389 Clarendon Street, Sth Melbourne, Victoria 3205, Australia (tel: 03 9696 9064—Visa, Mastercard & Bankcard accepted). A free catalogue of all our books is also available on request.